Calcutta Diary

Ashok Mitra

KOLKATA

Published in India in 2014 by:

Paranjoy Guha Thakurta

paranjoy@gmail.com

First Published in 1977 by FRANK CASS, LONDON

Revised Edition 2014

ISBN: 9789384439224

Typeset in Times New Roman 11/15

by Ram Das Lal, NCR Delhi

Cover design: PealiDezine

Publishing facilitation: AuthorsUpFront

For

Samar Sen

Contents

Section One

Section Two

Section Three

PUBLISHER'S NOTE

To describe Dr Ashok Mitra as a multifaceted personality would be more than an understatement. His career as an academic, an administrator, a politician, an activist and, above all, a writer of amazing eloquence and insight in both Bengali and English, have all meshed and merged so seamlessly that it is an impossible task to even attempt to cubbyhole him into specific categories. This reprint of a collection of essays he wrote originally for the *Economic and Political Weekly (EPW)* in the 1970s, with a specially-written foreword by eminent social scientist, Professor Partha Chatterjee, and a concluding commentary by the equally eminent historian of South Asia, Professor Ranajit Guha, is important because it recounts aspects of a unique and particularly difficult phase of contemporary Indian history—many of the essays were written during the infamous 21-month Emergency period between June 1975 and March 1977. This volume offers an unparalleled portrait of Calcutta (now Kolkata) in all its grime and glory in a way few writers have been able to capture life and longing in this infuriatingly memorable metropolis in eastern India.

After completing his graduation from the University of Dacca (now Dhaka) in 1948, a year after India became politically independent and was partitioned, he crossed over from East Pakistan (which became Bangladesh in 1971) to West Bengal. While he sought to gain admission to the University of Calcutta for a post-graduate degree in economics and even attended classes, he was refused admission after which he moved to the Benares Hindu University from where he obtained a master's degree. Thereafter, Dr Mitra joined the Delhi School of Economics that had then been recently established in the University of Delhi. He taught economics at the University of Lucknow for two years before travelling abroad to be associated with the Institute of Social Studies in Netherlands. In 1953, he earned a doctorate degree in economic sciences from the University of Rotterdam (now The Netherlands School of Economics) under the guidance of the well-known Dutch economist, Professor Jan Tinbergen (1903–94), who was the first to be awarded the Nobel prize in economics in 1969.

In late 1956, he returned to Delhi to join the newly-started National Council of Applied Economic Research (NCAER). He then went again to the Netherlands, came back to Delhi where he spent a little more than a year as Officer on Special Duty in the Ministry of Finance, before joining the United Nations Economic and Social Commission for Asia and the Pacific (ESCAP) at Bangkok, Thailand. Subsequently, in 1961, he travelled to the United States where he worked with the Economic Development Institute in Washington D.C. as a member of its teaching faculty. The institute had been started by the World Bank but was situated in a different part of the city and had no direct links with the Bank. Dr Mitra has been a vehement critic of the policies of the World Bank.

He returned to India and became a professor of economics at the Indian Institute of Management Calcutta (IIMC) that had been established as the first national institute for post-graduate studies and research in management by the government of India in collaboration with the Alfred P. Sloan School of Management (in the Massachusetts Institute of Technology), the government of West Bengal, the Ford Foundation and Indian industry. The institute had as its first director, K.T. Chandy, who, in the 1930s, was part of the young group actively associated with the India League spearheaded by V.K. Krishna Menon. Some of the members of this group later became important communist leaders in India. His joining IIMC was really an offshoot of what could be called the 'old-boy network'.

He went back to Delhi to join the fledgling Agricultural Prices Commission and was responsible for giving it shape. The Commission (now the Commission on Agricultural Costs and Prices), among other things, would calculate the minimum support prices of cereals like wheat and rice. In 1970, Dr Mitra was invited to take over as chief economic adviser (CEA) to the government of India in the ministry of finance, from which post he resigned in April 1972. While he was CEA, Dr Manmohan Singh (who went on to become prime minister of India) was economic adviser in the ministry of commerce and he went on to succeed Dr Mitra as CEA. His association with the then prime minister of India, Indira Gandhi, during the days when she rode high on the slogan of *garibi hatao* (banish poverty)—whose bitter critic he subsequently became—was used by Dr Mitra's critics to claim that he was hypocritical and had turned against those who had helped him, a claim he has always denied.

Returning to Kolkata, over the next three and a half years, he was a national fellow at the Indian Council of Social Science Research and simultaneously, a visiting professor at the Administrative Staff College of India at Hyderabad. This was the period when the essays in this volume started appearing in *EPW*.

He received an invitation to join the Institute of Development Studies at Brighton, UK, as a professorial Fellow for the year 1975–76. The Emergency was declared in June 1975 and the censors of the Indira Gandhi government clamped a ban on Dr Mitra's articles that appear in this volume. Dr Mitra recalls sending a letter to the *Economist* weekly published out of London complaining bitterly against the imposition of the Emergency and the 'horrors' that followed—the letter was promptly published. He was, nevertheless, able to proceed to Brighton without hindrance in October 1975. While in the UK, he wrote an article for the *Economist* on the completion of one year of the Emergency; the particular issue of the magazine was prohibited from circulation in the country.

After the Emergency was lifted in March 1977 and fresh elections conducted, later that year in June, Dr Mitra became finance minister of the government of West Bengal, a post he held for almost a decade till January 1986. During this period, he attracted considerable attention from the media, especially for his remarks against the Union government in Delhi and how it had economically discriminated against the eastern region of India in general and West Bengal in particular, especially in terms of investing in major public sector projects. By then, Dr Mitra was very much a part of the Communist Party of India (Marxist) which had led the Left Front government in the state under the leadership of Chief Minister Jyoti Basu. During his stint as finance minister, he once got angry with journalists who were questioning why the state government had abruptly removed a bureaucrat (S.M. Murshed) from his post, and famously remarked: 'I'm not a *bhadralok* (or gentleman). I'm a Communist!'

Though his personal relations with Basu (India's longest serving chief minister) remained cordial, Dr Mitra started having serious differences of opinion with him and the policies and programmes of the CPI(M)-led government in West Bengal. He decided to quit the government and be on his own, writing and speaking, for a few years. He was soon 'persuaded' by the party to move to Delhi to become a member of the Rajya Sabha, the upper house of India's Parliament. He served as chairman of the Parliament's Standing Committee on Industry and Commerce. During his six-year term as an MP during the mid-1990s, the government of India led by Prime Minister P.V. Narasimha Rao had embarked on its policies of economic liberalization under the tutelage of the then finance minister, Dr Manmohan Singh —policies which Dr Mitra intensely opposed in Parliament and outside it, through his writings and his utterances.

As in the case of his relationship with Jyoti Basu, despite having worked closely with Dr Singh in Indira Gandhi's government and despite their personal affinity, Dr Mitra was a trenchant critic of Dr Singh. Till he became Union finance minister in June 1991, Dr Singh was seen as an economist who had endorsed the 'socialist' policy framework of the Indian government. Even as the South Commission's secretary general in the late 1980s, he had articulated the economic aspirations of the developing countries and been critical of the International Monetary Fund and World Bank. He did surprise many when he espoused a sharp rightward shift in India's economic policy regime as finance minister between June 1991 and April 1996. Even as prime minister, Dr Singh has been perceived as among the more right-wing leaders of the Indian National Congress as far as his economic ideology is concerned. Dr Mitra contended in his book (*A Prattler's Tale: Bengal, Marxism and Governance*, Samya, 2007) that Dr Singh's appointment as finance minister in the Narasimha Rao government was on account of American pressure. This claim has, till date, never been formally denied.

While Dr Mitra has written academic books, including one titled *China: Issues in Development*, his short articles, first published in *EPW* and then in Kolkata's *Telegraph* daily, have been avidly read by a wide cross-section of readers in India and across the world.

Besides *Calcutta Diary* and *From the Ramparts*, two other collections of articles he wrote for *EPW* have been published: these are *The Hoodlum Years* (Orient Longman, 1979) and *The Starkness of It*' (Roli Books, 2008). His second book in the *Prattler's Tale* series with the subtitle 'Recollections of a Contrary Marxist', has been published in Bengali as *Apila Chapala*.

Equally proficient in English and his mother-tongue, Bengali, and in writing fiction as well as non-fiction, Dr Mitra was the recipient of the Sahitya Akademi Award in 1996 for his contributions to Bengali literature. He has written 20 books in Bengali on diverse themes. At the ripe young age of 85, he says he has the 'cheek' to edit, print and publish a Bengali fortnightly, *Arek Rakam* (or that which is different), which is going strong.

To return to the Emergency, when it was at its peak in 1976, he had two manuscripts ready for publication: *Calcutta Diary* and *Terms of Trade and Class Relations*. At that time, no publisher would dare publish him. It was at this juncture that Frank Cass came forward and offered to publish both books from London. The publisher paid him a 'token' advance of 250 British pounds for both books, which were published in early-1977, around the time the Emergency was lifted and the new Janata Party government was elected to power in March that year. The first print run of the book got exhausted in 1980 and only a few copies of the book were available by the mid-1980s. Even today, the original edition of the book can be purchased online. This new reprinted edition of the book should make it more easily available to readers.

On a personal note, I have had the privilege of knowing Dr Mitra from 1977 onwards. The first time I met him was when I had joined a monthly magazine called *Perspective* (now defunct) which had been edited by the late Dr Bhabani Sen Gupta, as a cub reporter and sub-editor, though I had been given the exalted designation of assistant editor. I later interviewed him for what was then one of the most popular English weeklies in the country, *The Illustrated Weekly of India*. Dr Mitra was always patient with me, occasionally chiding me for what he felt was my immaturity and impetuosity. Once, when I asked why he had given up his job as finance minister of West Bengal ostensibly to read and write, he asked me: 'Why can't I have the luxury of relaxing?'

I have visited his home in Sonali Apartments in Kolkata's Alipore area to interview him on several occasions. When I suggested that I interview him for a television channel since he had hardly, if ever, appeared on the 'idiot box', he recoiled in horror. He said he would never appear in front of a television camera. He added half in jest that he would develop a severe allergic reaction if a video camera was placed in front of him. Despite the eight and a half decades he has been with us, his mind remains incredibly alert, his memory amazingly accurate. I have a special relationship with *Calcutta Diary*. While I have reviewed at least a hundred books over the last 37 years I have worked as a journalist, this was the first book I got an opportunity to review. At the risk of appearing arrogant, I am reproducing the review (unedited) that was published in *Perspective* in the May 1978 issue. It took me some effort retrieving it from an old folder that I thought I would never find. In that folder were memories that returned, flooding my mind with nostalgia. In it were stories about a time that would never return and about a writer who wrote with such intensity and passion that his words will remain etched for posterity.

Perspective, May 1978

Books of the Month: **REVOLUTIONARY TRUTH ON THE WALL**

ASHOK MITRA—Calcutta Diary, Frank Cass & Co. Ltd., London, 1977, pp 206

Once upon a time there lived a chief economic adviser to the government of India under Indira Gandhi, who resigned from his job in 1972 and became her vehement critic. He had acquired a reputation for being a sound academic economist with a number of published works to his credit, but he was more than just that. His impassioned prose pieces read like revolutionary verse. He could write about the semi-feudal background of Begum Akhtar with as much power as about the Naxalite youth shot dead by the police. He seemed to be disillusioned about the left parties of India as he cynically described the " mela" that is a leftist rally in the Calcutta maidan. But we were in for surprises, for he became the finance minister under the CPI-M led Left Front government in West Bengal. The character that emerges is as puzzling as the city he describes with love and hate- the puzzle that is the city of Calcutta.

Ashok Mitra's *Calcutta Diary* is a compilation of 46 short articles. Except for two of these pieces which were published in *Frontier*, the rest of these articles appeared in *Economic and Political Weekly* since 1972 under the signature 'A.M'. Regular readers of *EPW* could not have failed to be impressed by the provocative column of Dr Mitra, and the present collection affords exhilarating reading to those who are uninitiated to his writings. Most of the articles pertain to issues of general interest (and hence have lost little reading value) and should appeal to most people – whether he be a layman or an academic economist- because they are well informed and reveal an erudition which comes from a clear appreciation of history.

The book is divided into three sections and encompasses a wide range of topics. Yet, the thematic unity is clear. The voice that keeps coming through is the voice of the oppressed and the downtrodden ; the cry for redress after generations of exploitation and the resulting abject poverty and deprivation. The words are very subtly executed, but the anger does not fail to show through.

An old refugee woman (Mother Courage, he names her) languishes in the backwaters of a subhuman existence. A landless labourer wallows in his defeatism, broken by the clutches of the landlord and money-lender. A "wizened crowd" wait year after year for their examinations to be held, only to succumb to the escapist fantasy world of Rajesh Khanna and Hema Malini. A lower middle- class family gets used to not seeing their revolutionary son again. The poets of Calcutta live in the delusions of their little magazines. Images keep flashing before the eye, juxtaposed one over the other , to form the totality of experience. Consider the article, "Calcutta Every Day":

Perspiration. The odour of it. A dilapidated CSTC bus emitting a morbid trail of black smoke. Burnt-out grass, dead grass, butts of crushed cigarettes, rags, pieces of paper, a quiet coexistence between the two parallel lines of the tram tracks…Revolutionary truth on the wall. Or at least a version of it. Beggars. A leper and his comely wife…Market place,the odour of fish, vegetables and unwashed human species. Some counter-revolutionary truth, this time plastered across a film hoarding. Hindi make-believe ……breasts suggestive of infinite plasticity ….More poets per square kilometre than even football fans. A newspaper kiosk, poetry magazines by the dozen, more revolutionary truth …A ration shop , the law of the Green Revolution …the greater the success of the Revolution , the higher the price of wheat. Aspects of dialectics, facades, speeches at the Maidan and negotiations over lunch at the Calcutta Club. Painted women whom history has not yet caught up with…pickpockets, policemen in worn-out uniforms, a hydrant leaking since morning.

Most of the articles in *Calcutta Diary* were written well before the Emergency. For those who do not look on Indira Gandhi's aberration in isolation but consider it as a logical culmination of events arising out of India's gross economic inequalities, will find more than an adequate vindication of this viewpoint in the book. The various economic maladies of the Indian polity, with its colonial hangovers, have been sketched extremely lucidly. One of the best articles in the book is the one entitled 'The New Obfuscators'. Mitra harshly derides the Indian economists for their impotent vacillation, and compares them to the ancient Brahmins who used to act as buffers between the masses and the monarch. In another context he writes: "It is pure Kafka:

wherever you go, whichever you turn, never mind which poor country you are currently in, there is no escape from courses and seminars on economic development".

In the third section of the book there are some interesting vignettes on some of the foreign countries, which the author visited . A businessman in Hongkong told him that you could judge the economic condition of Saigon by the price of its prostitutes . The poor whores spent a lot of money on plastic surgery to uplift their breasts and reduce the slant in their eyes, but unfortunately for them , the American soldiers left in a massive hurry.Then there is story about an ex-Nazi tourist guide in Rio de Janiero, who praised eloquently the city's soaring skyscrapers, forgetting to mention the slums that lay alongside them.

As T.J. Byres exclaims in the introduction to the book, " ... Mitra is very much a puritan. He does have an intense sense of responsibility for his conscience; a conscience deeply offended by the poverty, squalor, inhumanity and injustice which are rampant in India..."

Paranjoy Guha Thakurta
New Delhi
August 2014

ACKNOWLEDGEMENTS

When Ashok Mitra's *Calcutta Diary* was first published in 1977 in London, it was acclaimed by the British Broadcasting Corporation as the best book on India's Emergency. It was subsequently published in India by Rupa & Co. and went through a number of prints. It, however, disappeared from the market for a long while and we have arranged to re-publish it at the request of a number of social scientists and political observers.

Our grateful thanks to Professor Partha Chatterjee for writing a new Introduction to *Calcutta Diary.* We have also chosen to include, with Professor Ranajit Guha's kind permission, his discussion on *Calcutta Diary* which was first published in the *Journal of Peasant Studies* in July 1978 and is now included in *The Small Voice of History: Collected Essays* edited by Partha Chatterjee.

We deeply appreciate the help extended to by Gouri Chatterjee and Imanul Haque for ensuring this edition of *Calcutta Diary*.

FOREWORD

It is difficult to convey at this time my feelings when I first read Ashok Mitra's column in the *Economic and Political Weekly* forty years ago. For someone daily surrounded by the dull familiarity of beggars and pickpockets, policemen in worn-out uniforms, revolutionary truth on the wall, minor football riots, and too many red flags, reading the weekly 'Calcutta Diary' in the early 1970s was not just like looking at a mirror of everyday city life. It was much more. It seemed to record, even as it went along from week to week commenting on events and people, some truth of historic import that no one else was recording at the time, at least not in such a telling way. In particular, the reign of state-sponsored terror unleashed on the Left in West Bengal—the undeclared state of emergency before the declared one—which hardly drew a critical comment from the mainstream press at the time, was boldly and memorably described in his columns by Mitra. Reading these entries once more, I now see that there were four articles between 1973 and 1975 which dealt directly with this subject. I remembered them quite clearly but somehow thought they were spread over a dozen or so entries, so powerful was the impact they had made on me.

Of these four articles, the first, published in 1973, was explosive. 'You talk in private with senior men belonging to the administration,' it declared, 'from the second quarter of 1970 onwards, they will admit, the police were given summary powers to hunt down and kill undesirable elements.' People in

Cossipore-Baranagore in the northern fringes of the city knew this, of course, because early one morning they saw scores of dead bodies dumped in the open sewers or floating down the river. For the next couple of years, most neighbourhoods had their own stories of political killings, some reported in the press as 'encounter deaths', others going unreported. 'No need any more to conform to the droll literalness of "self-defence"; no need for the irritant of a proper search warrant and of regular witnesses, as was the wont during the days of the British; young people, once they have been defined as undesirable, could now be swiftly despatched to their deaths.' But Mitra did not just leave it at that. He went on to make an even more scathing ethical-political point. 'None in India are more intensely alive than the young men and women who are prepared to sacrifice—and have sacrificed—everything so that a new society could emerge. They must therefore die....' Contrast this with the official role of honour, he added. 'What is the number of nephews and nieces who are languishing behind the bars in this great liberal democracy of ours? Thirty thousand, forty thousand, fifty thousand? How many have been summarily shot, in prison or outside, so as to ensure that the house is not destroyed from within? But why bother about them; they dreamed, they do not deserve any better. While they are despatched to their fate, many of the unscrupulous ones, come 26 January and 15 August, will be honoured by the State. They may be rogues and scoundrels, but they enrich the system.'

The following year, Ashok Mitra wrote about a certain Kamal Bose of Bhowanipore who had been kept in prison for over a year and a half on one false charge after another, even as he was being granted bail and discharged by the courts. Mitra warned:

'Those wanting to stay out of prison in this country should beware. Liberty is not your birthright, nor your constitutional right, it is what your government and the police might occasionally like to bestow upon you.' The same year, he wrote about Prabir Dutta, also of Bhowanipore, beaten to death by the police at an open air theatre performance at Curzon Park. I remember attending the protest meeting a few days later at the same venue, addressed by the leading lights of the Calcutta group theatre movement and capped by the same play performed by Badal Sarkar's troupe. A few days later, I read Ashok Mitra's essay in the *EPW*: 'But one must be fair, one must not lose one's sense of perspective. A hundred deaths take place under the loving care of the authorities, it is only occasionally that a stray one is reported, such as Prabir's, because it occurs in the city centre, in the glare of a dazzling July afternoon sun. Moreover, all is well that ends well. Prabir is dead; there is one less unemployed to roam the streets of the city of Calcutta, one less speck of inconvenient statistics.' The sarcasm had an effect on me that was visceral, an excruciatingly painful mix of anger, laughter, dismay, frustration and utter helplessness.

Days before the declaration of the Emergency, Ashok Mitra wrote about two brothers, Pradip and Prabir Roy Chowdhury of Tollygunge. The two college students had been picked up by the police. The elder one, Pradip, was beaten and tortured to death in the interrogation centre of the Special Branch. The younger one, Prabir, was shot dead inside Howrah jail. All this happened while ministers and judges were daily declaiming on the imminent danger posed by fascist forces conspiring to bring down the progressive government of Indira Gandhi. Mitra offered the scenario of Pradip and Prabir's mother sneaking her way through security to present herself before the honourable judges. 'Would they—the guardians and upholders of the rule of law in this country—would they be able to return her stare and, composure writ large on their faces, assure her that, never mind her two sons, fascism shall not pass? Would they?' Indeed, in that summer of 1975, the question was loud and stark: was it the opposition that was behaving like fascists or the government?

More or less at the same time as this article was published, Jayaprakash Narayan came to Calcutta to address a massive rally at the Brigade Parade Ground. The Left parties agreed to join without their party flags. Ashok Mitra presided over the meeting on behalf of a citizens' committee. We in the crowd didn't know at the time—perhaps Ashok Babu didn't know it either—that his political career was launched that afternoon. A few days later, Emergency was declared. His friends were apprehensive that Mitra might be arrested for his leading role at JP's meeting. He left the country and spent the next year and a half on a fellowship at Sussex. *Calcutta Diary* the book was first published from London at thae time.

My memory of this book was clearly dominated by its resounding condemnation of state violence. Reading it again, however, I discovered several other gems that fully deserved to be remembered as well. The 1972 essay on freedom fighters—'tired, listless old men, a smattering of old women,' travelling to Delhi to be honoured on the twenty-fifth anniversary of Independence. 'How these old relics quarrelled among themselves to get into the list.... The fire has gone out, really and truly; these old individuals are tragic exhibits of their memories.' And then there is the essay on Nirmal Kumar Bose, perhaps the first of Mitra's unparalleled sequence of obituaries.

Bose was a scholar of astonishing range and ability. He was also a fully committed political activist, jailed more than once for his involvement in the Gandhian movement. But he was free of all cant and dogma. As Gandhi's secretary in Noakhali, he argued with him on science and morality. As a government officer, he disagreed with the government policy on scheduled castes and tribes. 'It merely reflects the state of barbarity this nation has reached in the course of the past quarter of a century that there was so little mention of his death even amongst men with academic attitudes. Newspapers salvaged their conscience by setting aside one or two brief paragraphs of obituary. The politicians, of course, could not care less.'

His essay on the writer Buddhadeva Bose shows the obituarist Mitra at his clinical best. He is fulsome in his praise for Bose's literary output: 'a complete littérateur.... If you leave out Tagore, no one else in Bengali literature has covered the total spectrum in the manner he did.' But obsessed with his search for a spell of undisturbed peace in which to write his critical tract on the Mahabharata, Bose began to churn out potboilers to save up enough money. In the end, he never got the time; the work remained unfinished. He was also politically gullible and was mobilized in the cultural battles of the Cold War to fight for the abstract concept of freedom. Mitra's elegiac style has offended many, for he does not shrink, out of deference for conventional politeness towards the dead, from making a critical judgment. But his note on Sadhana Bose, the screen goddess who died a pauper, ends up in a lament not just for the Bengali film industry but for the city as a whole. 'The film industry... epitomises the decadence which today defines Calcutta: I wait, you wait, they wait, everyone waits for the inexorable, melancholy, creeping death.'

I should also mention here that Ashok Mitra does not even spare the Bengali holy cows of poetry and revolution. After carrying out a tongue-in-cheek exercise for providing bank finance to fifteen thousand practising Bengali poets to publish their volumes of poetry, he concludes: 'Even revolution-mongering here has become a species of lyrical effusion; an excess of poetry has numbed almost all possibilities of activism.... Between the Scylla of lyricism and the Charybdis of economism, the Bengali poet will thus have to make an awkwardly difficult choice.' And the earliest essay in the collection, dating back to 1969, spoke of too many red flags: 'cadres must be taught my version of revolutionary truth, my revolution by definition is superior to yours.'

After these essays were published, Ashok Mitra, we know, was finance minister in the first Left Front government in West Bengal and was later a CPI(M) member of the Rajya Sabha. He became a critic of the policies of the party and government with which he was associated long before the fellow travellers began to jump ship. Even as he affiliated himself with causes, movements and organizations, Mitra has never been afraid to speak as the minority of one.

It is especially gratifying to me that Ashok Mitra invited me to write a foreword to this reprint edition of *Calcutta Diary*. I feel honoured to be given this opportunity to share with his readers the memories of my first introduction to the writings of one of the most articulate, courageous and upright intellectuals of our time.

Calcutta

12 July 2013 **Partha Chatterjee**

A PREFATORY NOTE

The pieces assembled here are the fruits of pseudonymous and acronymous journalism. The first and fourth pieces, written during 1968-69, are from *Frontier*, Calcutta; all the rest are from the *Economic and Political Weekly*—a random selection from A.M.'s weekly column in that journal during 1972-75. In the early part of 1975, friends had suggested the idea of a selection such as the present one. Even as the idea was assuming concrete form, Indira Gandhi's Emergency intervened. There was no question of a publication of this kind being allowed in the country during that period. A British publisher could however be attracted to the project. A matter of some historical curiosity, the London publication of the book coincided with the downfall of Indira Gandhi's regime in New Delhi in March, 1977.

But the nexus of the essays is that, at least in one part of the country—West Bengal—Indira Gandhi's Emergency started much earlier, perhaps from 1970 onwards. To read the pieces today is, for the author at least, to experience a kind of retrospective catharsis. And it could be that, for some others too, the worth of these essays is not altogether dissipated: perhaps there is a certain significance in recollecting the terror and inhumanity which were the staple of the regime that was then abroad. The collection represents, I believe, a climate of mind which is essentially Bengali, or, should I be even more specific, Calcutta-nurtured. Not all the essays concern Calcutta and its immediate environment. A number of them, included in Section Three, do in fact discuss remoter lands and peoples. Even so, the link, overt or otherwise, with Calcutta—and Bengal—is always there. The author of the pieces is a prisoner of Calcutta: this may be as much his pride as his tragedy.

There is nonetheless no particular need to feel apologetic about the biases and the idiosyncracies of the person who once wrote these essays. His biases are Bengali biases, his idiosyncracies too are of local vintage. He is a part of his people; he has been reared by the squalor which defines Calcutta—and Bengal. His loyalties are local, provincial, perhaps even sectarian. At the same time, he can hardly disown the other stream of consciousness which defines him—the consciousness of belonging to the great, awkward, fuzzy Indian nation. This nation is a medley of confusion, but the dominating fact is still that of acute social conflicts and crass class exploitations. Never mind the contradictions and heterogeneities, the ruling classes, the prime political decision-makers have a pervasive influence over the different segments of the country, including Bengal and Calcutta. This provided the backdrop, in the early Seventies, for Indira Gandhi's cynical maraudings. By 1977, however, even she had proved a point of substance, namely, that the process of history is determined not by the whims of tyrants and about-to-be-ones, but by the people themselves. During that phase between 1972 and 1975, optical illusion being optical illusion, this truth was not immediately obvious. Perhaps some of the essays included in this volume reflect that mood of uncertainty.

An Indian edition of the volume is now being arranged through the initiative of D. Mehra of Rupa and Company. On this occasion, I have to remember a number of friends who were responsible for the genesis of the *Calcutta Diary* pieces. It was Samar Sen who persuaded me to begin writing a weekly column, first for his *Now*, subsequently for *Frontier*. Hiten Chaudhury, the Managing Trustee of the Sameeksha Trust, and Krishna Raj, Editor of the *Economic and Political Weekly*, encouraged me to continue with the column in the *EPW*. Krishna Raj's colleagues in the *EPW*, Rajani Desai and Zawid Laiq, were early enthusiasts of the idea to put these pieces together. Others who had helped include Prabhat Patnaik, Govind Deshpande and Amit Bhaduri. It was however Hiten Bhaya who took the most trouble; he suggested the titles for each individual piece, which means that he had to go through the drudgery of reading the pieces over and over. Finally, two of my good friends, Terry Byres, editor of the *Journal of Peasant Studies*, and Ranajit Guha, of the University of Sussex, were instrumental, during those fugitive days of Indira Gandhi's Emergency, in persuading me that the pieces be published outside the country. Terry Byres not only helped me to locate a publisher, he was also generous enough to write a most sympathetic introduction to the British edition.

But, then, debts to one's friends generally belong to the unrequitable category.

May 1979 **Ashok Mitra**

Calcutta

Section One

1 Calcutta Every Day

Perspiration. The odour of it. A dilapidated CSTC bus emitting a morbid trail of black smoke. Burnt-out grass, dead grass, butts of crushed cigarettes, rags, pieces of paper, a quiet coexistence inside the two parallel lines of the tram tracks. A three-and-a-half storey building which perhaps had last got a coat of paint on the outside in 1938, a building which cannot quite decide whether it should crumble on to the pavement right now or three-quarters of an hour later. Revolutionary truth on the wall. Or at least a version of it. Beggars. A leper and his comely wife. Suddenly a tree, about twenty feet tall, thin branches all over, blushing with flowers. Home-bound schoolboys, pelting stones at one another. Market-place, the blended odour of fish and vegetables and unwashed human species. Some counter-revolutionary truth, this time plastered across a film hoarding. Hindi make-believes, possibly of Madras vintage, mini-*cholis* and mini-saris, breasts suggestive of infinite plasticity. Crows, statues with negative aesthetic quotient, statues which cry out for Lohiaesque removals. More poets per square kilometre than even football fans. A newspaper kiosk, poetry magazines by the dozen, more revolutionary truth. Revolution in the tropics, love in the tropics, insipid poetry in the tropics. The red triangle, the vulgar society, ethos travelling down from New Delhi. A ration shop, the Law of the Green Revolution, a morsel of another kind of revolutionary truth—the greater the success of the Revolution, the higher the price of wheat. Aspects of dialectics, facades, speeches at the Maidan and negotiations over lunch at the Calcutta Club. Painted women whom history has not yet caught up with, golf, Saturday nights, the oasis of shopping during the indolent afternoon hours around Park Street, cars installed with air-conditioners. Beggars, pickpockets, policemen in worn-out uniforms, a hydrant leaking since morning. A sharp nor'wester, flooding the streets, a couple of tired trees come down on top of the power line. Talk of over-utilisation of capacity, the civic facilities originally intended for eight hundred thousand now extended to eight million. Anti-thesis, human beings who are under-utilised, small engineering firms, retrenched labour, unabsorbed young engineers. Political parties who couldn't care less, incapable of caring more, the books speak of situations in Russia or China or Cuba, no clue to Calcutta 1969. Clenched fists, Mao's Red Book, violence in the air, to be met by matching violence, vapour, the meaning of meaning. Teachers in a procession, women with high fat content addressing shrill meetings, society for the protection of ersatz uteruses. Clerks equally incapable of maintaining the ledger or manning the barricade; lack of nutrition, yet the spouting of spitfire vocabulary. Wives alternating between kitchen and lying-in, several who die before reaching thirty, children who go astray. Lack of nutrition, but nervous energy comes marching in, nervous energy expended in abandon. Gang fights, the chasing of uncertain-looking, unsure girls, lack of food, but tea stalls abound, some migrate to local liquor. The youth have to be revolutionised, pocketful of Lin Piao, revolution in the revolution, other voices, other interpretations of insurrectionary truth. A bank gets looted, unscrupulous journalists, journalists parading as philosophers, journalists parading as statesmen, journalists who assume that between Tagore and them history was a vacuum. The law of revolutionary exposure, the more uncompromising a revolutionary the greater the hankering for space in the *haute bourgeois* newspapers. The other law, regarding the immutability of energy: the more you expend on fulmination, the less you have for culmination. Nobody really worries about culmination, the United Front is in Writers' Buildings at least for five years, all's right with the world. The gleam of 1972, from Hindusthan Park to South Block, from Siliguri to Srikakulam, young men in terylene trousers, the Red Flag, the hammer and the sickle, how many hammers and how many sickles, the emancipation of the peasantry, workers to down tools, workers hankering for transistor radios, workers who couldn't be bothered about whether economism is the opium of tired souls. Students who have scored seventy per cent or more to get admission to Presidency College, some join the Baker Laboratory, some sit for the I.A.S. Books, bookshops, the Coffee House agog with conspiratorial-sounding gossip, girls who combine poetry-writing with processing of plastic bombs, girls from refugee homes, boys on an uncertain equipoise between sincerity and unscrupulousness. Dusk, whining drizzle of rain, slush, mud and smoke. Is it hopelessness, or the lull before the insurrection, maybe again an equipoise. Dusk, Tagore songs amenable to many interpretations, a crowd returning from a football match, a minor riot, the hallmark of normalcy. A free fight, a bus overturned, some urchins run over, please, do not set fire to the bus or the approaching streetcar, your favourite leader has been informed, he is coming, he is going to address you, he would urge you to be calm. Revolutionary calmness, discipline above all, the cadres must be taught to be still and how not to be still. But too many red flags, ego colliding with ego, Bengalis—somebody points out—are three-quarters mongoloid. Eighty million of them across the border, robust peasant stock, three-quarters mongoloid. Never mind the tropical indolence, if the Vietnamese could achieve what they have done, why not you, three-quarters mongoloid ? Meanwhile, cadres must be taught my version of revolutionary truth, my revolution by definition is superior to yours. More revolutionary posters, more than half-hidden by others invoking votes for the Corporation election. Power grows, power grows in Writers' Building, power grows at Durgapur, power grows as the *bargadars* get settled on disputed and not-so-disputed land. Power grows out of the barrel of a gun, whose gun, what barrel? Power grows as a Hindu peasant refuses to break bread with his Muslim neighbour, it grows as a Hindu worker joins the rogues and the ragamuffins to demolish a mosque, power grows as a Communist Corporation Councillor presides over the neighbourly Durga Puja Celebration Committee, it grows as a party comrade draws up the battle plan for the capture of the Cricket Association of Bengal. Power grows in a zigzag ambivalence, power also had grown in Indonesia, at least till October 1965. Remember Mao Tse-tung's conversation piece, excellent. Comrade Aidit, you have now so many men in Parliament and in the army, *mais oui*, but when are you going to the mountains? Mountains of files, mountains of revolutionary literature, mountains of poetry. Poetry and drama and song and dance. Ah, where are the heroes of the Indian People's Theatre movement, they have not gone to the mountains, they have entered the jungle, the jungle of careerism, the jungle of money. You need money for a revolution, a revolution is for the even distribution of cash, money is life-soul. Another bank is looted, the ripple reaches the women of easy virtue, there are too many virtues at work, an excess of virtuous definitions. It is the interchangeability of virtues which should stop the crowd, enthral the crowd, one never knew about this rich proliferation of non-antagonistic contradictions. Anything goes, everything goes into anything else: communism, a government job, revolutionary speech-making, employment in an American advertising firm, producing a Bombay-type film, the Red Book, forming yet another Communist Party. Like proposals for a new bridge across the Hooghly, every day a fresh new party, the more the merrier. If so many try, never mind even if severally, we are bound to arrive somewhere. Let a thousand thoughts contend, each thought will have a representation on West Bengal's United Front, or on the anti-United Front, if only somebody cares to set up one such. The workers couldn't care less, the students couldn't care less, the clerks couldn't care less, the *boxwallahs* couldn't care less, the housewives couldn't care less. The housewives care for cheap novelettes and cheaper-looking morons who appear in films. Yet the bulk of them will vote for a version of communism, they cannot wait for the Revolution to commence; like the namby-pamby of an Almighty in the more atrocious of Tagore's poems, the revolution is all things to all Bengalis. Dust. Heat. Asphalt melting under the feet. Roads in a horrible state of disrepair. United Front or no, Kanu Sanyal clutching the Red Book or no, some people in Jorasanko—Jorabagan—Burrabazar—Bowbazar—Chowringhee continue to mint money, they will offer you a kerb quotation even for the revolution. It doesn't add up. Nothing does in Calcutta. South of Park Street, here and there, residual blotches of that peculiar cross of Victorian colonialism and Eisenhower America, Chinese stragglers manufacturing sad-looking shoes for years on end, pimps splitting the take with worm-ridden Bhutani prostitutes, of all things, a Hindi version of Ionesco before corpulent, 'upcountry' ladies in air-conditioned splendour. Suddenly, a procession. Suddenly the splinters fly. Suddenly, some blood-letting. You ask the hawkers, two people got killed on this very spot in the early afternoon, the hawkers couldn't be more indifferent. Nothing adds up in Calcutta. Neither revolution nor revisionism. Neither Satyajit Ray's alleged pretensions nor his acclaimed genius. Neither the poetry nor the experimental plays. Neither the potholes nor the glorious oleander trees. Neither the slum-dweller's listlessness nor the reputation of the social butterflies. It is a fearful, disturbing coexistence. Everybody mingling with everybody else, X running down Y in a morning editorial, X going to Y's cocktail in the evening. Altogether, too many revolutions in the revolution. Nobody can understand Calcutta, the incorrigible, the impossible. Summertime. One hundred and nine degrees Fahrenheit in the shade. A procession. A meeting. The Internationale. What Lenin said when. And why. My quotation is superior to your quotation. I am unemployed, you are unemployed, they are unemployed. I am a revolutionary, you are a neo-revisionist, they are with me, they have been temporarily hoodwinked by you. I quote the Red Book, you quote the Red Book, they couldn't care less. Yet they are the stuff of which revolutions are made. The blood is three-quarters mongoloid. You are confessing to your socialist instincts by referring to the blood count. But I can counter you, revolutions in the revolution...

1969

2 The Burnt-Out Cases

Quietly, one night last week, from Howrah, they took the train to New Delhi, about ninety of them altogether. Most of them past sixty, several of them much, much older. Tired, listless old men, a smattering of old women: who will imagine that they had, ever, the fire in them, the fire that had set so many rivers of revolutionary emotion ablaze? A measly-looking special train took them to the capital; they—the political sufferers of yesteryear—were supposed to be honoured there on the occasion of the twenty-fifth anniversary of freedom. It was a carefully selected list; there can, after all, be no dearth, particularly in this part of the country, of old men and women who had spent time in this or that British jail between 1905 and 1947, and who might still be alive and around. It will be less than fair to blame the Government: it could not possibly pay the passage to Delhi and back for thousands and thousands of these political sufferers; it would have been impossible to arrange for living accommodation either. Therefore, a short-list became unavoidable: the bunch of ninety decaying, dispirited souls merely represented a sampled cross-section of the patriotic heroes and heroines from the past. It could well be that those assembled on that rain-spattered night at the Howrah railway station were a biased specimen, perhaps the sample was not properly stratified, perhaps those who are currently leaning toward the ruling party made the list and those who are tilting in other directions were left out in the cold. And how these old relics quarrelled amongst themselves to get into the list: young brats trying to gate-crash into a crucial match between the two leading soccer teams in the city could hardly have been more acrimonious or seemingly lacking in dignity. The fire has gone out, really and truly; these old individuals are tragic exhibits of their memories, if perchance these still flicker away in some minds. Destitute, perpetually lacking shelter as well as funds, altogether unadjusted to the intricacies of an inflation-ridden, corruption-based system, scrounging a visit to New Delhi is now the core of their contentment. Honour them, they brought you independence. There is, besides, that scheme for offering a two hundred rupees a month pension to each and every political sufferer during the British regime. All one has to do is to furnish a copy of a document, duly attested by a 'gazetted' officer of the Government, to prove that one had in fact served time in a British prison, and for a political offence. What a flurry of activities amongst the former revolutionaries of diverse lineage: a gleam in their eye, and considerable running about, helter skelter, to obtain clarifications of the *modus operandi* for duly attesting the precious document. The gazetted officers are suddenly in great demand: the great revolutionaries of yesteryear, all legendary names, are imploring anybody, just anybody, in the official hierarchy: please, will you, give me an attestation, an attestation . . .

Is this the measure, then, of our achievements since Independence? Reducing the honoured revolutionaries into run-of-the-mill beggars? Do take a look at them, they remind one of those sad, morphia-choked circus lions: given the occasion, they are made to perform; the whip is raised, the sound of the lash, the whip falls; once the number is over, the lions recede, the tail between their hind legs, doped beyond redemption.

It is an insulting spectacle. But ask the Government, it is not at all rent by any dialectics of doubt, it is honouring them, those who brought us freedom. In their turn, hemmed in by penury and pestilence, what do these yesterday's noble patriots feel about these twenty-five years of freedom? Could it be that their cerebral reactions have exclusively got sublimated into this feeble lobby for persuading the Government to fork out, alas, some extra wherewithal for survival? Old people, they say, forget. But is it that their recollections are gone in their entirety? Bereft of ideals, bereft of emotions, the baggage of old bones is all that they have to offer?

Many of these ladies and gentlemen, when their days were on flame, used to dream of a classless state, of a pristine socialism, of a society where exploitation in any form would be taboo, where there may or may not be plenty, but whatever there will be, will be shared evenly and equally amongst all One feels like searching in their eyes. Do they think that that state of thraldom has arrived? Was this, was this the face that launched a thousand ships, and burned the city of Troy?

The memory haunts. The memory of early dreams, the memory of oaths devoutly undertaken, careers forsaken, temptations thrust aside. Thirty or thirty-five years ago, you could not walk down a lane or by-lane of any East Bengal town, be it Dacca, or Mymensingh. Or Faridpur, or Barisal, without somebody pointing out a house from where a son had been sent away to the Andamans, or interned in a village, or externed to a different province; a daughter who had been chucked out of college for picketing, or had done a term during the days of civil disobedience. It was a curious menagerie of ideologies which got grafted in those young hearts: stray readings from Bankim Chandra Chatterji and Tagore; a whiff of the declamations from Tilak and C.R. Das; now and then the message of Gandhi Maharaj as he was then endearingly called; the example of McSweeney the Irishman; the charm and charisma of Subhas Bose; smuggled documents scribbled and smuggled out by terrorists in prison or on the run; those early tracts on the wonderful, wonderful Russian revolution: Maxim Gorky, Lenin, Bukharin; here and there, some unassimilated bits and pieces from Marx. Thousands marched, thousands thronged the prison; a few took to the pistol; several, gradually, moved toward the Communist cause. Particularly this last called for a certain intellectual conversion. These young men and women generally came from a solid Hindu middle-class base, whose sustenance depended upon the exploitation of the lower peasantry, mostly made up of Muslims and those belonging to the depressed sections. For those who took to socialism, there was thus a question of acute choice, one's convictions cut athwart one's class interests. They gladly made the transition. Forsaking homes and old loyalties, they fanned into the countryside to organise the poor peasants, pioneered the trade union movement in Greater Calcutta's jute belt, radicalised the students. As famine stalked the land in the early 1940s and millions died; they, empathy writ large on their hearts, were again there, whatever little relief they could organise they organised with grit and ferocity. Perhaps what kept them going was their ability to dream, and their all-encompassing faith that, one day, their dreams were going to come true.

Partition, and the holocaust accompanying it, put paid to all that.Somebody's perseverence is always somebody else's opportunity. And the Bengali Hindu middle class got hopelessly caught in the contradictions of its position. With East Bengal suddenly torn away and a part of Pakistan, the correlate of terra firma was denied to the vast majority of the revolutionaries and political radicals. For a time, they tried to stay back in East Bengal and evolve new political patterns. The attempt did not succeed, and the trek to West Bengal began. The families of many of these political sufferers were caught in pincers; assets were lost across the border, the education of children was rudely disturbed, and even arranging a bare shelter posed problems. In truncated West Bengal, the content of political activity was gradually transformed. Refugee camps kept multiplying in and around Calcutta, alienation became as much the reality as the ideological theme, the prosperity which touched the top decile of the community passed by most of yesterday's freedom fighters, just as much as it passed by the overwhelming majority of the nation's population in these parts. Old soldiers do not die, they fade away. Bengal's crop largely disappeared in the alleys of the Left political parties of diverse shades. Some made good in polemics and intra-party feudings. But the bulk of them simply disintegrated into the anonymity of hard-up, peripheral existence. The hucksters took over the Congress party: several of the groupings on the Left too became heavily infiltrated by smart alecs and other opportunists who succeeded in carving a career out of parliamentary dissent. Yesterday's radicals and ideologues were pushed out: penury and oblivion claimed them. No Government has enquired of their fate during the past twenty-five years. Having sacrificed the best years of their lives for achieving the independence of a nation which could not care less for them, without any moorings of capital assets, without friends and connections in the right places, for these heroes and heroines of yesteryear, the quarter of a century of freedom has been a period of waiting and drifting, a period which has witnessed the total crumbling of the old world—and the old values. The offspring born to them would have nothing but contempt for parents who were so thoroughly incapable of cashing in on the years expended on patriotic fervour. Many of these children have slunk into the underworld. Some of the rest, like their parents, may have got themselves enmeshed in the politics of the Left, but that too may not indicate the assertion of any hopes, it would be more in the nature of a conditioned gesture. Once the lights go out of your life, you join the movement of protest: it is not really an act of faith as such, not even an act of defiance, you merely take the easiest way out and follow those who, tantalisingly, succeed in making dissent appear as a credible, viable alternative. At the slightest threat to life or limb, however, you would rat and join your class enemies.

The episode of Bangladesh has come and gone. For a few fleeting weeks, there was an emotional lift for these old men and women. The rivers and rivulets of East Bengal, the motor launches and boats, the railway junctions and the odd, as if half-heartedly constructed, highways, the mofussil towns with their schools, colleges, parks—for a few brief moments, a stirring of old memories, a return to one's old locales and dreams, a vicarious re-living of one's many exploits of heroism and valour.

The therapy could not last, and did not. These aged people, ever short of funds, squalor and hopelessness writ large on their wrinkled faces, are now entirely without co-ordinates. The India whose freedom from colonial subjugation is supposed to be past a quarter of a century this week, is altogether an unknown category to them. For consider the context. Precariously huddled in a near-collapsing Calcutta slum, rain water dripping all round, the stench of refuse and night soil, a general state of dampness in the air, undernourished, the children mostly gone astray, slouching on a creaking cot, they read bizarre news items. We can only savour a sample. A gentleman, who till the other day was a Finance Minister of Mysore, has demanded a crash programme for increasing many-fold the output of beer and for a drastic reduction in the excise chargeable on the beverage; beer, the gentleman has argued, is the common man's drink, and all efforts must be made to expand its production. Or take another piece of news, emanating last month from Bombay. The boys and girls in a college had launched a strike, the boys to assert their right to wear drainpipe trousers and the girls to assert their prerogative to wear mini-skirts with the daringest possible lift of the hemline. Even as these exciting events were unfolding, the Union Minister for Tourism and Civil Aviation was announcing a futuristic plan for developing the Capital's airport: glistening facilities, domes after domes, aluminium tapestries, hexagonal dreams piled one upon the other, sophisticated patterns to gladden the heart of Buckminster Fuller who, in fact, will supervise the construction.

As they alighted at New Delhi's ceremonial platform, somewhat unsure of their feet, a mixture of curiosity and apprehension in their heart, one wishes one could take aside some of the battle-worn political sufferers and ask them: please, was this the image of freedom in their minds, the socialism they had dreamed of ? Was this, was this the face that launched a thousand ships. . . .

1972

3 The Country Will Not Miss Him

There was no avalanche of flowers. The Bengalis were busy celebrating their Durga Puja. Quite early one morning during the Pujas, Nirmal Kumar Bose passed away—quietly, almost matter-of-factly. Nothing illustrated the personality of the man more than the manner of his death. Nirmal Kumar Bose hated formalism. He was scared of pedantry. He used to veto ceremony. He abhorred stuffiness, in politicians as much as in scholars. A totally unassuming person, he wore his learning lightly. Even in his death, he could not hit the newspaper headlines. Unobtrusively, one of that rarest breed—a civilised person—departed from the scene.

Meanwhile, buffoons with their interminable talk of the Central Intelligence Agency and other inanities trot on the stage. Shady specimens pontificate on the content of culture and the morphology of Indian tradition. Values are set by charlatans who dress themselves up as savants. Pots of silver determine the quantum of scholarship. Nirmal Kumar Bose was a man of immense civilisation. It merely reflects the state of barbarity this nation has reached in the course of the past quarter of a century that there was so little mention of his death even amongst men with academic attitudes. Newspapers salvaged their conscience by setting aside one or two brief paragraphs of obituary. The politicians, of course, could not care less.

Was he an anthropologist? Even if he were one, was he a pure one? Or was he what is described as a cultural anthropologist?

But since he had a background in natural sciences and encouraged even anthropometric studies, could not the physical anthropologists too claim him as one of their own? Then, again, go through his writings: will it not be inane to dub him a narrow anthropologist? Would you not call him a sociologist in the most liberal sense, in the widest expanse of that expression? Nirmal Kumar Bose defied, and consistently, set concepts. He strayed way beyond sociology and had observations to make, and contributions to offer, on art and religion, sculpture and musicology, philosophy and philology, or, at the mundane level, even demography and geological surveys. He surely had students ranging in over a dozen individual arts and sciences. He had time for each one of them, took pride in their success and achievements: each one of them, in turn, would proudly acknowledge the heritage.

But this man hated scholasticism. From Calcutta University's Department of Anthropology he moved with effortless grace to the Anthropological Survey of India, an organisation he created and nurtured with love and doting care. There can be no study of anthropology without a liking for man. Nirmal Kumar Bose was interested in human beings, human beings not just as museum and physiological specimens, but human beings who are receptacles and articulators of ideas and emotions, human beings who are moved by passion, who are struck by tragedy. But his eclecticism made him equally interested in tracing the history of human beings who were—and are—the victims of material, including economic, exploitation. Indeed, he himself was a most curious anthropological specimen: a disciple of Gandhi who did not mind breaking bread with lesser mortals; a Congressman who did not consider a Marxist to be altogether an untouchable. Here was a cultural anthropologist who knew everything about tribes and castes, but who had the catholicity to admit that castes do often break into economic classes. He was invited in his time by the Government to join them as the Commissioner for Scheduled Castes and Scheduled Tribes. But, despite his party alignments, he could not be prevented from speaking out the truth that, under the garb of kindness to these castes and tribes, the Government was very often their worst enemy, or that protecting the interests of these castes and tribes has become the portfolio of some self-seeking professional opportunists. Nirmal Kumar Bose did not, could not survive in the Government; but that is a blot on the record of the Government, not on his.

It is the spectrum of interests this fascinating man covered which is so awesome. Nirmal Kumar Bose was interested in scanning the commandments of Manu: he was absorbed by the exquisite aesthetics of the temples of Orissa; the behaviour patterns of the tribals in the Nicobar Islands gripped him just as much as the dance rhythm of the Munda women in Bihar. In all his activities, he never allowed himself to fall a victim of stereotypical responses, nor of specific sets of preferences. The philosophy of non-violence enthralled him, but the grinding poverty, the economic disparity and the social disorganisation of the vast metropolis of Calcutta nagged him no less: that hungry people would prefer to kill did not strike him as perverse. With all his faith in the abiding virtues of Hindu culture, he had the grace to admit that we have no indigenous tradition of science and have to borrow heavily from the Western sciences and historiography. All our commitments, he would aver, should be towards the liberation of mankind. But there was no trace of dogma in the assertion: the liberation of mankind, Nirmal Kumar Bose could not more readily agree, was amenable to multiple interpretations, and could be approached via multiple routes.

A couple of years ago, on the occasion of his seventieth birthday, a few of his admirers had got together and organised a seminar on the cultural profile of Calcutta. Surajit Sinha has lovingly brought together the papers and proceedings of the seminar in an impressive volume (*Cultural Profile of Calcutta*, the Indian Anthropological Society). Those who admired Nirmal Kumar Bose, those who loved him, those whom he loved and respected, will find many of Bose's ideas and predilections reflected in this volume. He believed in diversities; in his academic enquiries, he had an almost restless urge to break away from the shackles of monism into the wide, bracing welcome of pluralism. In this volume one finds, amongst others, Mrinal Sen and Mohim Roodro, for example, writing about the creativity and frustrations of Calcutta's artists, sculptors, movie-makers, musicians and dancers. Professional anthropologists discuss Calcutta's clash of dialects and linguistic diversities; others discuss the inter-group attitudes in Calcutta's vast social melting pot. There is a piece by the editors on the Kali temple, which no doubt Nirmal Kumar Bose would have fawned upon. There are yet others writing on Calcutta's elite, Calcutta's goondas, Calcutta's mentally disorientated ones, Calcutta's scientists, Calcutta's parasitic tribe of business executives. There is also a report on a typical Calcutta adda—something which Nirmal Kumar Bose used to gloat on—on Calcutta's problems. Finally, there is the text of a valedictory address by Bose himself, which is the quintessence of his values, of his humility, as well as of his precise scientific attitudes, of his pride in scholarly pursuits and of his affection for succeeding generations of scholars.

The country will not miss him; the politicians will cynically consider his death a good riddance: he, after all, was a witness to many hypocrisies. A noble human being however is, and remains, a noble human being even if no plaques are laid. If India still bumbles along, it is despite the politicians and because of people like Nirmal Kumar Bose who, like little islands, sustained in themselves the culture which makes India tick. The man with the wanderlust, the man who thought nothing of combining a roughly-hewn khadi *kurta* and *dhoti* with a pair of sturdy tennis shoes will not be around any more, but those amongst the humble ones who were privileged to get to know him will, jealously, cling to the memory of his many affections.

1972

4 Take A Girl Like Her

She cannot quite recollect her childhood days in the East Bengal village. For our purpose, it is irrelevant to know whether the village was in Dacca or Faridpur or what was quaintly known as Buckergunge. It was one of those typical middle-class families: a few acres of paddy land given to tenants and share-croppers, one or two tanks lush with fish, an orchard crammed with mango and jackfruit trees, the father not particularly interested in taking a job away from home, the usual quota of nondescript uncles and quarrelsome, gossipy aunts, the mother spending her time mostly in the kitchen or otherwise in confinement, the brothers, some given to kite-flying, one or two very bright in studies. The world as it was known till then came to an end for several thousands of such families between 1947 and 1950. There is a certain obfuscation of memory here, possibly because the mere recollection of events means re-living the mental and physical agony. The panicky decision to move, moderate assets left behind in entirety, the forced-upon, reluctant hospitality of near or distant relations in Calcutta, the scrounging for favour from petty officialdom, finally ending up in the colony, let us say, in Garia. There was always a vagueness in what the father was capable of earning on his own: that vagueness was soon removed. The mother's meagre jewels kept on disappearing fast: soon the nodal point of being becoming nothingness was reached. Some of the brothers went astray; if they were lucky, they were picked up by the political elements, so that there was a partial sublimation of their frustrations. Even those of the brothers who were bright in school had to break off studies for lack of wherewithal. They have become clerks in mercantile firms, one of them perhaps a messenger in Writers' Building; the one who was the luckiest—because, through the intercession of a relative, he could get into a vocational school—is now back home in the colony, in the two-and-a-quarter room tenement; he got retrenched last year.

But it is the sister one wanted to talk about. She turned out to be a miracle. Nobody through all these rough, rugged years paid any attention to her. She has been used to doing the chores ever since she can remember, rushing around in a tattered, discoloured frock. There was no milk for her ever, fish—a flimsy apology of it—perhaps once a week; as the succession of disasters and calamities unfolded for the family, she was a neglected member of the cast. There is no getting away from economic determinism: such instincts as love or affection or empathy are to a large extent a function of economic circumstances. Although the youngest in the family, nobody could spare a thought for her. Once the middle-class veneer is stripped away, the mode of intercommunication in such families is uncouth, horribly so. Maybe, a subterranean layer of emotion is still there, but it dares not come up—any such show of emotions will be considered rank bad manners. So the sister grew up, without love, without any future. But things happened. She was going to the girls' school abutting the colony; despite interruptions, lack of books, lack of adequate tuition, lack of time to study at home, she passed the high-school examination, and did surprisingly well. Another two years of intermediate arts in the girls' college three miles away—two extremely rough years, for the father died, one of the brothers, who got mixed up with a communist youth group, was locked away in prison, the last of the mother's jewels disappeared, chronic shortage of food because of the chronic shortage of money, because you are unable to run up even a credit, the only credit available is the sort of revolving arrangement you have with your equally impoverished neighbours in the colony. But, this time too, she got through in the first division. The college principal was kind, she arranged for a few tuitions which the girl could squeeze in in the mornings, which fetched fifty rupees a month. This stretch to the B.A. degree was the most critical of all: another of the brothers got killed in a police firing, the mother, by now a permanent arthritic, could no longer cope with even the very modest cooking; the usual problems which afflict a girl leading a privacy-less existence in a chattel came crowding in. Once more she came through. By now, the Durgapur brother was managing to send some money home, but that was neither here nor there. Whoever takes on the load of responsibility for once gets stuck with it forever. No question about it, everybody, mother included, took it for granted that the girl would go about earning the extra money. With a modicum of knowledge of typing, she could possibly try for the post of a lower division assistant. But she did not have any typing, and she preferred to teach. It was, however, necessary to have a teachers' training degree if you wanted to apply for a school teacher's job. So the girl piled on a few more tuitions, rushed cooking for the family, attending lectures during the day, on the wayback home another tuition. It was worth it. With a B.T., she has been able to secure a post in a higher secondary school: all told, an accretion of an additional two hundred and fifty rupees for the family.

Unfortunately, the school is way north in Dum Dum, but beggars cannot be choosers. The girl gets up between 4.30 and 5 in the morning: one brother leaves for work at 6.15, so whatever cooking has to be done has to be done by 6; after serving tea and some breakfast to mother and the other brothers, she hurriedly gets ready. Two tuitions have to be crowded in before 9. Luckily, both are in the neighbourhood, and she manages somehow. Hurrying back, she eats her lunch, arranges things for mother, with silent, rapid efficiency completes the bulk of the washing-up. A run for the bus stop; she catches it, gets a seat, has her first moment of leisure since morning. She has to change buses at Sealdah and this time it is very much more crowded, often she has to stand for almost half the way before a seat becomes available: whatever energy was recouped in the first thirty minutes of the journey withers in the heat and the jostle. By the time she reaches school, it is past eleven, she is fifteen minutes late. But the headmistress is understanding, she has been permitted to skip the prayer. Still, from then on, it is a crowded agony: but for half-an-hour's mid-afternoon recess, the shouting chore is continuous, and managing thirty-odd under-teen children for five hours can be an exhausting process. In between, her only nourishment is perhaps a banana carried from home, and a cup of watery tea. She catches the bus again at 4.30 and pushes her way out at Sealdah. Her third tuition of the day: some days the child's mother offers her a cup of tea, plus a few snacks; but this does not happen every day. It is dusk; she collects some vegetables and sundries at Sealdah, and now, fatigue and dust and perspiration, each nearly indistinguishable from the other, the bus to Garia. Back home, a brief wash, and the household chores left over from the morning. Feeding the mother, waiting for the brothers to return late in the evening, working out a version of an aide memoire about what lessons to teach in the class the following day, matching the sums of a budget which—every evening of the year—remains agonisingly impossible, stitching something or other, the dull, claustrophobic summer heat or the shiver of the northerly winds during the cooler months, the flimsy meal late at night; sleep, merciful sleep, if it comes, another day, another monologue with hopelessness.

No, there is no variation in the theme from day to day. She has nothing to look forward to, she has nothing to plan for, except the short-term arithmetic of how much to try to borrow from which neighbour or school colleague, this week, the following week, the week following the following week, and so on. There is no poetry or music in her life. The brothers are away in the evenings, she stays home in the tenement with the mother. The last movie she saw was perhaps eighteen months ago. The brothers go to the Maidan meetings, or join the processions; but for her, even such slogan-mongering is vicarious. There was one occasion some months ago when she went with the rest of the teaching fraternity to squat outside Raj Bhavan, but the direct experience of such thrills is few and far between. Occasionally, the brothers, in the company of friends, would waste money in a Chowringhee or Ballygunge restaurant—maybe the money earned by her, for she is the leading earner in the family, and the entire salary she meticulously hands over to the mother. Nobody cares to ask how many saris she has: her toilet equipment consists of a cheap hair oil, a still cheaper jar of facial cream, and a tin of nondescript talcum powder. Nothing to crow over her vital statistics: weight seventy-nine pounds, the haemoglobin count in the red corpuscles down to 71 per cent, chronic inflammation of the pleura. There is no question of marriage. Those first flurries of colony romances died down soon: you need a minimal glow of health even for divertissements like that. This Bengali girl is nobody's desire. No, she has nothing to look forward to, spinsterdom, give or take a few years, is going to set in early, an anonymous poem will fade and die, as unobtrusively as it survived. Or shall we say sub-survived?

Last month, the rains came. Water stayed in the colony for nearly nine days, the apology of the sewerage was washed away, each of the rooms of the tenement had water up to two and a half feet above the floor. The mother could be removed to a kindly relation's place; a trunk, full of clothes, was a total loss; a brother contracted pneumonia; she herself was running a high temperature; but, somehow, the cooking had to be done, money had to be borrowed; prices, already high, shot up even as the water was receding, rice cost much more than it did about the same time last month; some fish had to be had for the convalescent brother; the ever not-ending agony of the budget which refuses to match, and is incapable of matching.

Take a girl like her. Take just any girl like her, for there are several thousands. And please spare the part-time sentiments. Does the tragedy of her existence—or even her withering—count for anything at all? When we talk of a total transformation of society, do we include the import of her frail being in our calculations? She cannot recollect her childhood; mercifully, she does not react at all when the mother, all wistfulness, whines about her grandfather's suzerainty over eleven and a half mouzas in the district of Dacca, or Faridpur, or Buckergunge. If only somebody provides her with the moral suasion, she may yet succeed in stepping out of the shackles of middle-class semi-respectability. The uprooting of the existing class base will perhaps come one day, but it would be sheer cussedness to suggest that meanwhile she must wait. Her stepping out itself will be a blow for social transformation. Those who would want her to take her turn in the queue are irresponsible, and deserve to be condemned. Something has to be done, now, with a girl like her. She must not be wasted.

But maybe all this is airing of part-time sentiments. Do we rant against the mother, shower invectives on the brothers? Supposing they allow the girl—reluctantly, but nonetheless allow the girl—to run away to her own future, what will they do, how will they manage? Do we have the answer? And yet, with what face do we look up to a girl like her?

1968

5 The Song of Mother Courage

It is not absolutely necessary to invoke Bertolt Brecht to imbibe the Song of Mother Courage. If one is looking for grit, one can still find plenty of that quality even in this neighbourhood. The umpteen frustrations notwithstanding, little islets of fortitude, patience, courage spring up almost every day. If one has a spare morning or afternoon, it could be an interesting interlude to hop around the suburbs of Calcutta, and visit the vast congregations of camps and townships crowded by the refugees from what was till the other day East Pakistan. These specimens of sub-marginal existence have grown and spilled over in the course of the past twenty-five years. Whatever the reasons, they are the antipodes of the Punjab, the archetypal non-success story. At a low level, these colonies and shanty towns still represent a form of creativity, the creativity of passive acceptance, of the squalor and the filth and the hopelessness of it all. Life is crude and rude, and full of daily vicissitudes. A community of people, who lost practically their all across the border, have not been able to discover new moorings despite a quarter of century's shufflings. On the contrary, there will be an earful of complaints about how they have brought the precarious economy of West Bengal further down. Here and there, there are isolated cases of success. An odd boy from a refugee camp has done exceedingly well in the examinations, received grants and scholarships, landed a good job or joined the administrative service, and disappeared, from the camp, taking his parents and brothers and sisters along. An odd girl has demonstrated her natural talents in the finer arts, or has been discovered by a film director, and has suddenly emerged as a celebrity; she too, along with her people, has moved out of the colony. But for the vast multitude, it has been a story of monotonic squalor. Neither government subsidies nor individual initiatives have succeeded in ushering in any miracle. Poverty has piled upon poverty; joblessness and lack of assets have reinforced each other; slummy conditions of living have increasingly engendered a slumminess of the mind. The absence of gainful means of livelihood has gradually led to a steady loss of values. These colonies, there is little wonder, have provided a large chunk of the raw recruits for Calcutta's flourishing underworld. Boys from the refugee conclaves soon by-passed the short season of being in schools; they quickly learnt to break wagons, wield knives, throw bombs, do highway-robbing. In those halcyon days, they had mouthed the Maoist slogans, perhaps because of an accidental convergence between their operational preferences and a specific corpus of Naxalite practice. They have also been the first to fall prey to the enticements and bullyings on the part of the forces of law and order, and swelled the ranks of the so-called civic guards raised a while ago to suppress the Leftist tide in and around Calcutta. Again, it is these young people from the refugee camps and townships who have constituted the hard core of the lumpen groups who are now the standard-bearers of the Congress party's resurgence in this State. They are a totally amoral lot; morality in any case goes ill with lack of food. They will follow any flag, bash any head, break any strike, provided you dole them out the hard cash. At the sweet jingle of money, they can work themselves up to the most improbable heights of frenzy.

Trace the genealogy and you will discover that many of these young people have their roots in the erstwhile landed gentry of East Bengal; this is a community of high-caste goons. It has taken the space of a bare thirty years to reduce the scions of a proud, landowning aristocracy into the filthiest social scum. A certain gradualness has marked the process, but also a certain inevitability. Bit by bit, year after year, there has been a steady drop in assets as well as incomes; bit by bit, year after year, the standard of living has worsened, penury has become an acuter reality, conventional mores have given in to the compulsions of the daily reality. Since so little of the assets could be smuggled across the border, there was in any case little scope for living off capital. By and large, there were no alternative skills to the accidental one of land-owning. No surrogate means of living became available; after an interval of time, the boys went a-stealing, the girls perhaps kept their wits and, through various improvisations, managed to bring some extra cash home at the end of each month. By now this is almost a stylised story, and will cover the instances of literally thousands of households.

Depending upon one's attitude, this could be a saga of nobility—how a people, suddenly struck by lightning, have bravely negotiated through the turmoil of their fate; how, tucking in all false senses of dignity, the offspring of the upper-caste Hindu *bhadralok* have embraced the empirical correlates of the unfolding world. Alternatively, one can sum up this entire episode as part of the inevitable historical process: the feudal remnants are the victims of history's retribution; they are getting what they richly deserve on account of the follies and foibles perpetrated by their blood-sucking ancestors.

And yet, whatever one's point of view, it would be difficult not to recognise the singular courage which has often accompanied this unrolling of the historical process. Take a septuagenarian or an octogenarian lady in any of these refugee townships. She has seen history, telescoped history, being enacted in rapid motion before her nearly-incredulous eyes in the course of the past two scores of years. In the late 1930s or early 1940s, she was perhaps the proud czarina presiding over the household of the landlord who had ten or twenty mousas in Mymensingh, Dacca or Barisal as his fief. Life was placid and majestic; income was regular and easy; there was an unending cycle of ceremonies and festivities; family deities and family jewels cast a devastating lustre all around. There was no dearth of manpower and cronies; heads would roll even as the landlord would express his mildest annoyance at the demeanor of this or that group of individuals. The British were still very much the major imperial power, and the landlord was his direct agent.

Enter the Muslim League. 1947 was a tornado. In one mad sweep, it felled all: the land was gone, along with the jewels and the other assets. The husband was the lucky one, he died in good time. But the lady survived, the witness to history. As the pace of developments accelerated, the decision was taken, she left East Pakistan along with the children and grandchildren. She has since then negotiated each successive stage of immiserisation. Each stage can be clearly separated from the preceding one. Arrival in Calcutta and a brief stay with relations; renting a house or an apartment in the city centre; as the savings are drained, the size of the apartment grows smaller and smaller. All the while, the sons try to wangle jobs, mostly unsuccessfully: current income drops to zero. As savings are practically all exhausted, the family moves out of Calcutta proper and into a suburb. Soon, even a suburban flat proves too expensive, the family of the noble lord swallows its pride and settles in a refugee colony. Along with others, the family appropriates a puny plot of land, and builds a half-pucca structure. From then on, there is a sudden qualitative leap. Once you are reconciled to the destiny of being part of a collective whole, the family of the landlord forsakes its genealogy and becomes indistinguishable from the rest of the community of refugees. A common pattern of misfortunes begins to bind the families together. The grandson goes astray, maybe the girl goes a-whoring. But the Grand Dame lives through it all; she nudges aside the memory of her mansion and adjusts herself to the leaky, claustrophobic hut. Coping with the adversities, this one even more calamitous than the last one, has now become a habit with her. A philosophical calm has descended upon her countenance. Take her aside and engage her in gentle conversation. She has not got anything out of the country's independence apart from the inexorable slide toward pauperisation. Much more than any of the rest of the family, she is the one who has suffered the most. Yet, there is a certain inner reservoir of courage in her. She has been able to sail through the remorseless process of history much better than the rest of the household. Talk with her, there is no rancour in her heart. She has seen it all, has absorbed it all. Starvation, filth and cold pin her down. Miracles, she knows only too well, have had their day, and she will live her last flickering days condemned to the present squalor. So be it: she does not complain; she has not lost her faith either. Talk with Mother Courage, she has perhaps one or two surprises up her sleeve for you. What wears her down, you get to learn, is not that her grandchild has turned into an illiterate boor, but that he has turned into a common criminal. The old lady complains not of poverty, but of the wholesale erosion of values which the poverty has brought about. Her grandchildren, she argues, should have developed the courage to de-class themselves all the way and earn an honest living from manual work. Instead, they have chosen the life of wagon-breakers and knife-wielders. The tragedy, she will confess to you, is not that she failed to bequeath her legacy of riches to her grandchildren; it is that she failed to bequeath her legacy of courage. They, her own grandchildren, chickened out: instead of joining the working class, they have joined the lumpens. Is it her personal failure, or the failure of the society, she wonders. She will keep wondering till, one day at dusk, life ebbs out of her courageous heart.

1973

6 The Story of Indra Lohar

What follows is an authentic story. To every age its personalised sermon: protecting the little fellow, uplifting him, deploying the total weight of the administrative and judicial process so that the scales of justice could be always differentially tilted towards him, is the approved version of applied philosophy today. But does that at all disturb the placidity of real things and actual events? The story of Indra Lohar, a petty share-cropper, would suggest otherwise.

The rights and privileges of share-croppers—*bargadars*, as they are known in this neighbourhood—are spelled out in great detail in the West Bengal Land Reforms Act of 1955. The Act was amended twice in the very recent period—in 1970 as well as in 1971—to plug conceivable loopholes. The amended Act provides meticulous guidelines for regulating the crop share payable to the landowner: it also lays down explicit instructions for ensuring the security of tenure. The produce of the land cultivated by the share-cropper, it says, shall be divided between him and the landowner in equal proportion in those cases where plough, cattle, manure and seeds necessary for cultivation are supplied by the owner, and in the proportion of three-fourths and one-fourth in all other cases. The Act confers on the share-cropper permanency of tenure. The termination of tenancy is to be allowed only for bona fide cultivation by the owner himself, and only if the extent of land so resumed, together with any other land already under the latter's personal cultivation, does not exceed seven and a half acres and, further, provided the share-cropper is left with at least two acres. In addition, the share-cropper has now been blessed with heritable rights in respect of the land he cultivates; he is not liable to eviction on the ground of non-payment of rent: the orders for eviction on this ground are not to become effective if the share-cropper delivers the dues within such time and at such instalments as the designated authorities may specify.

Some cosmetics were added to the Act during the days of the President's Rule in the State in 1971. New Delhi really went into ecstasy over the progressive character of the latest piece of legislation; one even remembers an occasion when the highest in the land trumpeted to the world the revolution embodied in the West Bengal Act. Let us, however, turn to the story of Indra Lohar. Indra used to cultivate plot number nine of Mouza Tala, measuring roughly 4.97 acres, in the village Vora, coming under the jurisdiction of the police station Vishnupur in the district of Bankura. He had been cultivating this land for more than twenty years, under oral lease from Shrimati Annapurna Devi, the daughter of Bibhuti Bhusan Mandal. The veil of the daughter notwithstanding, Mandal was the landlord. Indra Lohar did not get his name recorded as tenant at the time of the last revisional settlement a decade ago. He did not do so presumably because Mandal would not have liked it. Indra was a loyal share-cropper, siding always with the landlord, staying away from the slogan-mongering Left parties, continuing to pay fifty-five per cent of the share of the crop to Mandal even though under the law he was required to pay only forty. The turbulence of the outside world did not affect his sub-marginal existence: he remained a timid, raja-fearing, self-effacing, petty share-cropper, resigned to his poverty.

Unfortunately for Lohar, Bibhuti Mandal passed away in

early 1971. The old order changeth yielding place to the new: while Annapurna Devi continued as the benami owner of Indra's plot, Mandal's son, Sachinandan, now took over as de facto landlord. Trouble started to brew. Sachinandan had heard of capitalist farming; somebody must have also told him of the wonders of I.R. paddy. At the completion of the aman harvest of 1971-72, he called in Indra and asked him to vacate the land. Indra prayed for mercy, and was prepared to pay the landlord even beyond fifty-five per cent of the crop. But oral lease was oral lease, and Sachinandan would not budge. Those whom God wants to destroy, he first turns them mad. Indra was gripped by madness: he turned to one or two political elements in the village, was told of the amended Act, and advised to move the court of law. The poor *bargadar* accordingly filed a petition in the court of the Sub-divisional Executive Magistrate, Vishnupur, under Section 144 of the Criminal Procedure Code, alleging that the benami landlord was trying to evict him from the land. The Sub-divisional Magistrate took cognisance and directed the Junior Land Reforms Officer of the area to institute an enquiry. The enquiry did not lead anywhere. Counter-petitions on behalf of Sachinandan followed, duly matched by yet others from Indra Lohar. The Sub- divisional Magistrate ordered a further enquiry by the local Agricultural Extension Officer, who reported that even though Indra's name did not feature in the record of rights, there was evidence of an overwhelming nature substantiating his claim as a *bargadar*. Meanwhile, however, it was already late February 1972, the elections to the State Assembly were a-coming, a-coming, and the Magistrate decided to postpone the hearing on the cases.

The elections were held. Contrived or not, a total debacle

overtook the Left parties. Once more, the old order changeth yielding place to new. On the morning of 18 April, the police raided the house of Indra Lohar and seized thirty-two bags of paddy, three kahans of straw and a certain quantity of unthreshed paddy. These properties, a subsequent enquiry revealed, were seized by the police neither in connection with any specific case nor under the orders of any court. There were not even any entries in the registers of the police station regarding the seizure. All that had happened was Nature taking its course. The elections were over, the protectors of the landlords were massively back in power, and the officer in charge of the police station considered it his bounden duty to teach the rascally *bargadar*, who had dared to file a suit against his landlord, an appropriate lesson. The fact of the seizure was reported to the Sub-divisional Magistrate, who called for an explanation from the police. While all this was going on, Sachinandan filed a title suit in the court of the local Munsiff praying for an injunction restraining Indra Lohar from proceeding with the case in the Sub-divisional Magistrate's court. The Munsiff readily complied with the request; the injunction was issued. Things moved pretty fast from then on. In the early hours of 22 May, Indra Lohar's house was attacked by a group of rowdies, he and members of his family were badly beaten up, and the residual stock of his paddy was carried away; Indra himself had to be moved to hospital. As the case came up for hearing in the Executive Magistrate's court, the landowner produced a certified copy of the order of the Munsiff preventing Lohar from pursuing the case. The Magistrate, apparently peeved, passed an order noting that the Munsiff's injunction was anomalous and amounted to an interference with the powers and jurisdiction of his court. The Munsiff was not one to take this lying down. He straightaway moved to the High Court, praying contempt of court proceedings against Indra Lohar, Indra's lawyer and the Executive Magistrate. The wheels of justice are supposed to move slowly—but not in this instance. The High Court of Calcutta has reportedly more than fifty thousand cases currently pending before it; that did not prevent it from taking speedy cognisance of the complaint of the Munsiff. A criminal case was lodged in August against the Executive Magistrate, Lohar and his lawyer. Shri S. Saha, Executive Magistrate, First Class, Vishnupur, tendered an unqualified apology before the High Court in October.

Indra Lohar and his lawyer did the same thing. The battle was over. Indra, physically crippled by the wounds inflicted upon him during the raid, is now sans land, sans his stock of paddy, sans any further courage to take the law of the land at its face value. The law of the land, the wretched fellow has learned from his somewhat traumatic experience, is only for the protection of the rich in society; the poor have no business to attempt to have recourse to it.

This case is neither gossip nor hearsay. Indra Lohar's story is narrated in a study which was undertaken for the Task Force on Agrarian Relations, the Planning Commission and the Working Group on Land Reforms, National Commission on Agriculture, by a group of State government officials. This is how, in the study, the curtain is drawn on Indra Lohar's story:

> When he was admitted to the hospital after being wounded, India's prognosis was uncertain. It is not so now. Persecuted by his Jotedar, assaulted and plundered by his hired hoodlums, harassed and intimidated by the police, restrained by the Civil Court from preferring his legal claim before the appropriate legal forum, hauled up by the High Court of Judicature at Fort William in Bengal for lowering the 'dignity and prestige'

of the Court, Indra Lohar lost his will to fight for his right. He paid rather dearly for his temerity to assert his notional rights embodied in law. Maimed and feeble, defeated and dejected, Indra has now bowed down before the majesty of the established order and stands dispossessed of his land.

Whatever legislation you pass, you can never circumvent the combined attitudinal biases of the bureaucracy and the judiciary. It may be rendering homage to cliche to talk all the time of the inherent deficiencies of the system, but can one deny that the entire burden of civil and criminal laws, judicial pronouncements and precedents, administrative tradition and practices is heavily loaded in favour of the socially privileged groups? Deep calls to the deep, and a judge or a police officer hailing from the propertied classes tends to bend the interpretation of the law to serve the interests of his class cousins. There are, one dares to say, hundreds and thousands of Indra Lohars in West Bengal, Assam, Bihar and Orissa. Socialistic pontifications will continue to be there, but it will not make the slightest difference to the reality of things. There might have been a difference if there were a living, pulsating, organised movement of the peasantry themselves, which could strike from below, apply pressure on the bureaucracy and the judiciary all along the line, and instil a healthy fear of the power of the masses in the minds of the police. But the ersatz revolution the country has witnessed has for the present put paid to all that. The political elements who advised Indra to go to court have disappeared, either picked up by the police or, in the transformed political milieu, liquidated by the landlord's goondas. Like it or not, the Indra Lohars of the country will have to wait a while before the tide of history will turn once more.

1973

7 All That Lives Must Die

These are cynical times, and the dividing line between sentimentality and ridiculousness can be altogether thin. This piece, nonetheless, is dedicated to slushy emotions. Toss it away if it nauseates you.

Mrinal Sen's *Calcutta '71* has a claustrophobic last scene, claustrophobic because it cuts across notions about what may or may not happen in our ordinary world of reality. Certain unnamed goose-stepping gunners shoot down a starry-eyed, defenceless young man against the vast expanse of a misty early morning in the Calcutta maidan. No bird chirps, the young man dies a writhing death, the sound of the shots is no doubt drowned in the seeming indifference of the heartless city. It does not matter though. About everybody knows the identity of the young man, and of the goose-stepping gunners. Everybody knows, but few will talk. You ask no questions, and you will be told no lies. Mrinal Sen has his difficulties. He has to have a cover, he must keep on making the kind of films he wants to make. The killers therefore remained unnamed.

But the film was hardly a parable, that particular episode hardly an allegory. You talk in private with senior men belonging to the administration: from the second quarter of 1970 onwards, they will admit, the police were given summary powers to hunt down and kill 'undesirable' elements. Dead men generally carry no tales, and the evidence of such killings is claimed by oblivion. The social and political philosophy of those in power determines the contours of 'undesirability'. Once these have been spelled out, the police have the *laissez passer* to go to town, really and truly, on a murder binge. No need any more to conform to the droll literalness of 'self-defence'; no need for the irritant of a proper search warrant and of regular witnesses, as was the wont during the days of the British; young people, once they have been defined as undesirable, could now be swiftly despatched to their deaths.

The other week in Rajya Sabha, a member was heard to wail: even though dubbed a terrorist, he had no fear during the British regime of being shot down in the street by the police in a sudden action to be subsequently described as an 'encounter', as has been the fate of a nephew of his in this city. A minister was quick to answer the member. Fighting the British, he explained, was quite all right, all of us were then together; now that the kingdom is ours, it is different; we have to do 'something' even if it be our nephews and nieces who try to destroy it from within. The 'something', obviously, is what the minister considers to be a polite euphemism for point-blank killing, under the open sky, of unarmed, defenceless young men and women. The British might have cavilled at this 'something', but not us. When we are dealing with our nephews and nieces, the rule of law is dispensable.

A rich farmer, whose cost of raising a quintal of wheat is Rs 40 but who sells it to the retailer at Rs 100, most assuredly does not destroy the system from within; he only realises a profit. A wholesale trader, who finances the farmers to the hilt so that they will keep back grain on his behalf till the price sky-rockets, does not destroy the system either; he is merely misbehaving, for which he is appropriately admonished, and maybe he can expiate his sin by contributing to this or that political fund. A chairman of a nationalised bank, in case the borrower happens to be a filthily rich specimen with whom he boozes in the evenings, may purposely charge a lower than standard rate of interest, relax the requirements for margin and forget to insist on collateral; there is no question of punishing him; he, it is to be assumed, is not destroying the system, but helping to strengthen its superstructure. An industrialist, who deducts the employees' contribution to the provident fund from the wage bill of the workers, but fails to deposit it at the right quarters, is guilty of unfortunate behaviour, but the Government will be aghast at the suggestion that he be shot without trial; he may be, at most, legally proceeded against. The act of an import-export tycoon, who has expanded his black operations through systematically under-invoicing exports and over-invoicing imports, is, come to think of it, something of a lark; kindly arrange, if you can, a party ticket for him at the next biennial elections to the Rajya Sabha. The senior civil servant, who diverts relief material intended for the refugees to the black market or arranges to give away scarce fertilisers or steel to the shady ones who grease his palm the most, and thereby vitiates the national priorities, may perhaps be warned or transferred to another job, but, since he is not a petty clerk swearing by some Marxist group or other, you cannot even invoke Section (2) of Article 311 of the Constitution to remove him; he is not a security risk. The merchant, who adulterates the cooking medium with a poisonous substance or adds stone chips to the rice, will, even if caught, be permitted to behave himself from now on; he is not one who, by any stretch of imagination, can be described as a saboteur of our system; he is not for burning. Take the politician who has used his official tenure to pile up a couple of crores of rupees by disbursing licences and suchlike, or the chief minister who lays out a guest house in New Delhi entirely at the expense of the State so that his wife, who happens to be a Member of Parliament, need not face any problem of accommodation in the capital; neither of them deserves to be stigmatised; they are following the norms. If a landlord wantonly kills a score of Harijan women and children before breakfast, let the creaky wheel of justice in due course take care of that; no reason at all to get worked up over such trifles. If a share-cropper is driven out of his field by the landlord's men and his family is reduced to starvation, must take it easy: the social revolution we are striving for cannot be ushered in in a day. Minority groups will suddenly be set upon, their houses razed to the ground, their properties looted; a few perfunctory arrests will take place, bail will follow, and there will be no occasion to demand any stiffer action against the criminals; they are not to be shot. Tycoons may conceal income and evade tax and keep cocking a snook at the Government machinery; no special measures will be recommended to bring them to book—they do not destroy the system from within, they will not be shot. Cheats, cut-throats, profiteers, speculators, embezzlers and worse rascals, none threaten the system from within: the rack-renter does not, the land-grabber does not, the stealer of public funds does not. For each crook or ragamuffin, there is the due protection of the law, the due process of the law; thievery and nepotism and robbing the poor do not harm the system, they do not destroy the house which the authorities are jealously mounting guard over, these are, almost, honourable professions.

It is a question of values. The operator in the black-market does not challenge the system; the crime he commits does not, in the short run, affect the life and living of those who constitute the authority; given appropriate arrangements, the latter may even come to share the profiteer's loot. Till as long as you pay the appropriate obeisance to the social foundations of the polity, you can get away with murder, or, which is the same thing, were you to commit a murder, the country's Constitution will lovingly protect you against executive excesses. The protection will be withdrawn the moment you begin to indulge in dangerous thoughts in the manner of Mrinal Sen's young man. It would be futile to try to sell the thesis to the authorities that such dangerous thoughts represent the purest species of patriotism. Given a certain hinterland of objective circumstances, sensitive young men and women will, despite the Defence of India Rules, the MISA and the Ministry of Home Affairs, continue to dream wild dreams, and to think grotesque thoughts. The central issue in patriotism, one would have thought, is the courage and the will to give up the lure of comfortable existence for the sake of an ideal. This is at least how the concept was defined, even along these shores, prior to 1947.

Barring the dangerous young men and women, try to name even one set of people in the country who practise the self-abnegation which politicians preach interminably. It is the cult of the self all over, beginning with the minister-politician down to the road engineer's overseer. Such is the moral code the authorities have succeeded in evolving over the years that if you are young, you are welcome to turn into a heroin-addict or a bum or a knife-wielder; but whatever else you decide to be, you must not turn into a dreamer of extravagant dreams, such as of transforming society through a revolution.

This measures the magnitude of the contemporary Indian tragedy. All that lives must die. None in India are more intensely alive than the young men and women who are prepared to sacrifice—and have sacrificed—everything so that a new society could emerge. They therefore must die, shot like dogs under the canopy of the open sky in concocted encounters with the police. And those who somehow escape death will be locked away, if not under the MISA, under a wild assortment of charges which bear the overwhelming hue of after-thought.

What is the number of nephews and nieces who are languishing behind the bars in this great liberal democracy of ours? Thirty thousand, forty thousand, fifty thousand? How many have been summarily shot, in prison or outside, so as to ensure that the house is not destroyed from within? But why bother about them; they dreamed, they do not deserve any better. While they are despatched to their fate, many of the unscrupulous ones, come January 26 and August 15, will be honoured by the State. They may be rogues and scoundrels, but they enrich the system.

1973

8 An Historical Parallel

The United States of America, the reign of President Coolidge, the regime of the Eighteenth Amendment formally enforcing prohibition. Chicago. Wednesday. 20 October 1926. Hotel Sherman, a stone's throw from the City Hall, the headquarters of the Mayor, and across the street from the office of the chief of police. A famous peace conference was on. It was being chaired by Maxie Eisen, racketeer extraordinary, to whom every push-cart peddler in the fish-market along Lake Michigan paid tribute, and who had the reputation of being an 'intellectual' in the Chicago underworld. Till the other day, his alignment was with the Irish gang. But the erstwhile leader of the latter, the florist Dion O'Banion, has only recently been despatched to his coffin by the gunmen of you-know-who, and, discretion being the better part of valour, Maxie had been increasingly liking the role of a peace-maker. Amongst the participants at the conference in the Lavender Room of Hotel Sherman was Alphonse Capone, ostensibly a second-hand furniture dealer (although once before a grand jury, asked to state his business, his response was: I must stand on my constitutional rights and refuse to answer anything particular about that), otherwise known as Al Capone, by common repute the head of the Neapolitan faction of the Mafia, now without question the monarch who had conquered nearly all he surveyed: sitting next to him was his crony, Antonio Lombardo, head of the dreaded Unione Siciliana, the name by which the Chicago Mafia is generally known. Next to Lombardo was Jack Guzik, the manager of the Capone bootleg syndicate and prostitution chain: next to him was Ralph Sheldon, boss of Capone's beer concessionaires and illegal distilleries. One could notice sitting across the table George Bugs Moran, the reputed burglar and gunpacker, and Vincent ('the Schemer') Drucci, premier jewel thief and rigger of elections; they were the surviving spokesmen of the North Side gang whom Al Capone had systematically annihilated since 1924. Next to them, sitting from right to left, were the delegates of the Irish gang: William Skidmore, ward-heeler and fixer of judges; Christian P. Barney Bortsche, well-known highwayman and blower of safes; and Jack Zuta, their leading armament specialist. Amongst the major luminaries, only Polack Joe Saltis, the beer wing of the South-West Side, was absent for circumstances beyond his control: he was in jail temporarily, because of a certain regrettable misunderstanding with the police.

Maxie the fish-market racketeer was relishing his new role as peace-maker cum brother-confessor. Bygones, he appealed to those who sat round the table, ought to be bygones. The Irish, the Neapolitans, the Sicilians and the Poles had lost as many as two hundred lives in internecine gang warfares since 1922. Their fights had been over the issue of establishing sovereign jurisdiction. It was a matter of dividing up Chicago and its suburbs into so many clear-cut spheres of influence within each of which a particular boss would reign supreme; he would, so to say, hold the charter for that geographical area for practically everything, including boot-legging, prostitution, drug peddling, election terrorism, judge-fixing, blackmailing, robbery, and so on. The egos had, however, clashed with egos, and the battle of annihilation and attrition had gone on for a long number of years. The original Neapolitan, Al Capone, had now managed to emerge as the major goon; the Irish had been almost totally decimated; the Sicilians were also in an equally bad way; so was the case with the Poles, with their leader Saltis very much on the run: Enough, Maxie argued, ought to be enough. The factional murders were giving the gangdom a bad name, the politicians, the legislators and the judges, who were on their pay-roll, were having trouble with the ordinary citizens and also with the Federal administration in Washington. It was thus absolutely essential that the gangs patched up among themselves. Maxie, accordingly, had taken the initiative to organise the peace and disarmament conference. He had already spoken to the Irish and the other gangs, who were more than willing to throw in the towel. He then spoke to Lombardo, who spoke to Capone. A few informal, preliminary meetings were arranged to sort out the modalities of the big conference. Finally, on 20 October 1926, the plenary session convened at Hotel Sherman. It was a stellar occasion; barring one or two unavoidable absentees, all the goons of the underworld were present. They spelled power and money. They controlled the corrupt politicians of Cook County belonging to both parties; they named the Senators and also the Governor of the State of Illinois; the mayor, Big Bill Thompson, was their henchman; the commissioner of police was a pal of Al Capone: and the judges were voted by their rigging machine. Here they were now assembled, in the manner of the Congress of Vienna, to carve up Chicago and the Cook County into distinct territorial zones, to impose and enforce their own law against the legislation of the society and the Constitution of the United States, and to declare dividends and decide stock options with the smooth assurance of, say, the board of directors of any major holding company.

The conference had not even proceeded five minutes when it became obvious that it was Al Capone all the way. The assembled delegates were seized by an atrophy of fear and reverence. Their readiness to agree with whatever Al Capone said was nearly pathetic. He dictated the basic terms of the peace treaty; most of them were accepted without demur. If there were minor grievances felt by individual delegates, they kept those grievances to themselves. For Al Capone had established himself as the supreme boss. His suzerainty was supreme on the North, and his power on the West too was by now beyond dispute. The South, from the Loop to the Chicago Heights, had also duly fallen to him. All that remained was mopping up operations. He had the line of communication with the police, the Mayor, the Senators and the judges. It was thus inevitable that, at the conference, whatever Capone said went. The terms of the charter of peace that was drawn up consisted of only five short clauses, namely, (a) general amnesty; (b) a moratorium on further murders and bashings; (c) all past killings and shootings to be considered as closed episodes; (d) all malicious gossip carried between the factions by meddlesome policemen, or presented through the medium of the press, old telegrams, letters and other documents, dated prior to the peace treaty, to be disregarded; and, finally, (e) leaders of the individual factions are to be held responsible for any infringement of the pact, and unfriendly activities on the part of the rank and file are to be reported to the delegates, who would then ask the respective leaders to initiate the necessary disciplinary measures.

Once the terms of the peace pact were agreed upon, the peace conference converted itself into a delimitation conference. The proceedings were in camera. Moran and Drucci were given the lease of a part of the northern segment of the city, consisting of the 42nd and 43rd wards. The territorial acquisitions, beer-selling privileges, and the vice and gambling concessions south of Madison Street were assigned to Al Capone, who was now formally recognised as the supreme boss of the entire West, from the Loop to Cicero, and on the South from the stockyards to the Indiana boundary line, and on down to Chicago Heights. The Sicilians were confined to their backyard in the south-western parts of the city. For the present, there was nothing for the Irish: they were on probation; once Al Capone was satisfied with their conduct, some concessionaires, it was implied, would come their way.

As the conference ended, all of a sudden peace descended upon Chicago. Up to October 20 during the calendar year, there had been sixty-two murders in Cook County. From that date till December 30, with the exception of a nondescript person, not identified as belonging to any faction, who got killed on December 19, no other killing took place in the city of Chicago. In subsequent history this interlude got known as the Seventy Days' Peace.

The historical parallel was irresistible. In the first fortnight of this month, on June 7 to be precise, at the end of a delegates' conference in Calcutta, a twenty-two point treaty of peace was announced amongst the different factions of the Congress party in West Bengal. These twenty-two points bear an eerie resemblance to the five-point truce which had been declared in Chicago forty-seven years ago following the conference in Hotel Sherman of the different gangster factions. Bygones be bygones, no retributory steps for avenging past killings and assaults; no more playing into the trap of agents provocateurs belonging to the police and other groups; in case of any infringement of the treaty by this or that individual member of this or that individual faction, a complaint is to be lodged with a co-ordinating committee on which would be represented the delegates of the different factions and which would be the final arbiter. Although not reported in the newspapers, it has also been agreed at the conference that Calcutta and the districts of West Bengal are to be parcelled among the different factions in terms of delimitation arrangements to be worked out by the co-ordinating committee. The committee is scheduled to meet in the very near future.

The citizens of Chicago were lucky; they could enjoy uninterrupted peace for seventy days. It is too early to say whether the uneasy peace thrashed out at the conference in Calcutta would have the same order of longevity, or whether the factions would resume their knifings and killings even earlier. The Chicago mobs fought amongst themselves over the concessions for boot-legged alcohol and beer, for the unrestricted right to kill and mug people in each area, for the right to collect the proceeds of blackmail and extortion in each area, to peddle drugs and cocaine, to corrupt the politicians, and to rig the elections. Here the concessions being fought over, one surmises, are about who will have the contract for moving rice from the surplus districts to the deficit ones; who is going to get the cut for importing mustard seeds from Uttar Pradesh and delivering them to the oil mills; who will have the right to name the new recruits for government jobs; who will get the bulk of the funds under the crash employment schemes or the emergency production programme, and who will control the money accruing in the exchequer of the state unit of the party. There will be other concessions, too, to be decided upon; for example, which faction of the party's students wing is to be given the monopoly of controlling the university examinations and collecting the tithe from the students for mass-copying arrangements; or which segment of the youth wing will be empowered to levy compulsory subscriptions on the public for organising community worships. There is some gossip that one faction has demanded the concessionaire for trafficking in girls from the refugee colonies in 24-Parganas and Nadia. This one is as yet unconfirmed: one must not, please, listen to rumours, which are bad for the morale of the people, and which also slow down the task of ushering socialism into, and eradicating poverty from, the country.

1973

9 The Emancipation of Kamal Bose

Meet Kamal Bose, son of late Surendra Nath Bose of 11 Surya Kumar Chatterjee Street, Calcutta; occupation: social service worker at Chittaranjan Cancer Hospital, 37 Syamaprasad Mookerjee Road, Calcutta: drawing a sum of Rs 343-45 only per month as salary and allowances: a citizen of India, head of household consisting of himself, his wife, and a child of two years.

Till the morning of 8 January 1973, Bose was a run-of-the-mill citizen, never having had any brush with the forces of law and order; no warrant of arrest had ever been lodged against him, nor had he ever been interrogated or interviewed by the police in connection with any case whatever. Things, however, changed from that fateful morning. Kamal Bose lost his liberty: he was arrested in connection with two criminal cases. Case No. T 454 72 dated 19 October 1972, and Case No. T573, dated 7 January 1973, both filed by the officer-in-charge of the Bhowanipore Police Station at Calcutta. Bose was duly produced before a magistrate, who granted him bail in both the cases. Bose, however, stayed where he was—namely, in prison—for, even as the bonds for the bail were being posted, the Tollygunge Police Station moved in with two further criminal cases against him: Case No. U/C 647 dated 19 October 1972 and Case No. U/C 650, dated 20 October 1972. Again, a petition for bail was moved before a magistrate: once more, bail was granted. After the fresh bail bonds were furnished, camaraderie among the police being what it is, it was time for the Narkeldanga Police Station to move in: Bose was taken into custody at the behest of the officer-in-charge of the latter Police Station, under order number PSP (3)-257 dated 24 January 1972.

The assorted calumnies spread by the enemies of democracy notwithstanding, the wheels of justice continue to move inexorably in our country. Since no evidence could be adduced by the hardworking policemen of the three aforementioned Police Stations, that is, Bhowanipore (located in Calcutta's south-central region), Tollygunge (location: city south) and Narkeldanga (location: city north-east), Kamal Bose was discharged in each of the five cases till then registered against him. But he could not be released from custody, for the Commissioner of Police, Calcutta, decided to exercise his discretion: by an order number 49(M) dated 24 February 1973, 'with a view to preventing him (Bose) from acting in any manner prejudicial to the maintenance of public order, in exercise of the powers conferred by Sub-section (1) (a) (ii) read with Sub-section (2) of Section 3 and Section 17A of the Maintenance of Internal Security Act, 1971 (Act 26, 1971), the Commissioner directed that Bose remain in detention. In terms of Sub-section (3) of Section 3 of the Act, the Governor of West Bengal approved the Commissioner's order through a subsequent order issued by the State Government's Home Department, Special Section (No. 2803 HS, dated 7 March 1973).

A writ of habeas corpus under Article 226 of the country's Constitution was moved on Bose's behalf before the Hon'ble Shri Sankar Prasad Mitra, Chief Justice, and his companion Justices of the Hon'ble High Court at Calcutta, Extraordinary Original Criminal Jurisdiction. While the habeas corpus application was pending, on the principle of 'the more the merrier', the Police produced Bose before the city's Additional Chief Presidency Magistrate and thumped down yet another case against him: No. A119, dated 15 March 1972. Kamal Bose was granted bail in this case too: since he was being detained under the MISA, there was, however, no question of his availing the order of bail issued by the ACPM: he continued to languish in Calcutta's elite prison, the Presidency Jail.

On 19 April 1973, the country's Supreme Court threw a spanner in the works. While delivering judgment in the case of *Sambhu Nath Sarkar vs. the State of West Bengal and others*, it struck down Section 17A of the MISA as being violative of Article 22(7) (a) of the Constitution. On 18 May 1973, the Hon'ble Shri Justices S.K. Bhattacharyya and S. Basu of the High Court at Calcutta ordered the Commissioner of Police, Calcutta, the Superintendent, Presidency Jail, Calcutta, the Assistant Secretary, Home (Special) Department, Government of West Bengal, and the State of West Bengal through the Secretary, Home Department, to set Bose at liberty 'forthwith' in view of the Supreme Court's decision. The Hon'ble Justices instructed that their order be communicated to the Superintendent, Presidency Jail, that same day by special messenger. The messenger arrived at the jail gate along with the order at 5.10 p.m.; but Kamal Bose was not to be released; the High Court's order could not be complied with on that day: Bose, it was blandly explained, had already been sent to the lock-up for the night.

Dawned 19 May 1973, Bose was taken out of Presidency Jail by the police, thrust into a waiting Black Maria and despatched to the office of the Special Branch at Lord Sinha Road. Bose's counsel tried hard to locate his client's whereabouts; he was ultimately informed by the police about what had transpired. Like the cat, the MISA too had nine lives: Section 17 (a) was struck down by the Supreme Court, but Section 3 remained intact, and Bose had been re-arrested under the latter Section of the Act. The police wanted to be even more thorough. These were uncertain times, you never know with wayward judges, and Section 3 of MISA was obviously not considered sufficient. So, on this occasion, the Beliaghata Police Station (city east) was pressed into service: an order of arrest was served on Bose by the officer-in-charge of this Station under Case No. PI47 dated 5 March 1972. The Special Branch transferred Bose to the care of the good and honourable custodians of law and order at Beliaghata. Bose's wife, Dolly, thought it would be rude not to match the police in tenacity: she, therefore, kept trying. She arranged for a bail petition to be moved on behalf of her husband in the Beliaghata case too. Once more, bail was granted, at Rs 1,000 by a magistrate. But, as you must have guessed by now, the moment the bail bond was furnished on 19 July 1973, Kamal Bose was rearrested in connection with another case. This time, the charge was registered by the Karaya Police Station (city east-centre). Case No. YI13, dated 29 June 1972. under Section 148 149 307 of the IPC read with Section 27 of the Arms Act. On 21 July 1973, Bose was produced at the court of the District and Sessions Judge at Alipore in connection with the case lodged by the Karaya Police Station, and an application for bail was moved for the umpteenth time. To the frustration of the police, he was again granted bail, once more for the identical sum of Rs 1,000. As Dolly moved about to arrange the bail bonds, she and Bose's lawyers could overhear the minions of the police openly discussing what would be the implications of furnishing the bail bonds. The suggestion was put across in a very friendly, informal manner: what, after all, was the point of elongating the suspense? Didn't Kamal and Dolly and Kamal's lawyers realise

that the moment the bail bonds were furnished, he was going to be rearrested in connection with some other case or cases? Why could not he and they, therefore, give up the ghost?
The pursuit of justice in this great land of ours is not only tiring, it is also an expensive process. Dolly saw the futility of it all; she and her lawyers relented, and the police heaved a sigh of relief. Bose went back to Presidency Jail, resigned to the fate of indefinite incarceration. The nation's Constitution, he had learned meanwhile, has many nuances: since what its Articles 19 and 20 give are taken away by Articles 352, 358 and 359, it needs quite an effort to stay at liberty. All Bose was able to achieve through six months' of sustained effort on the part of his wife and lawyers was a continuous shuffling between one Police Station and another and further on to the next one; to be confronted with nearly a dozen criminal cases in succession; to be granted bail in each of these: to be also discharged in each of these; nonetheless, once the police and the government had decided that he must stay in, he must stay in.

There the matter rested—until the introduction of Section 438 in the Code of Criminal Procedure in 1973. Under this Section, it is now possible for a citizen to move a High Court or even a district court for anticipatory bail. Hope springs eternal in the human breast. Dolly Bose, on behalf of her husband, therefore arranged to move a petition on 13 May 1974, before the Hon'ble Shri Sankar Prasad Mitra, Chief Justice, and his companion Justices at the Hon'ble High Court of Calcutta, Criminal Miscellaneous Jurisdiction, in which the State of West Bengal, the Assistant Secretary, Home (Special) Department. Government of West Bengal, the Commissioner of Police, Calcutta, and the Inspector-General of Police, West Bengal, were cited as respondents. The facts narrated in the preceding paragraphs were placed before the Court along with the plea that the police were acting in a mala fide manner and that they appeared to be determined to keep Bose in custody without trial as long as they could. The entire purpose of the police and the other respondents, the petition claimed, was to implicate the petitioner in case after case so as to thwart the orders of the various Courts for bail or for release. The modus operandus, it was explained, was to follow the sequential process: to disclose a case and implicate the petitioner in it only after bail had been granted in a previous case. He had reasons to believe, Bose maintained, that as soon as he furnished the bail bond in the Karaya Police Station case—till then the last one lodged against him in the very long series—he would be re-arrested on the accusation of having committed some other offence or offences: in the circumstances, he prayed that the Hon'ble Court might direct that, in the event of such re-arrest, he shall be released on bail.

The petition was heard by Hon'ble Justices N.C. Talukdar and A.N. Banerjee. After listening to the saga of arrests and re-arrests and re-re-arrests, the Hon'ble Justices suggested to counsel that maybe Bose should try it out at least once more: since what the Justices were saying was within the earshot of the representatives of the police, Bose could perhaps come back to the High Court after giving himself—and the police—another chance.

Kamal Bose and his counsel respectfully heeded the suggestion of the Hon'ble Court. The bail granted by the magistrate in the Karaya Police Station case in July 1973 was availed of on 14 May 1974. Bose walked out of prison, a free man for the first time in sixteen months. The police, perhaps still cogitating over the import of what the Hon'ble Justices had said, let him go.

Thus ends, for the present, the story of the emancipation of Kamal Bose. But you never know. Life and living have become extremely chancy under this Constitution, which we, the people of India, having solemnly resolved to constitute ourselves into a Sovereign Democratic Republic and to secure to all our citizens Justice, social, economic and political; Liberty of thought, expression, belief, faith and worship; Equality of status and opportunity: and Fraternity assuring the dignity of the individual and the unity of the Nation, adopted, enacted and gave to ourselves in our Constitution Assembly on the twenty-sixth day of January 1950.

As this piece is being written, Kamal Bose is still at liberty, but Dolly remains a much worried woman. In this great Republic of ours, by the time this piece gets printed, her husband may once more be gathered in. Whether the charge this time will be under Section 302 or 304 or 476 of the CPC she does not know: whether it will be lodged by the officer-in-charge of the Cossipore Police Station or the Burrabazar Police Station or the Muchipara Police Station, she does not know. Dolly Bose has never read Franz Kafka, but she and her husband, between them, can now furnish enough material for works that could put Kafka in the shade.

Those wanting to stay out of prison in this country should beware. Liberty is not your birthright, nor your constitutional right, it is what your government and the police might occasionally like to bestow upon you.

1974

10 Fascism Shall Not Pass . . .

Don't you read the newspapers, in this country fascism will not pass. All right-thinking people here are against fascism. A minister in West Bengal, famous for his plain speaking, has gone to the length of confirming that, in order to save the country from fascism, he is prepared to make the ultimate sacrifice: he will himself turn into a full-fledged fascist—and suppress, by well-known methods, those other fascists who dare denigrate the authorities: fascism shall not pass.

Fascism shall not pass, newspapers every day carry reports of meetings and conventions held in many parts of the country where the vanguards of democracy take stock of the situation, and warn the fascists: this far and no further. The collective conscience of our countrymen has been roused, fascism will not make any further advance. Different sections and groups are being mobilised: teachers, students, the working class, the peasantry, scientists, artisans, poets, you name them, they are all against fascism. Recently, in the capital, the lawyers chipped in. A boisterous gathering of the members of the legal profession declared themselves forever against fascism and for democracy and progress. The Prime Minister addressed them. There were other joiners, including a former Chief Justice of the country, who is currently Chairman of the Law Commission, and a number of incumbent judges of the Supreme Court and the High Court at Delhi. Queue up, whoever is not for us is against us, whoever is not with us is a fascist. Fascism shall not pass. At the rate things are progressing, wait a while, very soon, progressive elements amongst the police personnel too will be organising a convention against fascism.

Baburam Ghosh Road is a little alleyway down in Tollygunge on the southern fringes of Calcutta. It is indistinguishable from any other dirty lane in the city: slums, choked drains, stench of human and animal excreta, worn-out roads, non-existent pavements, rows and rows of dilapidated pucca houses crowding upon one another. Each such house is perhaps cut up into several dingy flats, dark, bereft of ventilation, lacking in basic sanitation facilities, an apology of an inner courtyard shared between a dozen families, perennially infested by termites and cockroaches. A handkerchief pressed against your nose, visit such an area if you want to know what the scourge of inflation has done to that ramshackle, moveable line of poverty economists talk of. The species of the lower middle class residing in these houses are fighting a losing battle: as prices rise, but their wages are kept frozen by the kindly and sagacious government, they are, inch by inch, pushed toward malnutrition and starvation. It is their kismet, they have to put up with this phenomenon of progressive immiserisation. In the Sixties, heads of such households, mostly clerks in government or mercantile firms, were often foolhardy enough to join the trade union movement and fight for higher wages. Now, since fascism shall not pass, they have been mostly silenced by the government's hired goons: they have also been told by learned people that any agitation on their part will be dirty 'economism'. For, after all, they—they too—belong to the top two per cent of the privileged sections of this country's population.

After such knowledge, there could be no forgiveness for any

stirring of discontent in the gloomy slum-houses on Baburam Ghosh Road. But, it is a funny business, life sprouts, despite the economists, even on Baburam Ghosh Road. Sadananda Roy Chowdhury, ancestry East Bengal, scion of a landowning family, current assets reduced to just about the double-barrelled surname which testifies to the feudal lineage, is a tenant in one of these dingy, dark, claustrophobic tenements. Fiftyish, a clerk in the office of the Accountant General, West Bengal, he long ago learned to chop and prune his ambitions. A clerk is a clerk, he must not dream, he must meekly return home every evening, he must learn to wither away. Yet life sprouts. Sadananda Roy Chowdhury had a small family, wife, two teenage sons, Pradip and Prabir. They were bright, alert, sprightly children: malnutrition, and the general frustration of Bengali lower middle class existence, could not restrain them. Life sprouted. The boys grew up, did well in the examinations, were loved by the neighbours.

The boys grew up. The elder one, Pradip, secured, against hard competition, admission to the Bengal Engineering College at Sibpore. Prabir, the younger brother, did even better; on the basis of his performance in the higher secondary examination, he obtained a scholarship and a seat in the prestigious Presidency College. Sadananda and his wife had reason to feel grateful at the way things were turning out. A clerk must learn to trim his dreams: even so, both the sons were up-and-coming, and somehow life began to promise a radiant glow beyond what the petty sky of Baburam Ghosh Road could offer.

Right here, a kink developed. Your conscience is a product of your environment. Pradip and Prabir, bright, alert, meritorious, were not capable of disowning their milieu. Young people are not capable of flouting their passion. Social realities intervened, and the rest of the tale has a familiar ring; so much so that there is a danger of its being treated as part of a worn-out cliche. To cut a long story short, their academic pursuits were rudely interrupted, a little more than three years ago both the brothers were picked up by the police. Thus ended the curtailed dream of Sadananda Roy Chowdhury, upper division clerk in the office of AG , West Bengal. This did not, however, set him and his family apart. You soon have to give up the count, for, in case you go round run-down neighbourhoods and colonies in Calcutta and West Bengal's smaller towns, there must be thousands of middle class parents like Sadananda Roy Chowdhury and his wife, whose dreams have similarly been scuttled in mid-course. And, as our academic economists would say, there is a certain poetic justice in this; these wretched clerks, who conjure up rosy and prosperous careers for their offspring, are in fact indulging in a variant of 'economism', do not waste any pity on them, let history take its own course.

Yes, it is important to be objective, the instance of Pradip and Prabir was not sui generis, thousands and thousands of college-going young men have, during the past five years, been picked up by the police and detained without trial; otherwise the nation would not have been safe for democracy. Few amongst these young people have had charges pressed against them in open courts. So it was with Sadananda's two children. In their case, the sequel was nonetheless slightly different, which is why this footnote becomes relevant, even if a wee bit tangentially. The elder brother, Pradip, died mysteriously in police custody shortly after he was arrested. He was being interrogated, for days on end, by the Special Branch of the state police; suddenly he passed away, reportedly because of heavy internal haemorrhage. Ask no questions of our patriotic police and you will be told no lies. Going by the gossip—no doubt subversive—as part of the democratic process of interrogation, a solid wooden plank was placed across his body, and hefty specimens belonging to the Special Branch took their turn to mount the plank and dance a tarantula. They mounted for roughly half a dozen occasions, each occasion stretching to five minutes or nearabouts. The police could have danced all night, but it was not necessary. Pradip's ribs as well as internal organs, according to the same gossip, were smashed to smithereens; he died. Some dances can be fatal.

Let bygones be bygones, Pradip Roy Chowdhury died accidentally while in the care of our progressive, anti-fascist government, but Sadananda and his wife had still that other child left, Prabir, the scholar at the Presidency College, who, after his arrest, had been lodged in the Presidency Jail, and of course there was no question of his ever being produced before a judge. A few weeks ago, along with some other prisoners, he was transferred to the jail in Howrah. And then it was the early morning of Saturday, May 3, the sun had yet to rise, the night soil was still piling up on Baburam Ghosh Road, there was a soft summer breeze, originating in the Bay of Bengal, wafting along the Hooghly river, some shots were fired inside the Howrah jail. Ask no questions, otherwise you will be deemed a fascist. The government story is as invariant as ever; some of the 'extremist' prisoners had attacked the security guards and were trying to escape; the guards, in self-defence, were compelled to open fire; five of the prisoners were killed, including Prabir Roy Chowdhury. He was supposedly shot by the guards while trying to escape, but, check with those who have seen his body, there were bullet wounds visible on Prabir's temple, forehead, windpipe and stomach. And the body was swollen all over, indicating the likelihood of blows from regulation lathis having descended upon it with a fearsome intensity. Whether the lathis came down first or were preceded by the shots from a revolver is a riddle one may now try to solve at leisure. The solution, however, will have little operational significance: either way, Prabir is dead.

But look at the brighter side of it. For Sadananda Roy Chowdhury and his wife, the ordeal is over, they will not have to worry about their children any more, both their sons are dead, having been most efficiently disposed of by the patriotic, high-minded government. The Lord giveth, and the government of the land taketh away, in a most sensible division of responsibilities. If you have children, children around whom you weave your dreams, children who are the cynosure of your eyes, children who are polite and brilliant and sensitive, just leave them in the safe custody of your law-abiding, law-enforcing, anti-fascist government, you will not see them any more, peace will descend upon earth.

Fascism shall not pass. Each day the news filters in of yet another convention of the conscientious ones against fascism. The Chairman of the National Law Commission, Justices of the Supreme Court and the Delhi High Court, they have stood up and been counted: they are against fascism, fascism shall not pass. But suppose Sadananda Roy Chowdhury's distraught wife takes a crowded train to the nation's capital, and, giving the slip to the guards and sentries, somehow manages to find her way to the chambers of these legal luminaries, who are against fascism. Suppose she lowers herself into a chair, and silently stares at them across the table. Would they—the guardians and upholders of the rule of law in this country—would they be able to return her stare and, composure writ large on their faces, assure her that, never mind her two sons, fascism shall not pass? Would they?

1975

11 Suffer Us Not to Mock Ourselves . . .

Suffer us not to mock ourselves with falsehood. The format is always the same. For the reports always emanate from the same source. Three dangerous 'extremists' have been shot dead in an encounter with the police; a dozen of them have been nabbed; five of them have been injured—three fatally—when the border security force were compelled to open fire in self-defence; two of them have been killed while attempting a jail break; the body of a dead 'extremist' has been found in an abandoned house. Day after day spokesmen of the police feed such reports to the Press; day after day, newspapers faithfully reproduce the version. Corpses are incapable of issuing rejoinders.

If someone killed in cold blood by the police is described as an extremist, that is only a description. All one can say is that another life has been confiscated by the representatives of law and order, and the corpse has to be given an unsavoury name. Once you identify a corpse as that of an extremist, that by itself is a retroactive justification of trigger-happiness. In this country of six hundred million, human lives are cheap: shoot a couple of bodies before breakfast, another foursome between breakfast and noon, two or three more before sundown. Weariness has entered the soul. As long as it is not myself, I cease to care who becomes the police's prey. The young ones whose lives are taken were in any case up to no good; they were, in any case, the products of indiscretion on the part of their parents—fifteen, twenty, twenty-five years ago. Let them answer for the folly of their progenitors. This is open season for killing young men, this is lynching land: so much the better that everything is neatly organised under official auspices.

There is thus little point, perhaps, in elaborate descent from the general to the particular. Nevertheless, it will be a shame if one or two of the more intriguing episodes do not make it into the chronicles of our times.

It happened on July 20 last. Prabir Dutta, twenty-three, was an unemployed young man. His father is an invalid, his mother works for the Life Insurance Corporation of India, a younger brother is in school, the sister is still younger. The family belongs to the standard category: refugees from East Bengal, middle-middle class, every day being pushed down toward greater immiserisation, every week a focal point of accumulating economic crisis, unpaid bills, shrinking horizons of hope, bitterness welling in a vacuity defining work and activities. Prabir, the eldest offspring, was taken off his studies: a not particularly meritorious student, it was pointless to waste money to keep his name on the roll of a college, where anyway hardly any teaching ever took place; the examinations, too, had meanwhile been reduced to a farce. So there he was, without a craft, with a bare background of secondary education, perfunctorily looking for a job, enquiring of parents of friends and of relations about the possibility of some openings somewhere, enquiring fitfully, not with much hope, but as part of a conditioned ordering, as if the grammar had laid it down that he should continue to look for a job even when he knew there was none. He was—he must have vaguely realised it himself—an inconsequential speck of a statistic. In the city of Calcutta, there must be at least a couple of million like him, seeking jobs, but bereft of technical or professional equipment, and without social—or, which is almost the same thing these days, 'political'—connections. Such young people roam around, aimlessly most of the time. Time hangs heavily around them. To cheat the boredom, some of them write poetry, mostly of the indifferent nondescript type. Prabir did too. Some of them compose songs—and sing; Prabir did too, occasionally. Those who do not write poetry or compose songs scrounge for some money—from mother or elder sister—for a vicarious outing, now and then, with Hema Malini or Mousumi Chatterjee; or perhaps they learn to wield a knife and join the Youth Congress. There are too many of them by now to try to enter the latter either: there is standing room only, even in the underworld.

Prabir would roam the city's filthy streets, generally purposelessly. One doubts whether he had any political convictions: his feeble attempts at writing poetry belonged to the genre of effusive-lyrical, with certainly no trace of any political ideology. July 20 was a Saturday. Prabir took his meal at nine-thirty in the morning and left home, the dingy two-room ground floor apartment in Bhowanipore in south-central Calcutta. He walked. It was a Saturday. Most of the offices which are not fully closed on Saturdays empty themselves by lunch-hour. Right at the city centre, as Chowringhee Road meets Lenin Sarani, lies the stretch which once upon a time acquired the appellation of 'Esplanade', but is now a mere turnstile for the tramcars. There used to be a patch of greenery in a corner of this stretch, but it is now almost obliterated; till 1947, that patch was 'Curzon Park'; since then, it has become Surendranath Park. Surendranath

Banerjea was the great orator: come Independence, in the world of nomenclatures, the tory British governor-general was supplanted, formally, by a Bengali ham. But the old name has stuck. Curzon Park has shrunk in territory in the past 30 years. Still, you can find practically every species of humanity—decrepit or otherwise—milling around in that narrow strip of land from early afternoon till after dusk. Vendors of all descriptions, students, young college teachers, beggars, lepers, prostitutes, cardsharpers, pickpockets, straightforward rogues, brokers, magicians, clerks doing their last bit of shopping before rushing home, political aspirants, poets, lovers in droves—they set up a milieu, compose an environment, establish a community with a corpus of its own, an equilibration unique in style. Everything is improvised at Curzon Park, but somehow everything, every day, appears to be part of a pre-arranged ensemble. The ensemble dissolves by the time the last tram cars flock to the depot. It miraculously re-forms the next day.

Curzon Park attracts would-be play-makers too. Calcutta consists of an unending stream of drama groups. Playwrights, actors and actresses, amateur plagiarists, *et al.* who cannot scrape the funds to hire a hall but have aspiration written across their hearts, congregate at the Park. They do it every afternoon, but do it with greater gusto on Saturday afternoons, when the crowd collects quickly. The themes of the plays vary, some are vapid-social, some are roaring revolutionary, but nobody minds. A small group of watchers gather across Raj Bhavan, a makeshift podium comes up, the players perform, the prompters prompt, the playwright improvises, the audience applauds.

July 20, apart from being a Saturday, was Vietnam Day as well. One particular group, full of revolutionary bubble, was mounting a play expounding the heroism of the Vietnam peasantry. The crowd was swelling; some slogan-shouters, proceeding from the east, were converging towards the spot where the play was on. The police always mount a patrol around Curzon Park: they did so on that day too; their presence was taken for granted; the lathis were, as usual, agleam. The revolutionary play was moving to its climax; the slogan-shouters were on the point of joining the main bunch of watchers; it was four o'clockish in the afternoon, Prabir Dutta was in the crowd, watching and listening; suddenly something went wrong.

What went wrong cannot be precisely unravelled, because the archives of the police are a closed book. The police claim they discovered in the crowd a dangerous 'extremist', against whom several warrants were pending, and that they moved in to apprehend him. The organisers of the play assert that it was the culmination of an official conspiracy to crush their venture to present revolutionary poster-plays for the masses. Anyway, the police charged, pandemonium ensued, people began to run helter-skelter; several among those trying to get into trams or buses, or forming the queue outside the cinema showing *Bobby* for the twentieth week, claim to have seen the regulation lathis of the minions of law and order being brandished in the air and going up and down, several times. What is not disputed, even by the police, is the fact that several young people got arrested, and a number of them had to be moved to the Medical College hospital, one and a half miles away, either by private parties or by the police themselves, for treatment of injuries suffered during the incident. The body of Prabir Dutta was found lying outside the Emergency Ward of the hospital at around five o'clock or thereabouts. It had been brought there from Curzon Park, in a cab, by some passers-by. There were quite a few marks of injury on his body, and a particularly deep one on the rear side of the skull. The left wrist, according to some reports, was hanging limply. Soon, the police moved in onto the premises of the hospital. Once the doctors of the Medical College certified Prabir to be dead, the body was moved post-haste to the morgue next door.

It took a while to identify the body; Prabir's mother could be contacted only pretty late. Earlier in the evening, prominent individuals associated with various theatre groups in the city had reached the hospital. They kept insisting that the post-mortem on the body should be done by a non-official doctor, or at least by a doctor attached to the Medical College; if Government rules were inviolable and the police medical examiner had to be present at the postmortem, a second doctor, with no connections with the police, they urged, must also be there. Each of these suggestions was turned down. A cryptic press note was issued from police headquarters; yes, the young man was dead; yes, there were some marks of injury on his body; yes, one of the ribs of the young man was found fractured. But there was also a nice, trim, explanation for each of these. The police had wielded no lathi at Curzon Park, the bruises found on the body of the young man were mostly self-imposed. The police had moved in to arrest an extremist seen in the crowd, there was commotion, Prabir fell down in the rush and was trampled upon by others: that was how his rib got broken, it was undoubtedly sad that the young man was dead. But his death involves no foul play. As he fell to the ground during the melee, some of the food he had consumed seven hours earlier rushed back from the stomach, unfortunately the food came up the wrong way and choked his windpipe; he died. This diagnosis was, it was given out, confirmed by the official medical examiner who performed the post-mortem. The report of the post-mortem was not released. There was no foul play, but the body was not handed over to the mother or to any other relatives. The police did not even allow the body to be taken home. It was taken straight to the cremation ground in an official ambulance; the last rites were performed under direct supervision of the police. All this, despite no foul play.

But one must be fair, one must not lose one's sense of perspective. A hundred deaths take place under the loving care of the authorities, it is only occasionally that a stray one is reported, such as Prabir's, because it occurs in the city centre, in the glare of a dazzling July afternoon sun. Moreover, all is well that ends well. Prabir is dead; there is one less unemployed to roam the streets of the city of Calcutta, one less speck of inconvenient statistics. It is so cosy, that food, the measly food an unemployed youth from an impoverished family took at nine-thirty in the morning, still managed to come up the wrong channel seven hours later. There is a certain indigestibility in the ingredients one tries to absorb in Calcutta; and it is to be welcomed: without it, the tales served up by the police will be difficult to swallow. Suffer us not to mock ourselves with falsehood.

1974

12 A Brief Whiff of Hope

It was a meeting, called by assorted political organisations, to press a charter of demands in support of the unemployed. The charter included a demand for dole for all those who are out of work for no fault of their own, but on account of, allegedly, 'the imperfections of the economic and social system'. The details of how this dole is to be organised were not spelled out in the resolution passed at the meeting. Perhaps the resolution and the charter of demands were merely a peg. As prices keep rising, discontent, under cover for the last few months, is beginning to bestir itself. Alongside this, the Left parties, which had been in near-hiding because of you-know-why, are also slowly rediscovering their innate militancy. But more than the declamations at the meeting, what was interesting to watch was its morphology. A meeting is not a meeting without an assembly of people. To this particular one, impressive numbers had in fact flocked. It is no longer possible for activists from the mofussil towns and villages simply to get into a train and arrive in Calcutta to attend a Left rally. To travel without a ticket is, of course, totally to be ruled out, but instances are not lacking where even those possessing tickets have been pushed out of the train at intermediate stations in case it was apparent that they were on their way to join a leftist gathering. Trucks too are allowed to carry people into the city only if they are of the right sort, namely, if they are proceeding to a meeting to be addressed by some of the ruling party stalwarts. For other parties, trucks and lorries are prohibited. There is, besides, the question of finance. For the Left parties, the days of dazzle and glory are, for the present, over. They have to count each penny and make it travel the utmost possible length. The kind of quasi-pomp one witnessed at similar rallies in the past is now a mere matter of memory. These problems notwithstanding, thousands still did come to this particular meeting. It was an extraordinary compilation of episodes and emotions, of glistening enthusiasm on the part of some, tempered by a quiet casualness displayed by others, a carnival spirit lighting up some faces next to deep furrows of worries lining some others.

It takes all sorts to constitute a political meeting. People converge in processions, with festoons flying, snake-dancing across the wide and not-so-wide thoroughfares. People come, walking alone, or in twos and threes; here a college teacher, there a journalist or an unemployed artisan. Young housewives with the bindi agleam on their foreheads, the faint fragrance of a cheap face powder blending with the zeal of a school brat. And you can see hordes and hordes of factory workers or farm labourers from 24-Parganas, Howrah or Hooghly. Few and far between, lost in the swelling crowd, you might also find one or two affluent types, who drop in either because they just feel curious or because they discover a thin emotional link with what is going on. But, by and large, the meeting belongs to the poor, the very poor, the down-and-outs and those on the way to becoming down-and-outs, interspersed by a fair cross-section of what will pass as the lower middle class: dressed in tatters, hardly any suggestion of warm clothing, torn shoes, a rip in the dhoti or the blouse, stains of betel-nut juice across the shirt front or on the sari. For a brief three or four hours, they take over the vast stretch of flat land in the maidan. The meetings are a great democratiser, for everybody squats—the very poor next to the not-so-poor, the not-so-poor next to the reasonably affluent, and the reasonably affluent next to the altogether affluent. Maybe next to you is a police informer, but he too is squatting. There is the atmosphere of a country fair all over. The speeches from the distant rostrum go on and on. Everybody has one eye turned to the speaker, but the other eye is usually roaming. It is a somewhat bizarre spectacle, for while grim sentences blare out of the loudspeakers and a good number do listen quite intently, there is also a certain facetiousness in the way the crowd behaves. Perhaps the people do believe more or less in what is being asserted from the rostrum. Even if they do not understand all of what is being said, such as the evil tentacles of monopoly capitalism and their consequence, they are vaguely aware that those friendly gentlemen up there are emotionally with them, they are part of one common movement. It is their own welled-in dissatisfaction, they realise, which is finding its voice through those speeches. If the leaders on the rostrum ask them to march, give up one day's wage as contribution to the cause, on occasion offer food and shelter to some activists, they will readily do so. They have, after all, come to the meeting because they want to gain back self-confidence, they want to share and share alike the warmth of the assurance which a vast collection of individuals can provide to one another: it is almost a kind of social security.

Yet, at another level, there is a lightheartedness almost bordering on frivolity. Quite a number—those who can afford to do so—buy party literature, dig into their pockets and come up with one or two bits for this or that group of workmen who are either locked out or have been the subject of police victimisation.

At the same time, they keep up an interminable small talk amongst themselves. College students or school teachers greet one another; people from one village enquire about the state of being of those who come from another area or village. And some amongst them keep buying snacks, munch away at groundnut, vada and other savouries, treat themselves to a soft drink or a cup of hot tea. All the time, vendors wind their way through the squatting crowd and do a brisk business. In some corners, while the daylight is still there, you could even spot small groups making up a tight circle and playing a quick game of cards, either bridge or something less pretentious. You will also find a stray boy pumping merrily away at a mouth organ, or a slip of a girl, a bright ribbon tied to her hair, jumping up and down, up and down, repeating a slogan she has picked up only a moment ago. Sitting next to her, her elder brother keeps up a running banter with another gentleman barely five yards away, or maybe exchanges some office gossip or some disquieting piece of news about a common acquaintance.

Little islands of people who come together for a brief span of three or four hours. They represent a fairly faithful melange of Bengal's fast disintegrating middle class and its emaciated proletariat. There is a thread which strings them together, brings them to this evening's sharing of the burnt-out strips of grass which the maidan is, just as they share the prospect of a bleak present slowly fading into a bleaker future, a future where jobs are scanty, food is dear, housing is atrocious and the day-to-day existence is a continuum of nightmares. For some, there is the sharing of more particular adversities: of sons or daughters being locked away in prison, or killed by ruffians or the police.

Undoubtedly, for many, there is also a sharing of ideology. It is, however, not so much to vocalise ideologies that they come to the meeting. They listen to the speeches, they clap with devotion when the more popular leaders start performing, but most of them know what to expect from the speeches; most of them also know that the resolutions you pass are not of much operational significance: these only provide an outlet for emotions. They come to the meeting primarily to enjoy one another's presence, to gather courage from the fact that they are not alone, they come in the belief that the moment individuals come close together under one segment of the sky, a transformation takes place, one gets into the spirit of the collective personality. Perhaps a fair chunk of the people also come because in their pattern of living there is so little variation, so little occasion of departure. Never mind whether they have a spare paisa: never mind whether at the end of the month they will be badly missing the money they have spent on train or tram or bus fare to come to the meeting; never mind whether, on their journey back from the meeting, they will be waylaid by thugs belonging to the landlord's party; they still care to come because this is their only diversion. Such meetings entertain the impoverished, provide them with a precious half-dozen hours of fever and excitement. There need, therefore, be no sense of guilt or shame if they listen to the speeches with only one ear, while the rest of the faculties are deployed to soak in all that is happening, in the course of the evening, around them. There need be no sense of guilt at keeping up the small talk, at spending money on a cup of tea or a packet of spiced murmura, nor need there be any feeling of guilt that while the leaders talk of the inevitability of the social revolution, you cast eyes on the bright, young girl sitting hardly two rows away from you.

It is little use feeling snooty about the character of such

political congregations. Where existence is only sub-marginal, you do still need a little light in your life, an occasional touch of brightness, a brief whiff of hope. The manner in which the poor enjoy themselves is the least capital-intensive of all kinds. Soon after sundown, the leaders will climb back from the rostrum, the crowd will start to melt away. Some of them will, once more, form into processions, but the vast majority will be stragglers. They will disappear into the night and will be engulfed by the worries of daily existence, but they will have carried back a few morsels of cheer from the meeting. The social revolution may or may not be round the corner, the leaders may or may not have been talking bosh. A single day's outing may have exhausted resources which could otherwise have lasted for several days, but you ask these poor and hapless people, they have no regrets, they feel adequately recompensed. Come the next occasion, you can rest assured, they will all return; they will spread their dirty handkerchiefs or pieces of newspaper on top of the dirty, unkempt grass, make themselves comfortable, buy some crisp murmura or groundnut, and munch away fiercely even as the performing leaders talk of the miracles that have happened during the last thirteen years in some distant land which goes by the name Cuba.

1972

13 The Planes Do Not Land Here Any More

How they wail, the newspapers in Calcutta. Almost all the foreign airlines are shunning the city. This cannot be, they must be brought back. It was perhaps all right for the airlines to have deserted Calcutta a few years ago when the abominable communists were on the point of taking over. But, look, Calcutta is no longer the pestilential city; we have thrown out the communists; we are reviving the investment climate; big business has slowly started to trickle back; a massive urban renewal programme is under way; Haldia is round the corner; the Calcutta port itself will once more hum with activity once the Centre sees reason and permits the unfettered flow of water downstream through the barrage at Farakka. The international airlines must therefore be made to come back.

There is no frustration which can compare with frustration at high places. In this city of filth and squalor, one and a half million every night try to scrounge a space merely for sleeping under the open sky; you can see men, women and children rummage through piles of foul-smelling garbage in search of a stray morsel of food and, perchance, some discarded rubbish which could have a resale value, maybe adding up to a few coins. In this city, half an hour's smart downpour, and the major arteries disappear under water, public transport comes to a standstill, hordes and hordes of humanity are stranded, for hours on end, where they are. In this city, watch how people travel: a public bus would be overloaded three or four times over, persons sitting on top of others, standing on top of others' toes, forming flying pyramids at the entrance and the exit, outside the bus, in the rear and on the sides, miraculously discovering supports which you would never imagine could have existed. Or take the suburban trains, loaded on top, loaded on the sides, nearly every day one or two accidents, someone either getting electrocuted by an exposed, over-hanging electric wire, or getting his brains smashed as the head hits against some iron post or other. Try to think of the enormity of exasperation on the part of the collective mass at the delays, breakdowns, jostlings, pickpocketings; at the daily, monotonic repetitions of the experience of smell, perspiration, flying of tempers, and the utter hopelessness of it all.

But, as we were saying, all this can abide the question, it is the frustration at high places which agitates the newspapers. Judging by the near-paranoia at the reluctance of the international airlines to return to Calcutta, it must be, currently, the dominating frustration of those whose sentiments the newspapers reflect. In this competitive clime, the non-return of the flying Shebas is deeply wounding to the ego of Calcutta's business and executive community. Till a few years ago, one could hop away, from Calcutta's airport, at one straight go, every day in the week, mornings and afternoons, either to Europe or to the Far East—and beyond. This is no longer possible: the milk trains do not stop here any more, not every day, not every morning or afternoon; very often, for a connection, you have first to travel to Delhi or Bombay. Nothing could be more hurting to the pride of the local snobs. Why cannot the airlines be just like them? Now that the nightmare is over, they have returned to Calcutta! Why cannot the airlines?

Ask the men and women, standing for a bus to take them home at the end of another claustrophobic day, ask them even as the queue lengthens to nearly a quarter of a mile or thereabouts, do they care at all whether the airlines return or not; ask the suffocating crowd in a tram-car at the peak of office hours, or those perching precariously on top of a suburban train, expectantly heading toward home, sweet home. Like it or not, here are the masses on whose toil the economy that is the city is based; one need not travel all the way with the theory of surplus value to perceive the simple truth that, by dissociating itself from the masses, no superstructure can hope to survive for long. Calcutta's industrial and managerial class thought it to be otherwise. Leave aside the Rajasthani community, who could never take kindly to the clayey, alluvial soil of Bengal. Leave aside even the remnants of the British, who, during the past quarter of a century, almost exclusively concentrated on how to disentangle themselves, in terms of both emotion and finance, from this place which they had, once upon a time, built in a fit of imperial absentmindedness. Take only the brown sahibs, who took over the industrial and commercial firms from the British; take also the case of those other characters, who have drowned their conscience in the service of Rajasthani equity; or even the native Bengali industrialists, who, at different points of time, have dabbled in such diverse activities as textiles, light engineering, electronics, steel-rolling, pharmaceuticals and what not. There may be minor variations in the pattern, but, ever since 1947, these people have existed in this city, revelled and fornicated here, in total disdain of their surroundings. Clubs and parties, golf and horse races have been the staple of their existence. For them, it has been a separate, esoteric world: they would slink to the office, nursing yesternight's hangover, at around 10.30; by 11.00, coffee will be served by dainty secretaries; one or two perfunctory meetings concerning office chores, one or two letters for dictation; come 12.30, the chauffeur-driven cars will be summoned, and the sahibs will migrate to the clubs, aperitifs will be followed by yet other aperitifs, indolent gossip about other people's jobs and wives, a languorous luncheon, a slovenly, contented reappearance in the office around 3.00 or 3.15; but, by 4.30, the sahibs will call it a day, some will head toward a few hurried rounds of golf, others to luxurious bungalows or apartments for a brief rest and recreation before the gruelling round of boisterous cocktails and parties commences in the evening.

No, this is not a caricature, nor is it intended to be. For a few hundreds belonging to Calcutta's managerial and industrial section, this is how living was defined, and was—and is still—played out. Given such a lifestyle, there was, and is, little scope for reading or thinking or doing any piece of serious work; you heap your woes on the government or labour, organise occasional 'in-group' sessions to discuss the crushing burden of taxation, and the rest is one uninterrupted alcoholic stupor. Somebody had successfully sold to these people the notion that they were the true inheritors of the British; they fell for the joke; it was relatively easy to take over the externalities of British living, the haw-haw accent, the club-mongering and occasional stealing of each other's wives,the tennis and the golf and the safaris, but nobody told them that the British slogged hard to build an empire exclusively on mercantilist pretensions; nor that, despite their toil and labour, history finally caught up with them. Calcutta's boxwallahs were—and are—not even neo-literates;

they were—and continue to be—unadulterated illiterates. The humdrum of Bengali middle-class society, the grim reality of Calcutta's squalor and poverty, the political process which was gradually finding expression in the working-class movement, none of this touched them; as profound theists, they thought that these irritations would pass them by. When the gheraos broke to provide a rude, rough jolt, the boxwallahs, a frightened, demoralised lot, started shrieking for support. Now that the horrendous interlude is seemingly over, they are reverting to form, in attitude as much as in manners.

One has only to compare this sorry lot with similarly-placed professional and business groups in Bombay or Ahmedabad. In neither of the latter cities are the industrialists or the executive class so totally uprooted from the cultural and social milieu: you will find them involved not just in the political field, but, much more intensely, in assorted social, cultural and humanitarian activities. Also, what is perhaps most crucial, their manner of living is not as totally alienated from the average level of living as in Calcutta. There is a certain moderation in the enjoyment of the good things in life, a certain consideration for the feelings and sensitivities of the less affluent ones, as also a certain realisation of the perils of extreme selfishness, attributes so altogether absent in their counterparts in Calcutta.

The insensitivity of the Calcutta crowd shows even within narrow confines. The management institutes at Calcutta and Ahmedabad were set up almost at the same time; today, the Ahmedabad institute has an imposing building and a campus to match, most of the funds for the construction having been contributed by the local managerial and business groups. The Calcutta institute maintains to this day its precarious existence in cramped, borrowed premises: the government had arranged for several hundred acres of levelled land for its campus way back in 1964; but the great leaders of industry and commerce here could not be persuaded to put up the funds necessary to start of the building.

When one talks of low productivity of labour in this state, must not one therefore ask: how do you measure, how do you separate the setback to productivity because of the incompetence and inefficiency of the managerial class from the adverse consequences of inefficient labour input? If you own and control the newspapers, if you rule the roost over the political elements, you can certainly shift the blame and slander labour, but the process of history is going to catch up in no time.

The other day, the government took over, with much fanfare, the management of the Indian Iron and Steel Company. There will be many others in the private sector which are about equally badly managed, and the alibi of labour indiscipline will wear thin. Even assuming that several of these now pass on to Government hands, what *modus operandi* will be there to nurse them back to health? To assume that persons from the existing managerial set-up, with a little shuffling here and there, will succeed in restoring efficiency to these units is not just a mistake; it is much worse. If there is any single group which fits Nirad C. Chaudhuri's description of the bronzed-out ones, it is the brown sahibs of Calcutta. They deserve liquidation, not salvaging; summary treatment, not compassion. It is an altogether laughable idea that they will be the catalysts of industrial revival in this part of the country. These may be harsh words, but all they are capable of is wailing, from the dump heap of history, for the planes which will no more touch Calcutta.

1972

14 A Revolutionary Handshake

Success shakes hands with the also-rans? Calcutta's international airport has little custom these days, but Fidel Castro's plane, returning from Hanoi, stops for a while. Despite the short notice, a sizeable crowd gathers to greet him. It contains the usual sprinkling of what in the United States would be described as bobby-soxers. That was bound to happen. In this city which cannot quite get rid of its, if you will, revolutionary pretensions, there is still magic in Cuba's name. Che, no doubt, would have been a bigger draw, but, in this lean season, Fidel will do.

The assortment of the various shades of the Left are all there, besides some of the indubitably non-Left. A truce is a truce is a truce! The polemics are forgotten for the narrow space of half an hour at the airport, they all queue up in quest of Fidel's eminently shakeworthy hand: it is big and strong and supple. He has come through, we have not. We have not made it, he has; the revolution keeps on eluding us, he has authored one of his own. Its lustre has dimmed somewhat in recent years, the circumstances have made almost a tepid conformist out of Castro, he has been leaning much toward one particular Mecca for the last three or four years. But, there you are, the rough has to be taken with the smooth. The maker of a revolution, one who has flouted, and successfully, the conspiracy of American imperialism. None of us has met Lenin, who in any case has been dead for fifty years; Mao Tse-tung will not touch India's shores, our rulers will be scared stiff if he does; Fidel Castro is the only other one who has made a revolution on his own, with not one iota of help from anybody else. There could be no more authentic hero of our times. True, Che would have set ablaze more emotional prairies. But, then, he is buried in a remote, unmarked, Bolivian grave. Meanwhile, Fidel is here.

As they shake Castro's firm, friendly hand, as they scan Castro's slightly bemused face, what thought passes through the minds of Calcutta's stalied, stymied leftists? They are quite a representative crowd of old sloggers, most of them have given their all for the sake of the cause, and yet, the goal today seems to be as distant as ever. What is the catalysit that causes a revolution? How does one start a prairie fire? Castro's elocution, as with American any Latin, is almost autonomous; has the revolution, too, something of that autonomous attribute—it happens when it is time for it to happen, you cannot induce a revolution, you cannot push history?

For, going by objective conditions, you would have thought the revolution ought by now to be knocking at your door, clamouring for immediate entry. Conditions of famine have reappeared after these thirty years. Food is short and dear and unevenly distributed. Hunger-marchers are, with every day, crowding into the city. About a hundred crores of rupees have supposedly been spent on Calcutta through the CMDA in the course of the past three years: that, however, has not prevented things from continuing to fall apart. Jobs are hard to come by: seventy per cent of the city's population have no income at all. Civic amenities are on the point of total collapse; a pig's sty will put to shame Calcutta's slums. Transport is choked to the full. The people, even those who manage to obtain some food, lack in calories, in iron, in vitamin, in protein. If it is social oppression, the exploitation by a few of the multitude and pursued through the decades, which sparks a revolution, there is no dearth of it around this neighbourhood. What is it, then, which has stalled the process of history, turned back the revolution? The fact that you are part of a much bigger polity, and the part is never bigger than the whole? Or that your organising ability has never quite transcended petty-bourgeois rigidities? That you have been bogged down by an excess of economism? That all you have done, despite the many individual sacrifices, despite the hundreds of martyrs, is merely playing at revolution, and the movement has never been touched by the magic of steel? That your thought has never integrated with your practice? As they greet Fidel, Calcutta's veteran leftists must be sifting the puzzle. Granted that you can neither export nor import revolutions, what do you have to learn from Fidel's success, and, let one add, Che's failure? Or is it simply a question of random occurrence—it is not just the objective conditions, but, along with them, perhaps putting them into the shade, the stochastic accidents which decide the contours of history?

Fidel, in his turn, what thought does he hide behind that enigmatic, half-amused smile? As he lands at Calcutta, he is perhaps, inevitably, reminded of Lenin's famous prognostication. Does he chuckle unto himself? In case he does, is it because Lenin, in retrospect, has been proven such a nincompoop as a soothsayer? Or is he detained by the irony that he is received with open arms not merely by the Left, but even by the heinous capitalists of bourgeois, comprador-colonial Calcutta, yet his plane will be denied an effusive welcome in Shanghai? Or would it be that he does not chuckle at the thought; instead, rues it? What memories will he carry back from Calcutta's forlorn airport? Memories of underdevelopment all right, but what species of underdevelopment? Will he have any thesis to expound back home to the crowd in the vast outstretched cane fields? Will that thesis be about how some people will be denied their revolution because the leaders fall prey to capitalist vices, because they refuse to take to the hills, because the modality is not yet perfect? Or will he be a stickler for form, be as polite as he is at the moment at the airport, shifting all the blame for Calcutta's indescribable squalor on the ghosts of yore, on some distant imperialism and colonialism?

Does he genuinely believe that the misery unfolding before him is the consequence of a lagged series, that the history of the past quarter of a century is an irrelevance, or is it that, two hours hence, he has to shake hands with Madam Gandhi and cannot let himself go? Could it be that uppermost in his mind is the fact that he has to sell his sugar and get things in exchange, that, under present circumstances, he can sell his sugar only to some people and not to others, that the susceptibilities of the latter have to be respected? What image will he carry back of Calcutta's motley crowd of leftists? Is he just another Jesting Pilate, and can only behave in the manner of an Aldous Huxley let loose amongst an improbable crowd consisting of a group of Surti Parsis? Or, as he sequentially shakes the hands lined up in a demure queue, does he feel that he is in the midst of comrades, brothers engaged in a common struggle? Addressing the curious crowd, does he have his faith in international brotherhood confirmed, does he obtain that extra bit of assurance that Cuba will live even amidst this crowd of Indians? As somebody makes a mention of Chile and Salvador Allende, does he light up inside: fascism shall not pass, despite the grim news from Chile, we shall overcome?

The half hour ends soon. Fidel makes the typical gestures, with his arms and with his snub-nosed cigar end. There is a flurry of leave-taking, interpretations into and from English, into and from Bengali, the flavour of the torrential hyperbole, at each end, gets lost in the translations. The bobby-soxers never felt happier: the handsome six-footer, with the red glow all over, has beamed at them, waved at them. Fidel, ambling easily across the ramparts, reaches the staircase, ascends, turns round and waves again, withdraws into the dark interior of the plane. The plane is revved up, soon it is airborne. The enchanted crowd waves for a while, waits indeterminedly, then melts away. The question still remains. Is the revolution a-coming, what makes a revolution tick? As you drive back to the city, you see the huddle of the hungry ones who have slowly made their way from the villages in search of food. Quite a few of them, give or take a few days, will die. Their deaths will be fitfully mentioned in the newspapers; in parliamentary proceedings, these deaths will be ascribed, not to starvation, but to malnutrition. Once the festive season is over, the leftists will launch into another of their incessant agitations. But the puzzle will remain. What is the pay-off from the revolutionary handshake? Does one know at all how a revolution is put to shape? We scoff at our own humble strivings at setting up one, but, the half hour with Fidel notwithstanding, who amongst us is the lucky one to stumble upon superior surrogates?

1973

15 The Legacy and the Led

May Day is a paid holiday in Calcutta—and in West Bengal.In the afternoon, unending processions of the labouring classes converge on the maidan: they are entertained to passionate speeches by the leaders, the brotherhood of the international proletariat is full-throatedly proclaimed. But something sticks out, something at least mildly uncomfortable. The declaiming leaders all belong to a particular slot. Scan their names: irrespective of whichever Left party they might swear by, each one of the names is high caste, high-breed Hindu. There are maybe thirty incarnations of leftism in West Bengal. None can thrive without being shepherded by upper-class Hindu ministrels.

This, it may be argued, is unfair banter, since the malady touches all political parties, and is not specific to the Left. But this precisely is the point. If the Swatantra party is studded with glamour boys and glamour girls from high society, that ought not to constitute any news. A party supposed to defend the interests of feudal elements, filthy capitalists and the rest of the bourgeoisie must in any case be led by the hegemony of the upper class. What baffles is the persistence of the motif even in groups and parties preaching the international brotherhood of the working class and the tenets of violent revolution. One can, of course, analyse the reasons. Once upon a time, those who constitute the top echelon of the Left leadership were in the mainstream of the so-called national movement. They are the offspring of the bourgeoisie, the offspring of the landowning barons. After Independence, the national movement splintered and they drifted to the Left. Their ideology got oriented, but, you cannot rewrite heredity, the class and caste bases were incapable of being altered. Therefore, whether meanwhile you make fun or do not make fun, there they are, guiding the destiny of Bengal's Left. Now and then, an occasional aberration, the scion of a working class family has come to the fore, but by and large the roster of names straddling the entire spectrum of the Left leadership follows a set pattern. Begin with the Dasguptas and the Lahiris and end with the Mazumdars and the Chatterjees: all impeccable high-caste names, either Brahmin, or Vaidya, or Kayastha.

This may not be so unique. Perhaps if one travels all the way to Maharashtra and Gujarat, the phenomenon will be repeated. In the Bengali milieu, however, a further dimension gets added. High-caste Bengali Hindu names are invariably also pristinely feudal names. You hardly have to go very far back. It could be that, barely fifty years ago, either the father or the grandfather of this or that eminent Bengali Left leader was a flourishing landowner in North or East Bengal. The offspring walked away from their feudal moorings. They walked away from the memory of the attitudes and the mode of life which permeated their early upbringing. But is the transformation altogether total, does not something still linger on? Feudalism, after all, used to sustain itself on feuds. The ego of the lord was the heart of the matter. It was this ego which drove the master to keep collecting more and more fiefs and revenue by squeezing the poor and helpless peasantry or, alternatively, by capturing, through war and litigation, the land of other feudal lords. To dispute, to contest, to join battle, made up the ethos of existence. Intolerance was the credo: I matter, nobody else does: only I deserve to survive and prosper, the rest must either pay obeisance to me or be liquidated. The other side of intolerance was jealousy, all-consuming jealousy. He who has come up must be brought down, by hook or by crook. By now, one associates this attitude of petty backbiting with drab, petty-bourgeois values. This is without question, though, a feudal legacy.

One walks away from one's feudal past; one tries, consciously or otherwise, to declass oneself, but, in the stream of consciousness, something persists. However hard they try, the leaders of the Left parties find it nearly impossible to shed, totally, their heritage, the heritage of egotism. Thereby is unfolded a two-stage tragedy: the parties of the proletariat have not only to be led by quasi-feudal quasi-bourgeois specimens, what is a much greater calamity, these specimens import into the Left parties some of the fixations and mannerisms that are products of their heritage. Feudalism insists on feuds, it idolises intolerance, it transmogrifies petty jealousy. Take a look at the cross-section of the allegedly revolutionary parties infesting West Bengal. Cannot one say that one of their major staples is intolerance of each other, envy at the prospect of one of them stealing a march over the other? This bland fact will, of course, never be admitted. The intolerance will be cloaked in tough ideological jargon. The subjective differences will be given the garb of historically incontrovertible objective differentiation. Ordinary petty bourgeois jealousies will be dressed up in the claptrap of the philosophical line and tactical rationality. The Hegelian process of thesis-antithesis-synthesis will unfold ad infinitum in an archetypal Bengali Hindu middle-class setting. From the snakepit of intolerance and jealousy, the antithesis will rear its head. But since, for long-term survival, the revolutionary groups have perforce to cling together every time the authorities launch an onslaught, a kind of synthesis will in no time occur; this will soon again give way to a further bout of tension, and a further bout of mutual name-calling, till the announcement of the fire next time. And so on, till dawn does not usher in the revolution.

The pattern has stuck, and continues to repeat itself. With all the animosity of the Centre, with all the other indiscretions committed, individually and collectively, by the different Left parties, the second United Front Government in West Bengal could perhaps have continued till this year, and the course of history around these parts could have been substantially different. But it was jealousy and hatred and suspicion of one another which turned out to be the determining variable. To keep the United Front going would have been to allow one amongst the Left parties to come to the fore. Who knows, that party, given its superior clout, could soon have swallowed the others. Such a thing could not be permitted to happen: it was better that the Left, the great revolutionary Left, rather ceased to be in government. Talk to each of these parties today. Some of them would assign broader national considerations for their not agreeing to the continuance of the United Front in 1970. Some others would mention the big-party chauvinism developed by one of the partners. Yet others would complain that the rules of the game were not being properly observed by any of the parties. A few would read a tract on how it was necessary, at that juncture, to liquidate the United Front in order to cleanse the Left of the stench of sterile parliamentarism. But smokescreens are smokescreens. What motivated them was fear—fear that one of the parties might get way ahead of the others; fear bred envy; while there was still time, the rest of them must therefore do in that party. They tried to do it in, and therefore the overall leftist cause in 1970, and continued to do so till 1972. It is only following March 1972 that the intolerable pressure of external circumstances has forced the revolutionaries to rediscover the good points in one other.

You think the malady is confined only to the conventional Left parties enamoured of the parliamentary path and still encrusted in quasi-feudal quasi-bourgeois ethos? You have a shock coming your way. One has only to refer to the umpteenth divisions into which the Naxalite movement is now splintered. Learned theses are still smuggled in and out, from this or that hideout, from this or that prison; they find their way into newspapers and journals, go to great lengths to explain how these splinters are consequential to fundamental differences in philosophical attitudes and tactical lines. Are they really? Scratch the surface, behind the facade of earth-shaking tactical lines would emerge the ugly face of commonplace, no longer even feudal, but essentially crass, petty-bourgeois bickerings. The bickerings could be as much over philosophical visions as over the disposal of funds or over who must wangle a trip to China at whose expense. And this despite the fact that, on the individual plane, there are, and have been, magnificent displays of courage, devotion to the cause and willingness to suffer.

History is supposed to make pace in this manner, through the deus ex machina of parties with greater historical relevance determinedly pushing out those whose lines and tactics have become obsolete. One would like to believe in the proposition and play along—if only one were sure that the spectre which is haunting the entire Bengal scene is not, to a considerable extent, the spectre of ordinary, common or garden village feuding.

1974

16 A Wizened Crowd

Call it a waiting of quality. One meets hundreds of young boys and girls who were supposed to sit for the university's final examinations in 1972. It is, the calendar says, July 1973, but the 1972 examinations are yet to take place. With luck, the university may be able to organise the ritual toward the whining end of the year; the results, again with luck, may be announced some time around the middle of 1974. This has gone on, year after year, with each year's examinations, and will, bless you, continue to go on. There is a certain elongation of the allegedly academic process in which each of the parties concerned—the university, the students, the teachers, the paper-setters and examiners—have quietly acquiesced. Between holding the examinations and not holding them, between passing the examinations and not passing them, between deliberate speed and excruciating delay, the intersection of the timeless moment stares you in the face. Not a shadow intervenes; the concept of time has been shed of its corpus, additions and subtractions and multiplications and divisions, each and all, are reduced to a species of total indifference.

Or perhaps not. Perhaps a few shrewd calculations inform the decision to put up with the apparent absurdity of the current happenings. Who knows, in this particular instance, there could have been a converging judgment that a quota of speed and efficiency, a hustling of the process would be a less than optimal arrangement. For as long as the examinations are not held, technically these boys and girls remain students, and, therefore, by definition, cannot be considered as part of the job-seeking working force. For as long as they are students, these boys and girls can postpone their worries, and help postpone the worries of others. They themselves know it, the university knows it, the Government is equally aware of the droll truth. Given the absence of adequate capacity in the system to absorb the young men and women into productive occupations, it is a superior solution to offer them a simulated extension of their tenure as students. The psychological wear and tear involved in such a solution is negligible, and even the outlay in terms of real resources for the nation as a whole is much less than what would be necessary if one were to mount a determined effort to place them in employment. As the jargon-toting economists would say, the opportunity cost of not holding the examinations is so little as to be laughable.

So they wait, this throng of the young ones. They are a wizened crowd, wise much beyond their years. If you came this way, they will inform you in matter-of-fact non-poetry, starting from anywhere, at any time or at any season, it would always be the same: you would have to, rest assured, put off sense and notion. Between passing and not passing, between claiming a first-class degree and not claiming one, there is hardly any differentiation to be made: when jobs are in such short supply, the fact of an additional university degree—or the lack of it—can be, and usually is, brushed aside. How does it, therefore, matter if the examinations run two years behind schedule, or, when they are finally held, are reduced to a farce? Since degrees have long ceased to be legal tender, how does it matter if the practice of unfair means is organised in the manner of large-scale military operations? Live and let live, pass and let pass, for you all belong to the same vast fraternity, the fraternity without hope, that morose constituency of the would-be-without-jobs. A premium is deservedly to be placed on devices which can put off the date of the formal entry into the rolls of the constituency. For as long as one can still describe oneself as a student, there is a postponement of the despair, a tentative moratorium on the agony of feeling responsible: please allow them to remain as students as long as it is decently feasible. The authorities agree with an unprecedented alacrity, the arrangement suits everybody fine. Each time the examinations get postponed, it is once more a lofty illustration of the splendour of the zero-sum game.

And since nobody knows the precise shape and contours of the future, or when the examinations will be announced, the boys and girls flock to the Bombay films. These have been a great leveller: the snooty Bengalis too have been completely bowled over. Even a Satyajit Ray film will run for a bare four to five weeks in a Calcutta cinema; in the nooks and corners of the mofussil, it will last for much less. But specimens of Rajesh Khanna-Sharmila Tagore mish-mash will go on for months on end. These outpourings from Bombay are crude, vulgar, absurd. So what; the more absurd they are, so much the better, so much more is their allure. The young men and women, awkwardly poised on this or that side of twenty, are already aware of the darkness awaiting them. A whiff of Scott Fitzgerald may still cling to the air: tender, one would be told, ought still to be the night, it is a little too early to put up the shutters. But, there you are, no feasible alternatives can really be worked out; these young people will, sooner or later, have to be told that they are a condemned lot; they already have a hunch of that, give or take a couple of days, or weeks, or months, or years, they know that they will be duly informed. Waiting for the summary gloom which is going to overtake them, they choose to escape into the absurdity of the Bombay film. No tithe yet on wild dreams or proxy adventures. They therefore absorb the fantasies; they, vicariously, rush into the luxurious embrace of a near-ethereal Sharmila Tagore; equally vicariously, they go through the thrills and excitements which accompany the exploits of a Sashi Kapoor or a Shatrughan Sinha. They scale all the impossible heights, mount all the impossible horses. In that technicoloured, slushy, gooey revue, for a spell of a brief one hundred and fifty minutes, they experience a certain transformation of even their physical sensitivity; the fare served up is cheap at the going price. Once you step out of the cinema hall, outside, it may be, and is, squalor, joblessness, degradation, hunger and the rest of it. But let another couple of days pass, once you are able to scrape another couple of rupees, you can hop back into the languid amour of the cinema hall and be transported back to the melody of the soft clouds, luscious heroines, fantastic good looks, limitless money.

Somebody in New Delhi must have studied with a fierce diligence the formula of the Bombay movies. The latter have accomplished two great distinctions. First, they have managed to place the accent on the subterranean unity which is pervasive in the diversity that is India. They have ended the quest for the lowest common factor in India's life and part of it. Whether it is the Punjabi farmer or the artisan from Uttar Pradesh or the Santhal share-cropper from Bihar or the clerk from Bengal or the nomad from Nagaland or the bank accountant from Tamil Nadu or the professional agitator from Kerala, none can escape the aphrodisiac which the Bombay film is. The animosities of language wear down, the little local chauvinisms are contained the moment the crowds huddle together before the magic screen and the vamp of a Helen begins her acrobatics. Certainly of much greater significance, the Bombay films have also taught the people the great art of total oblivion. That dreams could be an impeccable, one hundred per cent surrogate of reality would not ever have been believed unless they had arrived on the scene. Between the sham and the genuine, the Bombay films have convinced the young men and women, there is no distinction worth making; in fact, the real thing belongs to the never-never land, which is all the greater reason to prefer the ersatz.

Somebody elsewhere grabbed at the lesson. Beginning with 1969, what is happening in the Indian polity is only a grotesque, daring version of the archetypal Bombay film. Serve up the most extravagant promises, utter the most absurdly ridiculous pronouncements, condition your audience to a state of dotage by feeding them a bunch of imbecile prescriptions. The formula has worked, will work. It has happened any number of times since pre-history, that the amateurs have, after a while, altogether ejected the professionals from the arena. They should watch out, the tribe of Helens and Sharmila Tagores; they are in great danger of losing their bread-ticket.

1973

17 A Reserve Army of Poets

It is always the weighted average of your guess and my guess and our next door neighbour's guess, but, according to one set of statistics, there are at present nearly five hundred poetry magazines and fifteen thousand practising poets in West Bengal. Determining the current number of poetry magazines can be a matter of semantic exercise. For some of these may appear only once in five years, or appear just once and fade into oblivion. A whole lot of others are supposed to be monthly, bi-monthly, or quarterly publications, but their periodicity varies with the financial straits of the managing editor at any given moment. There is that other specimen, representing a genre of passion which is a cross between love of poetry and love of entertainment, for example, the daily poetry magazines which usually assert their existence every year during the week or fortnight when Calcutta celebrates Tagore's birth anniversary. In one or two stray years, one has also heard of hourly poetry bulletins. The births, deaths and periodicities of these magazines are afflicted by an acute stochasticity, and bands of budding mathematician economists, if they are so interested, can have a whale of a time trying to fit a simulated Markov process or some such thing to the phenomenon.

But even when frustrated by the random nature of the data concerning the number of Bengali poetry magazines, one is perhaps on much firmer ground while estimating the number of practising poets. There is a definitional problem here too, but the problem can be got over by adopting the point of view that a practising poet is one who has at least a dozen poems published in journals or magazines around the year. Alternatively, he could be one who, while appearing in journals only rarely, still manages to publish at least one volume of poetry every two years or thereabouts. Since an average issue of a poetry magazine carries poems by fifty poets—give or take a few—even allowing for overlapping and multiple appearances, there is a kind of coherence between the estimated number of poetry magazines and that of practising poets.

In the room serious people come and go, talking of Keynes, Marx or Pareto. But, meanwhile, what does one do with this furious rash of poetry, what does one do with West Bengal's reserve army of poets? Is it at all impossible to convert this obsession with poetry into an economic proposition? Even in a society violently gone over to the pursuit of economic growth, it would be worse than philistinism to question the role of poetry. Poetry enlarges the stock of imagination for a nation: investment in poetry, therefore, along with investment in other branches of literature and philosophy, ought to pay off by enlarging this stock. It is this stock of imagination which helps a country to produce brilliant engineers, brilliant technologists or brilliant planners. One can thus make a perfectly economic case of the State taking an increasingly positive role for expanding the availability of poetry in society. And if it could be shown that, given organisation and goodwill, the publication of poetry is viable even on narrow financial terms, to vote for the poets would become respectable even without recourse to shadow prices and social rates of discount.

Assume that roughly half of the fifteen thousand practising poets would have a volume ready for publication every year. That is to say, if finance were not the stumbling block, as against the current average of three to four hundred, seven thousand five hundred volumes of poetry could have been published in West Bengal. Even if demand is assumed to stay put at the estimated current level, it should be possible to sell six hundred copies of each volume. Since about one hundred extra copies are to be kept for complimentary distribution, a print order of seven hundred copies would be called for. Given the estimated costs on the basis of accepted specifications, including specifications pertaining to the quality of paper, layout and get-up and the average length of a volume, an expenditure of approximately one thousand rupees would be necessary to print this number of copies. For seven thousand five hundred volumes, therefore, the cost would come to around Rs 75 lakhs. If the average price is fixed at Rs 2.50 sales should net Rs 1.25 crores. If the Government or the banks help the authors with marketing outlets, the cost of distribution could be drastically pruned from what it is at present. Even were a fifteen per cent margin allowed for distribution, one should be able to end up with a rate of return of around thirty per cent or more from this venture into organised publishing of poetry. If this return is now evenly spread between the poets and those who would finance them, the latter would still end up with a rate of return of fifteen per cent, which should be able to meet the test of nearly all the dogmas—including the corniest one among them—with respect to project evaluation.

A tongue-in-the-cheek exercise? Leading the good-intentioned ones up the slippery path of lyrical vacuity? One can straightaway list the difficulties in the way of pushing such a project through.

For instance, it would be said that if seven thousand five hundred volumes of poems are to be published each year, even the impossible Bengalis would reach the point of surfeit; diminishing returns would fast set in; beyond the third or fourth year, the number of copies which could be sold would register a sharp decline. This would be a fear without basis. There is no end of poetry in the world, particularly in this part of the world. There is, similarly, no end to generations of poetry-lovers; they follow close upon the heels of one another. As population expands, so does, at least at a proportionate rate, the number of poets, and the number of readers who read what the poets compose. The crucial problem is organisational: educating the poets into the economics of it; persuading them to agree to band together in co-operatives so that they could negotiate, in an effective manner, with the banks or whichever other institution would finance them; taking care of problems of production and distribution; cajoling the financial bodies to forget their standardised notions about collateral. These institutions would have to be persuaded to accept the published copies as collateral and to forget the rest of their dehydrated regulations. With kindness in their hearts, they would also have to conduct the poets to the strange universe of accountability and economic viability, and, where necessary, organise them into marketing co-operatives so that distribution does not suffer.

Ultimately, it is a matter of judgment. Financing the poets is merely an illustrative category: there could be umpteen other creative activities which could be shored up if only some investment is thrown their way. Many multiples of seventy-five lakh rupees are being frittered away every year by the banking establishment here, there and everywhere. It could well be that one or two volumes would turn out to be what the Americans call lemons, and sell badly. But there is an elementary statistical proposition concerning the inertia of large numbers; seven thousand five hundred is a pretty large number.

There would be other objections, though. For one watching the current scene in West Bengal, the realisation may suddenly strike that the pity is in the poetry. Even revolution-mongering here has become a species of lyrical effusion; an excess of poetry has numbed almost all possibilities of activism. In these circumstances, to preach the notion of poetry as a marketable commodity could be akin to offering hostage to revisionist fortune. Between the Scylla of lyricism and the Charybdis of economism, the Bengali poet will thus have to make an awkwardly difficult choice. And, in the resulting frustration, he might perhaps end up by producing some more poetry. Which is where we came in.

1973

18 A Small Funeral

Last month, the court dancer took the final bow. It was a Sunday morning, rain was lashing the streets and lanes; Sadhona Bose, that heart-throb of the Indian screen in the distant 1930s, passed away in a run-down Calcutta apartment building. For most of the recent years, it was a wretched existence for her; the death was equally wretched. She died a pauper, uncared for, a lonely, prematurely old woman whom the world had forgotten. There was a small funeral procession; few cared to join, fewer even enquired who it was who was dead. No flowers for the court dancer of yesteryear: she did not belong any more.

There is material here, in the manner of her living as much as her death, of a rich, dense tragedy. A granddaughter of Keshab Chunder Sen, who married a grandson of Romesh Chunder Dutt, flouted the established conventions, played an avant garde role on both the stage and the screen, danced and sang her way into the hearts of millions, minted money once upon a time in Bombay. But, soon, the autumn leaves gathered, ups and downs intervened. Sadhona Bose returned to Calcutta, the leaves fell, a gradual fading into penury, oblivion and desolate death, an unfolding of history which is remorseless, but somehow also representative of the descending gloom.

Is not something similar happening to the Bengali cinema? For weeks on end in this city, you will find it awfully difficult to go to a Bengali picture even if you desperately wanted to. Of the eighty-odd cinema houses in Calcutta, not more than four show Bengali pictures on a regular run. The rest have mostly gone over to the gyrating products coming out of Bombay and, sometimes, Madras. If you take a census of the nearly four hundred cinema houses in the entire state, the position remains unchanged, not more than fifteen per cent of these will be exhibiting Bengali movies, and that too only on a spasmodic basis. A bare handful of Bengali pictures are produced each year these days; still worse, there is a long queue before they can be released, the halls are mostly pre-empted by the Hindi ones. No flowers for a dead Sadhona Bose, no demand for Bengali movies even in Bengal, and this despite the fact that, at the margin, Satyajit Ray and Mrinal Sen continue to be the rage. Whatever pictures they produce are instantly released and run for a respectable number of weeks. When their regular run is over, they are beckoned by the international circuit; some are also bought by the foreign television chains. Who knows, there is perhaps a bit of inverted operational logic here: because Satyajit Ray and Mrinal Sen have been discovered elsewhere, a reserve clientele is ensured for them back home. Even so, their takings will be small beer compared to what the average Bombay movie makes.

The plight of the majority of the Bengali pictures which manage to get released is much, much worse. These are supposed to be potboilers, but in fact are able to boil very few pots. Four decades ago, Calcutta was the hub of the country's film industry. There was no dearth of capital, no dearth of talent either. Apart from the great New Theatres, there were at least three or four other studios which enjoyed a brisk existence: pictures were made not just in Bengali, but in a dozen other Indian languages too, including, of course, Hindi. Geniuses and soldiers of fortune, from Prithviraj Kapoor to K.L. Saigal, flocked here in search of a career—and sudden, dazzling fame. In their wake arrived the musicians, the technicians and the rest. The old order has now changed beyond recognition. The banquet hall is deserted. Calcutta's ramshackle studios are empty. Work goes on, listlessly, intermittently, in one or two. The rest are on the point of closing. The number of unemployed directors vies with the number of assorted unemployed and underemployed technicians and actors. Some of the smart ones among the directors have migrated to Bombay; so too have some of the actors and actresses, scenario writers, composers and technicians. But, at any point of time, only a limited few can escape, the rest have to stay—and encounter death. The film industry, in short, epitomises the decadence which today defines Calcutta: I wait, you wait, they wait, everyone waits for the inexorable, melancholy, creeping death.

No distributor in his senses will agree to touch a run-of-the-mill Bengali film, and for very good reasons. In terms of box office appeal, they are non-starters. Just as a good Bengali movie—a Ray or a Sen—can be very, very good, one of medium quality can be a bore, and a bad one can be quite unbelievably bad. The non-Rays and the non-Sens are either straightforward tear-jerkers or inconsequential slapsticks or apologies of historical costume-dramas. None of them click. The tear-jerkers are shoddily produced and incompetently acted; they also stick to a formula which is now well-worn. The slapsticks, the outcome of a poor compromise between Bombay vulgarity and Bengali qualms, never really come off. The historical extravaganzas, invariably under-capitalised, betray a shoddiness in production; they cannot even begin to dream of taking custom away from the Bombay films.

The losers take nothing. They potter around, a morose crowd, blinking at the ever uncertain future. One or two lucky ones get a break. A slip of a refugee girl, making a debut in an unpretentious Bengali picture, is spotted by a talent scout from Bombay and is spirited away. In about a couple of years, she earns as much as five lakhs of rupees per picture, this much in 'white' and this much in 'black'. One or two composers are able to exploit their past connections with other composers already in Bombay, and get away; so do one or two technicians. The rest are the luckless ones; they lack connections. No hope for them; they stay and stagnate.

For a while, hope flickered; maybe, with the emergence of Bangladesh, the market for Calcutta pictures will expand. That could not have happened, and has not happened. Bangladesh has its own problems: its excess supply of producers, directors, actors, technicians and the like is no less than here. In terms of quality, the pictures made over there are perhaps even sloppier than the average Calcutta output. There is therefore little chance that the film industry there will allow free entry to the West Bengal products; they too have to survive.

From time to time, proposals are mooted about how the government could take a more activist role, pump funds into Calcutta's film industry, and ensure that more movies get produced. It is not, however, a mere question of production. Persuading the distributors to agree to release the pictures through their circuits is about as important. Distributors do their homework, they have their own market surveys. If a proportionately greater release of Bengali movies is going to ruin their profit margin, persuasion is bound to fail. And in case you press too hard, you run the danger of infringing this or that article of the Constitution.

Why Calcutta lost out to Bombay is an involved story; or

maybe it is not. One should really proceed from the general to the particular. What has gone wrong with the Bengali film industry is broadly the same as what has gone wrong with Bengali enterprise as such. One is face to face with a phenomenon for which no ready explanation can be found in either Alfred Marshall or, for that matter, J. Steindl: stagnation has come even before maturity. This has been seen to be repeated in different spheres of economic activity: in pharmaceuticals, in engineering, in book publishing. The moment a Bengali enterprise has reached the threshold of indivisibilities, it has faltered. Further expansion has hinged upon coalescing with outside elements and raising additional capital, but the Bengali has played hooky, and the shadow has begun to fall. If an invective is to be deployed, the appropriate one is perhaps petty bourgeois-mindedness. The Bengali industrialist has claimed to be an entrepreneur, but he has never really broken away from his domestic moorings. The more he has failed to enlarge his assets, liquid resources and technical capability by taking in outside funds and expertise, the more helpless he has felt in the face of the growing complexities of the world. His defence mechanism has consisted of an increasing withdrawal within his shell. Each of this has happened with the cinema industry too: in the initial phase, the opportunities all came knocking to Calcutta. They were not availed of, or were muffed. Calcutta's ennui became Bombay's great breakthrough.

All that now remains is a garish epilogue. You hear perfunctory talk every now and then: Bombay is all borrowed plumes, Calcutta has native talent; what Bombay can do, Calcutta can do even better; let the fog lift, Calcutta will flood the market with Bombay-type movies, packed with songs and cabaret dances and fights and acrobatics and wish-fulfilment and other insulting-your-intelligence ingredients: Bombay will be beaten at its own game. This again is petty bourgeois fantasy. You cannot make up for three decades of lagged investment in a jiffy: however hard you try there will now not be enough funds available in Calcutta to turn the production of motion pictures as lavish as it is in Bombay and Madras: Calcutta will be unable to recover from the initial disadvantage, the razzle dazzle will be missing. At the same time, call it the consequence of Bengali snobbery or Bengali intellect-mongering, even in terms of essential coarseness, Calcutta's pictures will continue to fall short of what Bombay or Madras are able to offer. There lies the rub. If you want to be a vamp, you have to be a vamp all the way: if you have mental or cultural reservations about playing the role, you will flop. The motion picture-going public, at least a large mass amongst them, have gone over to the banalities of the Hindi movie, but Calcutta's directors and technicians are still in two minds. They want to make money, but they also want to talk of Antonioni, Ozu and Wajda. This is preposterous. They must therefore suffer, and await death.

1973

19 The Nationalisation of Akhtari Bai

That was a different kind of world. Calcutta, the early 1930s, the era of Subhas Bose, J.M. Sen Gupta, and ersatz self-government which was the Calcutta Corporation. Nobody had heard of the poor, or bothered about them; they, or at least the bulk of them, were peasants—and Muslims. Kazi Nazrul Islam was all right, he was as good as being one of us; he had even married a Hindu girl. But pampering of the Muslims would not do. Somebody must tell Gandhi; Jinnah must be told off: the antics of Fazlul Huq must not be tolerated any more. The Congress, after all, was three-quarters solid Hindu *zamindars*. They had their beautiful mansions down Camac Street and Lansdowne Road. It was the nadir of depression, but so what? The Permanent Settlement had built-in virtues, the peasantry suffered, not the landlords. The landlords' real income in fact went up, as also the real income of the fixed income-earning middle class. Those were the days that were: Calcutta still had class; Begum Akhtar was still only Akhtari Bai—slip of a girl, singing, before the taluqdars at Lucknow, or the *zamindars* down Camac Street or Lansdowne Road in Calcutta, mostly light-classical.

On occasion, the terrorists would break loose and create news. Some silly girl would take a pot shot at Sir John Anderson, one or two police agents would get assassinated, there would be some comment in the newspapers, the despatches between the Secretary of State and the Viceroy, and between the Viceroy and the provincial Governors, would intensify. The Congress leaders would be torn by ambivalence: disapproval of the doings of hotheaded young people would be combined with agitated condemnation of British obtuseness. After a brief while, the racket would die down. The Muslim peasantry would continue to be pressed down upon. The landlords would supervise, through their umpteen agents, the efficient collection of revenue. Come December, the Viceroy would address the Bengal Chamber of Commerce. The *zamindars* would be in their full regalia. In the evenings, Akhtari Bai Fyzabadi would perform. During the day, there would be cricket. Remember all those names who constituted the core of the Calcutta and Ballygunge Cricket Clubs? Longfield, Belirend, Van der Gutch, Hosie? Rabindranath Tagore would be in Santiniketan, and all would be right with the world. The Bengali poets were a considerable community; they would be short of funds, but no matter; in the early 1930s they would always somehow manage to bring out avant garde journals which, though as a matter of principle against Tagore, would publish as their opening piece his long letters praising or castigating them. The Bengali young men, that is, those who were Hindus, would divide themselves in two easily identifiable goods; would-be terrorists and would-be poets. Sometimes would-be terrorists would outnumber the would-be poets, sometimes it would be the other way round: here and there there would be some overlap. Every now and then, this or that odd professor would quote from Lunacharsky or Leon Trotsky. What the Russians were doing unto themselves would be the staple of some infrequent discussion or other. But barely anybody would lose his sleep because of the distant thunder which was Moscow or Leningrad. The poor were quiet and submissive, they were mostly peasants, and they were Muslims. All one had to do was to tell blighters like A.K. Fazlul Huq where to get off; the rest would be peace and tranquillity. The Metro Cinema would perhaps have on a Janet Gaynor film, and there would always be Akhtari Bai to listen to at this or that *zamindar's* place. There would be no occasion to chant in mournful numbers that life was one long empty dream. It was not, it could not be, the poor were not around, and Akhtari Bai was performing in the evening.

Came the War—and the Partition. It was a terrible wrench for the Bengali Hindu *zamindars*. The next thirty years they have continued their desultory attempts at rehabilitating themselves—spiritually as much as physically. There was an end to indolence: the houses on Camac Street and Lansdowne Rood caved in, the revenue disappeared, the Hosies and the Longfields departed—maybe to Australia or to Canada—but they also took with them a certain style of living. The surplus was raised in the paddy fields of north and east Bengal, though it used to circulate in Calcutta. The British had set up the arrangement, the Hindu *zamindars*, lawyers and doctors gave corpus to it: luncheon at the Firpo's, fruitcake and other patisserie for Christmas, illumination at Chowringhee and Park Street, gala ball at the Governor's house: the Calcutta Club would be agog, the Viceroy would be at the Belvedere, he would receive the gentry from nine in the morning till late in the afternoon, the realities of poverty and pestilence would fade into the dark background. Bade Ghulam Ali would be in town, so would Akhtari Bai, then a slip of a girl.

As the war ended, and the country was split in two, this style of life was dealt the coup de grace. Other modalities for the circulation of surplus value had to be thought of. The problem was not in the germination of surplus: in our land the poor are for ever, they are always squeezable. But there could have been—as they love to say in economics—a 'realisation' problem. The disappearance of the filthily rich could have heralded a cultural crisis. The new class of industrialists did succeed in filling the vacuum, but only up to a point. For, meanwhile, even culture had proliferated—with its thousand promenades and cul-de-sacs. The wretched of the earth remained the wretched of the earth; culture flourished, however—and grew. What the industrialists on their own failed to accomplish, they left for the State. Those who, ensconced in comfort, had once read Leon Trotsky on proletcult, suddenly felt elated. The State stepped in, and the realisation crisis was over! Akhtari Bai blossomed forth as Begum Akhtar.

Thus, at the Centre, a Ministry, supposedly charged with the responsibility of looking after Education, also took over Culture. The 'Akadamis'—not academies—came into their own. Culture was nationalised, and a policy of discriminating pricing came into operation. It was both monopoly in the product market and, simultaneously, monopsony in the factors market. What favours to dispense to which artiste or singer or playwright or painter or poet became the prerogative of those in authority. And the distribution of the works of the poets and playwrights and artists also became the subject of centralised decision-making. Till as long as Jawaharlal Nehru happened to be around, the supplanting of the taluqdars and the *zamindars* by the State did not perhaps make a difference—after all, Nehru's style of operation was hardly distinguishable from that of a nineteenth-century Hindu overlord. In the sphere of culture at least, his intervention ensured a continuance in the character of patronage. Akhtari Bai was transformed into Begum Akhtar, but there was a whiff of past memories in the modulations of her voice; from time to time, the slip of a girl would attempt to rush to the stage and dislodge the doughty dowager which Begum Akhtar had become.

As you look around, first to this side and then to that, it is a queer mixture of a set-up: slapdash semi- and quasi-feudalism co-exists with degenerate mercantilism and gawky-eyed capitalism. The nationalisation of Culture, spell it with a big C, could not but give rise to a series of oddities, and a large portmanteau of outrages. Culture was taken over by the State. But the nature of the State being what it has been, the masses have been doled out only droll tunes, expatiating on the virtues of family planning through the community wireless sets; occasionally, supplementary meals have been served too—such as how, through the heroic endeavours launched and guided by whoever happened to be in power, this noble land was saved from the designs of the nefarious Chinese. But all the while, the good things of life were reserved for the rich—the ruling class, who alone had entitlement to listen to Begum Akhtar or watch Yamini Krishnamurthy on State-sponsored occasions.

The slip of a girl made good, she transcended her humble origins, she became rich and famous, she, Akhtari Bai Fyzabadi, became Begum Akhtar, recipient of many State awards. And she travelled outside the country—a cultural ambassadress, spreading the gospel of India's aesthetic refinements. In other words, she was captured, became a cog in the machine. When she was not rich and famous, she would come down to Calcutta, the clientele of affluent landlords would of course be there, but she also had a different category of admirers. Young people—and some of the old—from middle-class homes would ask her to sing for them free of charge; and she would agree. Even before the I.P.T.A., there was therefore this—howsoever tepid or feeble—effort to sing for the masses. Once the State took over Culture, it was altogether a different proposition. Akhtari Bai was nationalised. She became Begum Akhtar. She had little time to spare for ordinary people. After catering to the whims of those in authority, whatever little leisure she had went for the edification of the rich. Akhtari Bai, Begum Akhtar, died in harness. It is a pity she could not be liberated before her death: the nightingale, as long as she was around, remained chained to the cage.

1974

20 An Ordinary Man

Home is the sailor, home from the sea. He was an ordinary man, belonging not even to a species, but a genus. He had his early schooling in Santiniketan: but that was a mere episode, long-forgotten, even by him. An ordinary man who, a while ago, had crossed his sixtieth year, with archetypal Bengali Hindu middle-class affinities and alignments, hopes and aspirations, scuttled beyond redemption by the rampaging inflation. A homeopath by profession. He died last week.

An ordinary death. The homeopath was suffering, for the past few months, from various ailments common to hard-placed, undernourished old men. He shuttled between hospital and home a number of times, his health did not improve; despite medication and care, the complications grew, and his general condition continued to deteriorate with every week. Last week, he died. It was an ordinary funeral. A small circle of friends gathered. They remembered the hundred kindnesses rendered to them by the man. spanning over many, many years; they remembered his warmth, his generosity, the magnificent grace which defined his personality; it was a moment of empathy and commiseration, mutually shared and offered. But a moment like this is always brief. It was an ordinary funeral, the funeral of an ordinary man, it did not take long. The friends dispersed. The family is now left to its loneliness. It is not just the loneliness which follows the departure of a close and dear one. There are, inevitably, major economic implications of the death of the head of the household. The vacuum left by an ordinary man's passing can indeed assume extraordinary proportions.

An ordinary man. Even as a homeopath, he was perhaps just about ordinary. Till his very last days, he remained somewhat overawed by the skill and proficiency of better-known eminences in the profession. He had, besides, that innate modesty: deference to the views, and sometimes idiosyncracies, of others was second nature to him. An ordinary man, who never asserted himself, whose professional opinions too were always expressed mutely. An ordinary man who was professionally popular, but not 'successful'. Success is measured in terms of rates of return. The homeopath could barely make enough for his family. In more recent years, as his health began to fail, the state of finances became increasingly more precarious. But this again identified him as being only one of a genus. The number of professional men, whether in medicine or law or teaching, for whom in this clime living is an unceasing struggle to scrape a minimal of income, is legion; Calcutta and the mofussils are literally strewn with such specimens. You can spot them by the pallor of their faces, by the trace of chronic malnutrition in their physique, by the cynicism and bitterness which keeps intruding into their vocabulary.

The homeopath, until a few years ago, kept the bitterness within himself. He succeeded in discovering sources of serendipity. Call it love for your neighbours, call it social conscience, he considered it great fun to medicate, free of charge, for the poor and needy in working class slums. The coarseness of commerce never intervened. There was no fanfare. The homeopath's chamber was bare, commonplace. It would have been atrocious had it been otherwise; an excess of dazzle would have put off his clientele. Sometimes he would be paid a token fee; most of the time there was no question of a fee. Odd calls here and there, now and then, would fetch some income; these were chancy and altogether too infrequent. But you telephone him, he always had time for you and your problems; he could not afford a car, but he would trudge on foot, or push his body into the frighteningly overcrowded public transport and arrive where you wanted him to be, tired but cheerful, full of solicitude and courtesy. Doing a good turn to others was for him a cerebral impulse. The sum of such impulses was his life. And, all the while, money would continue to be short. But you would never guess by looking at him: graciousness had little to do with the presence or absence of money.

Even an impoverished homeopath, though, has his dreams. Perhaps our quiet, gentle man had a greater claim to dreaming dreams. Most of the time, he dealt with the down and out; percentage-wise, there are more honest and good human beings amongst the tramps and the destitute ones than amongst the filthy rich who travel to private nursing homes for the treatment of their maladjusted egos. The kingdom of the poor ought to come, and soon, the homeopath must have felt. But you have to work for it, the filthy rich deserve to be dispossessed, there will never be a voluntary abdication on their part; there must be a movement, a political movement, a movement which begins at the grassroots, so that the kingdom of the poor could come.

The homeopath was an ordinary man, a quiet man, but he had his passion, his own convictions. These were not quite explicitly stated in all seasons. Here was a polite man; despite the fact that the crowd he treated consisted mostly of the poor, the Bengali Hindu middle-class tradition made it inevitable that he straddle a wide enough social spectrum in the course of his daily perambulations. He was firm in his views, but rudeness did not come easily to him; who knows, perhaps he considered it better strategy to camouflage his political predilections when visiting the camp of the enemy. But the devotion and allegiance remained. He was not exactly a part of the political movement; yet it would be preposterous to suggest that he was not. He and the likes of him have always been around, giving flesh, ever since 1905 or thereabouts, to deep-stirring political concepts. They have shunned the limelight, but no movement worth its name could have developed without the sustained spadework put in by them. All along, they have acted as catalysts between people and ideas. A dream has to be brought home; a star has to be cajoled to make a landing. An enormous lot of anonymous perseverance is called for in this task: hard unobtrusive slogging, day after day, in different spheres of social existence. Party leaders and party cadres play their parts: but an almost equal contribution is made by a handful who remain outside the domain of established party structure, genuine volunteers, who shun prominence, do not sign manifestos, refuse to join a delegation or, for that matter, a procession, but for whom the dream remains no less the real thing. Lawyers, doctors, teachers, they constitute the great tribe of catalysts, the moulders of mass sentiments, the non-loquacious, non-demanding organisers. They do not proclaim it from the housetops: their identification with the cause is nevertheless total. For its sake, they sacrifice their time, their opportunity for money-making; completely integrated individuals, they straightaway perceive the link between the context of the dream and their mundane, immediate, chores. The rainbow of a bridge joins their life with their dream. The great silent army of dreamers marches along.

The homeopath was one such dreamer. He was an ordinary man; ordinariness defined his being. He had no great personal ambitions. He remained loyal to his friends, loyal and affectionate and generous. But, alongside, he remained loyal to the cause of social and political change. He was a sympathiser, not a cadre. But the grammar of nomenclatures can be a pretentions portmanteau: instead of revealing, it can obfuscate. In his modest, silent way over the years he signed in his contribution. In such matters, there is always a problem of toting; once the memory of a few people is obliterated, none will remember the specifics of his sacrifice. Those who seek anonymity easily come to it. It is a superior choice in most cases. The more civilised ones themselves do not want their names to be bandied about. So it happens. Through the ages, the silent ones remain the silent ones, unknown, unacknowledged, unlisted. But the law of human dynamics would have been immobilised without them. History does not inscribe their names in its scrolls, but history will hardly ever dare to negate them.

The homeopath, kind, solicitious of the welfare of neighbours, did not suffer from any crisis of identity. He loved to tend others, including the large number of the poor who were unable to pay him, either for his visit or for his medicine. There was a certain community of affection between him and those whom he treated, free. Maybe, because he loved them, they also came to love his cause; they came to the awareness—more by instinct than by tuition—that his cause in fact was theirs: he would not have even bothered to work for the cause, if it were not for them.

A hero in his own manner, but there will be no record of his heroism. The last few years made a sombre chapter. Suddenly the cause seemed to be more distant than ever; externalities came to loom large in the calculus of possibles and probables; confusion rent the air. These were years of a certain sadness; it was as if while the cause remained as it ought to be always, some unscrupulous elements had walked away with the props of one's faith. Disease and illness one can put up with; it is much harder when one's zest for life is gone.

An ordinary existence. The ordinary life of an ordinary man. And now an ordinary death. But all these do add up, otherwise history would be a fraud. It is the ordinary men who shape the modalities of history, despite the fact that the scrolls do not mention them. Ordinary men, great in their particular manner. The homeopath, Amal Sen, slipped away, last week; an ordinary death, the hunter home from the hills. Amal Sen, an ordinary man, nevertheless a great man. His greatness will enrich history, even though history will be barely aware of it.

1974

21 The Quashing of Many Dreams

This is an inexorable process, and the shortage of paper claims victims in remotest quarters. The little magazines are in danger of extinction. The ones with pretensions of monthly appearance have converted themselves into quarterlies; the quarterlies have turned into biannuals; the biannuals have ceased to be so, they have become so much chancy statistic. And all of them have thinned down.

Thereby, a certain richness of life is being rubbed out. Call it a transmutation of the libido, call it the burning of not-altogether-sparable calories, the little magazines represented an archetypal heritage of the Bengali middle class. There is this continuous tussle between mind and matter; these magazines were great duels in the sun: the mind challenging matter. Take any cross-section of clerks, school and college teachers, the unemployed. At any given moment, they are without funds; the sum of these moments is their collective existence. Nonetheless, at any given moment, a fair number amongst them were wont to indulge in the luxury of a little magazine. The range of themes such magazines would cover boggled conventional imagination: flaming prose; flaming poetry; poetry as much of the revolution as of the cloister; Jean Genet and the theatre of the absurd; alienation and young Marx; personalised essays, some harping on the nostalgia of life in Presidency College circa 1949, some dilating on the epic heroism of an obscure woman partisan in Vietnam, another one perhaps analysing the agony of a cricket enthusiast on the eve of a test match; a number exclusively given to short stories: Utpal Dutt and the crisis of Bengali drama; Baudelaire and the concept of hell; nineteenth-century Calcutta tapestries; a discourse on whether Titu Mir was a revolutionary or a charlatan; neo-fascism, fundamental rights and the elections of 1972; translations of three, or six, or eight French slapsticks; annotated commentaries on Antonio Gramsci's prison notes; a heavily footnoted dissertation on the Central Intelligence Agency's roster of alleged activities in South Asia since 1946; the McMohan Line and Neville Maxwell's India war; is Rilke relevant in the post-EEC European context; a pistachio of an issue running down, evenhandedly, the CPM, Satyajit Ray and the up-and-coming Davis Cup player. And the magazines would come in all sizes and shapes. The pages would be replete with naive snobbery; occasionally, there would be name-dropping aplenty; gushes of lyricism would follow twenty pages of spouting of revolutionary fire; crass dishonesty would coexist with all too obvious integrity. The writers would run each other down; adversaries would be called the vilest of names; opportunism would snugly creep up and make a niche for itself next to the fearless outpouring of invective against well-known establishment figures.

Good, bad, often indifferent, together they still constituted a climate. A mirror to Bengali middle class life, you could say. Insufferable egotism, matinee-kind sentimentalism, wide-eyed sensitiveness, incorrigible nihilism, malice stemming from close, claustrophobic existence, the imagination full of audacity, the courage to dream impossible dreams, the courage to compose incredibly sensuous lines, the total indifference to the even bare rudiments of economics and finance, dangerous survival from day to day. Some of the contents might have appeared to you as prize specimens of elongated adolescence, some others to be atrocious beyond words; but suddenly, in the melee, one would come across a piece, either short or long, describing with meticulous care the sociological foundations of nineteenth-century French cuisine, or a profoundly moving, strikingly original tract on Albert Camus and the notion of decadence.

Take it or leave it, these little magazines were a composite whole, an assertion of the leftover life of the Bengali middle class now fast a-dying. Economic opportunities have long passed them by. A combination of follies and circumstances has ensured that, in money matters, they will remain inept forever. Often the Centre will be blamed, with or without reason, for all that has happened or has not happened. Now and then, a more perspicuous piece would appear, perhaps in one of these magazines, drawing attention to the native deficiencies of the Bengalis themselves: it would be hard-hitting, mercilessly objective, not mincing a word. But while hard words do not break bones, they do not alter the face of reality either. Some of Bengal's young people have thus sought sublimation in revolutionary death, some have disappeared behind prison bars: some others have taken to Bonnie-and-Clyde quasi-adventures, but with little of pure romanticism percolating in them. All of that, however, still leaves out a considerable number.

These latter do not quite know which way to turn. This is a confession they would hate to make even to themselves. The Bengali ego remains the Bengali ego. Woefully lacking in funds, deficient in calories, the Bengali youth—parochial, impossible—would still like to imagine the rest of the world to be lying at their feet. They might be without food, the only nourishment since morning till late afternoon might be a few tepid cups of tea or coffee, the animation would still not quite go out of their constitution. At this time, and at all times, every one of them is a hero unto himself. The hero would launch a little magazine.

Perhaps nothing would ever be set on fire. Perhaps the course of a little magazine was always pre-determined, predictable, as predictable as the volatility of Bengal's youth. Perhaps to an outsider, idly leafing through the pages of these magazines in a street-corner stall, the contents were excruciatingly tiresome; perhaps when you got to know a couple of them, you had known them all. Even so, it would be no move towards the direction of Pareto Optimality if these shut down, as might soon be the case with most of them if the cost of paper becomes increasingly prohibitive and the all-round inflation raises other costs alongside. For it would then be a world without catharsis. As Aristotle sayeth, it is not gnosis, but praxis must be the fruit. To grant each his own gnosis is not enough. The ego must have its outlet. The decrepit Bengali youth, bereft of co-ordinates, cannot prosper in business; they will flounder in industry; the land-man ratio will keep them away from agriculture; they by now have neither the inclination nor the aptitude to join the various administrative services in their hordes. Binomial causations are at work, and these youngsters, even if they wanted to, will no longer be able to catch up with the remorseless turns of history. Economic opportunities are a function of asset-holdings. It is altogether futile to speculate whether the distribution of asset-holdings, as it has come about, has a built-in bias against these young people, or whether the nemesis has been brought about by the Bengali's passion for iconoclasm and vacuous romanticism. Maybe; the latter of the propositions has an element of truth in it. But a purposive endeavour to rid the Bengali of his core of cynicism-alternating-with-romanticism might hardly do much good either. Take away their little magazines, and several of these youngsters would be deprived of the privilege of the only praxis they know. The closure of the magazines would not automatically lead hem into the ante-rooms of money-minting companies, nor into the cosy parlour of the government. The issue of asset-structure is not a mere matter of psychological obsession: it is very much a concrete entity, and cannot be demolished at short notice just because some alleged idlers have their fiddling instruments confiscated. Those who are in with the assets would resist those who are out; the would-be gate-crashers, the overwhelming majority of them, would return empty-handed. What would they do then without their little magazines?

It is only a thin dividing line separating the hilarious from the tragic: A world without little magazines could, according to some, appear to be a world with some less trash. If you happen to be a cost-benefit megalomaniac from the ravines of economics, the disappearance of the little magazines might even appear to be a crucially significant development, bottling up a 'non-priority' activity, with so much saving of precious paper. Nobody seemingly is bothered about the opportunity cost involved: quantifying that might mean venturing to look beyond one's nose, always an inconvenient exercise. By shutting down the little magazines, you would of course kill many loves, quash many dreams. But, what should be more relevant, you would be shutting off a modality of expression: the emotions which belong to a dangerous span of years would henceforth keep simmering, but would not be able to simmer over. A complex of urges would grope around in search of an outlet. The libido must have other alternatives for its sublimation. If there is not going to be any letting out of words, who knows, there might be a whole lot of extra letting of blood.

1974

22 Cometh the Goddess

Once more, the onslaught of the festive season. The season has now been captured, almost in entirety, by the urban classes. Gods and goddesses are fast shedding their rural roots. The poor over there do not have the wherewithal to worship divinity, and the rich still feel insecure enough not to turn the season of the Durga into an exercise in lavish exhibitionism. Gods and goddesses nevertheless have to survive, they have to for the sake of the parasites who make a living out of the business of community worship. The commercialisation of the Bengali pantheon, one could almost say. And commercialisation and urbanisation go hand in hand.

The resulting process is akin to creating value from circulation. Put the squeeze, put the squeeze, skim the fat off the rich householder, the shady-looking businessman, the income tax-beating professional; let the funds flow. But, on the other hand, also put the squeeze on the poor school teacher, the struggling clerk, the harassed wife of a lowly-placed pensioner. Rosa Luxemburg's 'third persons' are very much on the scene; they will use the alibi of the worshipping season to levy an impress upon you, irrespective of your absolute or relative economic position, and thus come to money. Do not ask them how the money is going to be spent. Who does not know that conventional account-keeping is a hang-over of the past colonial days? If you insist, an annual general meeting of the committee of festivities will be convened; a report from an established firm of accountants, meticulously listing the validated heads of income and expenditure, will be made available to you; the vouchers and cash memos will be all there. These are constituents of the general pyrotechnics of third-person existence. The tribe of parasites will continue to flourish—and rule. The world belongs to them.

There is a certain heartlessness in the gaiety that ensues. Command music and ersatz glamour make up the stock-in-trade of festive occasions. Suddenly, the scarcity of power is no longer a relevant variable. Illuminations dazzle the eye; the drums beat, rising to a crescendo; 'cultural programmes' become a compulsory appendage to the public worship of the deity; the incurable politicians make their appearance; true to the cultural norm, they 'inaugurate' even the worshipping. The 'third persons' have an intensely busy time: as money jingles, they look busier, more intense, they feel more smugly self-important. This is all part of the game. There is a certain heartlessness in it all. The inexorable law of survival is the inexorable law of survival. Each is for himself or herself. The 'third persons' could not care less if the hungry crowd keep pressing against the enclosures where the worship is being organised. Business is business; the business of worship could not possibly be suspended because a few unfortunate ones have run across some little, local difficulties—they being unable to secure the food which could ameliorate hunger. Ah, well, have you not noticed that this year, under disbursements, we have introduced a special additional item: famine relief? That should take care of the problem. In the meantime, ladies and gentlemen, you will be glad to know that in tomorrow's cultural programme, we have been able to add a further item: Shrimati Bhimpalashri Basu has kindly consented to a recital of Kathak dances.

A total dissociation from the realities of life is thus proclaimed. These proceedings, besides, are not taking place eight hundred, a thousand or fifteen hundred miles or kilometres away, these are aspects of reality from the immediate neighbourhood, that woman is imploringly begging for a morsel of food in a lane hardly a hundred metres away from the park where the community worship is being held, the rickety children who stare vacantly at the dazzling image of the deity are as much a part of the objective correlate as Shrimati Bhimpalashri Basu. But, there you are, commercialisation extracts it all, the process of civilisation is denuded of all traces of subjectivism. Society is rendered into one vast marketplace: it is only the cry of prices which matters here, the cry of prices backed by effective demand, reserve as well as of the normal sort. The other cry, the cry of the needy, leaves no impress: money talks, the lack of money is a fatal deficiency, the consequences of this deficiency will visit those who are afflicted by it.

It is little use to argue in terms of the aesthetics of it, either. Aesthetics has been, through the ages, always class-based. The blood sport the Romans used to indulge in did not attract any opprobrium on aesthetic grounds from any of the contemporary critics; it was just so much good, clean fun, including the ritual of throwing the slaves to the lions. In your unguarded moments, you may begin to feel somewhat uncomfortable that saturated talk on egalitarianism, socialism and frugal living could still be combined with the phenomenon of unbridled merriment on the part of the upper classes even as people are dying in the streets for the altogether mundane reason of lack of food. But this, after all, is what *laissez-faire* is about, you have to take the rough with the smooth, you live and do not particularly care whether the others do, too. Aesthetics, unless properly tempered by pragmatism, remains an abstraction. And pragmatism duly takes into account the realities of class alignments while formulating a system of aesthetic values.

Thus it is that hardly one politician will be around if you ever take it upon yourself to run down the institution of community worships. The slightly more sophisticated specimens among the politicians might even attempt to educate you: the business of such worships activates the circulation of surplus value, to discourage them is to condemn oneself to a bleaker regimen of dull work and duller profit-taking. The surplus value per se, however, is not something to which one would claim a natural right, it arises because of the advance of petty, scheming men, who do not mind if people go hungry as long as they themselves can have a rollickingly good time. After all the sophistication is assembled, all the dissembling that is to be done is done, all the words that are to be gurgled out are gurgled out, the hungry and the starving continue to voice their feeble entreaty for food, while Shrimati Bhimpalashri Basu, exhilaration in her feet and limbs, dances all night. Or, is it a new phenomenon, this slide into insensitivity? The old-fashioned virtues of simplicity and benevolence have been rendered into curiosities; they have been substituted by a species of smart-alec-ism, which believes it can combine a lip service to socialism with the pursuit of untrammelled private gains. Such is the legacy of the more recent years. Fixers and commission agents, 'third persons' par excellence, are an inevitable adjunct to the system that has come into being: fix a job, fix a speech, if the public media are under your control, you can even fix a famine. The objective correlates, as they are called, may then appear in an altogether different light:

for you can even fix the definition of objectivity, and duly take care of the poet or the editor or the social scientist who demurs from your definition. Festivities and carnivals fit snugly into this arrangement. They exude and propagate the air of middle-class normalcy: they are the agents fixing the environment. The festive season is on, the drums beat, the chanting of the ethereal mantrams, the affluent flaunt their jewels and livery, Shrimati Bhimpalashri Basu's feet and hips pulsate to the rhythm of the onrushing Kathak number, the organisers of the gala worship push their way through the crowd, they never looked brisker, the politicians feel assured. Everything is under control, the famine has been fixed, the cry of the hungry is not cognisable, and has not one of the country's ministers already assured the Americans on his honour that not one person has died here on account of famine? Let the drums beat a brisker space then, there is an eerie upsurge of excitement in that recital of the Kathak, the season of festivities will soon be over, but, never mind, perhaps we will have other excitements forthcoming, if not exactly a pie in the sky, at least an indigenous version of the sputnik, and, who knows, perhaps to be followed by a general election?

1974

23 Totems Are All

As economic distress spreads, people in all walks of life discover their own escape-hatches from reality. Once the obvious solutions to life's umpteen problems fail, attention is diverted to the lure of faith-cure. Obscurantism displaces coherence in thought. Individuals begin to look for a sudden, magical turn in their personal affairs. Social solutions, they conclude, are not available: so they scrounge around for improvised modalities.

If one strolls along the thoroughfares of Calcutta, the phenomenon hits one in the eye. Alongside the proliferation of community worship, there has emerged the hegemony of spiritual leaders. Never has there been a larger ensemble of deities. Obscure gods and goddesses have been dragged out into the public domain. However, they do not come cheaper by the dozen: quite the contrary. Compulsory levy on the populace, enforced through political clout and brandishing of the dagger, leads to the accrual of a sizeable revenue each month in the different areas of the city, ostensibly for the purpose of arranging the worship of the deities. Unemployed youth have hit upon an avocation which makes it possible for them to combine religiosity with the earning of not inconsiderable pocket-money. A correlation of a sort has thus got established between the community worships and the mounting box-office success of low-grade Hindi movies. Next to the deities, and having almost equal significance, are the faith-healers who are mushrooming all over the place. They will cure your cancer, they will turn your brass into gold, they will get you a job, they will ensure your promotion in service, they will swing the contract in your direction, they will make you a minister, they will find a good match for your daughter.

Instant solutions to seemingly intractable problems are dangled before you. As nothing else has clicked, quite a number argue among themselves, why not, for a change, take recourse to a guru? This is a tantalising, slippery path. All you have to do is let the taboos and totems take over. A sizeable cross-section from among the poor as much as from the petty bourgeoisie, therefore, keep hopping between alternate poles. Militant mass action has not yielded any tangible dividends: let there be an interregnum: the interregnum of the guru.

So you come across layer within layer, trend within trend of Bengali fixations. To many who are temporarily or otherwise disenchanted with the efficacy of political struggle, a spiritual leader offers soothing balm. If, at any point of time, the political leader fails to deliver—or is found out to be, a false one—never mind, you still have the stand-by syndrome of spirituality. As happens with any collection of entrepreneurs, some of them are genuine, some are dross. A people whose awareness of the economic roots of social issues is yet heavily admixtured with emotional fizz, finds it difficult to isolate the true from the ersatz. Depending upon the circumstances, this allows the pretenders and the charlatans to carve a niche for themselves on the display of their razzle-dazzle. But this is a chancy occupation, with a high rate of turnover caused by frictional factors. Accidents take place, and the gods keep failing, all the while to be replaced by other gods. If one dada is found out, people do not necessarily turn away from the whole breed: rather, they go on trying, in desperate sequence, the other ones: in the process, many end up as paupers, because the dadas and those around them also have a way of making you part with your income and your assets.

Several of the religious operators have learnt to blend American business practices with a namby-pamby philosophy. There is a certain catchiness in their articulation which, in the short run, is confused with profundity. And legends can be made to spread easily. Unless, therefore, economic circumstances change qualitatively, the spiritual leaders are likely to continue to receive a steady custom. The propensity of some of them to combine spirituality with spirituous-ness may not be a State secret: but what are you against the multitude? The people will continue to flock to those who promise instant deliverance.

The process that is on is marked by a peculiar non-reciprocity. Disenchantment with the efficacy of political action induces members of the middle class and the poorer sections to rush to off-the-counter faith-healers. But even when faith fails to cure once and for all, there is no automatic movement towards the barricade. Even if there is a return to the political arena, traces of tribalism persist. Faith in organised mass action remains in discount; the intermediary of a charismatic leader is jealously clung to for attaining economic and political ends. The fascination which Subhas Chandra Bose holds for the Bengali mind was not dimmed even during the halcyon days of the communist movement. The invocation of Chairman Mao by the Naxalites, it is possible to conjecture, had also a similar rationality: the urge to abdicate one's doubts and questionings before a father-figure. And Indira Gandhi's meteoric rise in popularity, following the vanquishing of the enemy in Bangladesh two seasons ago, had a similar root in totemism; Nehru's daughter emerged as Durga the Destroyer, who also held out the promise of filling in as Bhagavati the Preserver.

For those who think that the current goings-on in these parts are an aberration, and that, sooner or later, indeed sooner rather than later, the political battle will be joined once again along classical lines, on the basis of sharply delineated class issues, a major disappointment could well be in store. The charlatans currently exploiting the people in the name of faith are merely symptomatic of a deeper malaise. A kind of tribalism has set in, and will claim its share of victims before there can be a restoration of rational political activity. As long as intermediaries cast their shadow between the people and the issues, the struggle for the realisation of economic demands will be in abeyance. In a way, the presence of such intermediaries cannot but cause a setback to economic growth. For, while totemism rules, the impression will persist that, just as there could be an instant solution to one's personal economic problems, national economic issues, too, could be similarly resolved. The quest for a financial wizard, by no less than the Prime Minister of the country, is an indication of how far the notion of faith-healing has extended: the laws of economics, mathematics and physics are harsh; so avoid them, and opt for the prowess implied in the preternatural and the supernatural. The decision has been taken; henceforth, the dadas and the babas are to be the nation's emancipators. And, if sometimes the local ones fail, then we will go out and import surrogates from abroad—maybe on fifteen-year tenures and instalments!

1973

24 Guernica's Children Remember

To each his own Pablo Picasso. For some, the excruciatingly enchanting Blue Period; for some others, perhaps, the countless instances of Cubist scaffolding. There are many others for whom meaningfulness is represented by the days when Picasso was still a Fauve. Or would you rather vote for the slightly eccentric, enormously rich Pablo, installed in France's Cote d'Or, the restless dilettante with the twinkle in his eye, shuffling about from pottery to sketches to sculptures?

For yet others, Picasso was Guernica. Guernica was Picasso: the artist who knew that there was no art without life, that art was a transcription of one's experience, that art was war, and that the artist was the activist. Guernica was, and remains, primal emotion, the ringing protest against the depredations of men against other human beings; but it was, and is, also the assertion of life: it was, and remains, indignation and empathy, despair and hope, hatred and love.

Resistance collapsed in Spain, the combatants—those amongst them not left behind, dead and often unburied, in the battlefield—dispersed. But the passion lingered. Spain could not be saved, but there were other causes. Fascism had to be fought in other lands, in Europe as much as elsewhere. Inevitably, despite Spain, death came to fascism in almost every other country. The Soviet Union came through, Picasso was around. Even as the Second World War ended, there was, however, a re-gathering of reaction. Winston Churchill did not wait for long to deliver his Fulton speech. Bertolt Brecht was hounded out of Hollywood, the House Anti-American Activities Committee strode on the scene, and could Joe McCarthy be far behind? The Rosenberg couple went to their heroic death, there was the unleashing of General McArthur in Korea, the Ho Chi Minh trail came alive. Soon, Dien Bien Phu was round the corner. Pablo Picasso was still engaged, the doves of peace began to flutter all over, in the motifs of your dreams, even in the handkerchief of your betrothed; the days continued to be the days of faith, of dedication, of enchantment.

Very few were aware that it was already late. The Twentieth Congress was a great saboteur; idealism never quite recovered from the shock administered by it. Even were one to by-pass the urge to analyse what caused it all, the consequences of Nikita Krushchev are there for all to see. Guernica, the doves of peace, Picasso, each was a symbol of the international brotherhood of toiling peoples, of a camaraderie of fighting idealists. The Twentieth Congress liquidated that camaraderie. It was the death-knell of great universal causes. From then on, John Osborne's hero could only look back in anger.

Old age brings oblivion because of natural factors. But the fact that there was so little occasion, in recent years, to return to the theme of Guernica, or to mention its creator, is part of a greater malaise. In a world given to sectarian self-seeking, idealists are an embarrassment. Picasso became an embarrassment to a large number of his past patrons. Art was being supplanted by craft: the erstwhile idealists were being taught, assiduously, the blessings of deviation. The Red Flag and the Internationale were reduced to rituals: Pablo Picasso became an irrelevance. A man with a tremendous reservoir of Gallic wit, he tucked himself in. Of late, one used to hear so little about him.

Yet, did this withdrawal from the limelight really matter? A destitute Calcutta slum-boy, or a rack-rented Adivasi farmer in a remote Purulia village, never heard of Picasso. Nor was Picasso ever conceivably aware of the specific conditions of their living. But he was a shrewd operator: exploitation, he had no difficulty in recognising, has a quality of ubiquitousness: you run across time and space, the form of exploitation changes, its content hardly ever. It may seem altogether far-fetched that the problems and sufferings of a black American in a New Orleans ghetto, or of a Mexican cotton picker in the vast open tracts next to Ciudad Obregon, or of a political activist languishing in a West Bengal prison, or of a Vietnamese child whose human form the American napalm has despoiled beyond recognition, are bound by a common thread of narration. It is, however, largely a question of faith and empathy. An international movement is born the moment several far-flung people come to claim a common heritage, and come to declare a community of goals. Faith, after all, is the end-product of ascription. We ascribe, therefore we create.

This is precisely what Pablo Picasso the activist did. By a single piece of Guernica, by his exuberant scattering of the doves of peace, he created, on his own, a common fury, a common idealism, a common fire of indignation, a common tension. He did not conform, he refused to define himself in terms of pre-ordained formulae. This fact notwithstanding, none could ignore the fierce activism of his art. Since the grammarians could not lick him, they joined him; perhaps that was their strategy to make him join them. He did join, but only in his kind of way. Picasso could not, for example, ever be persuaded to sign a statement running down Mao Tse-tung.

What the quaint little man has left behind will continue to be the subject of wild disputations. The many women in his life will fight over the earthly spoils: MGM will, for all one knows, soon launch on a full-length cinematographic biography; almost for certain, the Communist Party of France will air its proprietory rights over him, and the battle will no doubt be taken up by the far-out radicals: Jean-Paul Sartre and Simone de Beauvoir will feel impelled to join in the fray: mountain-loads of polemics will pile up along the Left Bank. The unemployed artisan in Howrah, and the destitute day labourer in Bankura, will have never heard of him: they will be no part of his direct legacy, the quality of their daily travails will remain what it has been. Irrespective of whether the Government takes over the collieries given to slaughter-mining, the miners, crammed in hellish hovels, will continue to live, and die, like expendable beasts. At the dead of night, the landlord's men, in the company of the constabulary lent by the officer-in-charge of the local police station, will swoop on the decrepit hut of the share-cropper and take away his grain by force. The assassin's knife will suddenly herald the end of the throbbing idealism of a young college teacher who, in his folly, considered it to be part of his birthright to read, and in turn let others read, the literature of the Revolution. Organised trade union activity will remain the subject of venomous attack on the part of those in authority: every now and then, confrontations will continue to take place between the struggling workers and the forces of law and order who, it can be taken for granted, would, invariably, give vent to the whims of the capitalist owners. Prices will soar, profiteers will make their pile, but if you want to raise your voice in protest, you will be put out of harm's way.

This is a world altogether remote from the tranquil fishing

village where Picasso had ensconced himself for the past two and a half decades: there were few occasions for him to return, overtly, to the theme of international camaraderie: rich American dowagers would drop in; fat commissions for sculptures would arrive from all over. But the heritage of Guernica is the heritage of Guernica. It cannot be disowned. Even if it be in one's subconsciousness, the doves of peace will keep fluttering. Whether he is at all aware of it or not, the Calcutta student, who chucks a bright academic career to disappear behind the bars in order that the country's 'security' may remain unimpaired, is carrying in himself a bit of Picasso. The flame of Guernica will burn. We are all Guernica's children.

1973

25 He Had Picked the Wrong Target

One rages, helplessly, against the dying of the day. Buddhadeva Bose could not make it. During the past few years, he had been scrounging for money, some extra money which would see his household through while he resumed his magnificent opus on the Mahabharata. The annotation of the epic was turning out to be the quintessence of his creative genius. The once-and-past enfant terrible of Bengali literature had entered the zone of tranquillity; yesterday's stormy petrel was almost unrecognisable. These pieces on the Mahabharata were poetry and philosophy rolled in one; their chiselled prose had a severe beauty; their canvas bore witness to an overwhelming imagination.

But there it was. This man had remained, over the span of nearly half a century, a complete litterateur. Literature was, to him, much more than passion: it was faith, his only allegiance. It still failed to ensure for him a reasonably comfortable livelihood—despite his having authored something like one hundred and fifty-and-odd volumes. If you leave out Tagore, no one else in Bengali literature has covered the total spectrum in the manner he did: you begin with poetry, and go on to list short stories, novels, essays, literary criticism, plays, travelogues, belles-lettres, children's tales, nursery rhymes and translations—not to mention his great contribution as editor. But money was always short. This is a much reduced Bengal, and in more senses than one. With the splitting of the country, the market for Bengali literary output has in any case shrunk.

An even more basic factor has been at work. Buddhadeva Bose was a punctilious writer. He was finicky not only about the words he used to sculpt, but also about how his volumes were produced, and under what auspices. However, quality is a forgotten premise in a milieu where hucksters have invaded literature. Finance capital conquers all that it surveys; the industry of literature, too, has been taken over by it. Unless you are prepared to act as a lackey to one or other of the newspaper combines, your livelihood is in danger. Literary success is now a derivative of propagation. Your volumes sell only if one of the leading newspaper establishments is prepared to act as your patron, not otherwise. If it condescends to do so, it is roses all the way; sales of your works begin to climb, and newspapers underwrite your victuals.

In his years of innocence, Buddhadeva Bose, the great fundamentalist who would never compromise on standards, used to make gentle fun of those ensnared by the newspaper chains and writing for dubious journals brought out by the latter. Yet, by the time he died, the wheel had come full circle. He had to turn for his daily bread to persons whom he used to detest—the vulgarians of the newspaper world, the unscrupulous lot who could not care less about literary ethics. Fundamentalism was given a quiet burial. Buddhadeva Bose had to compromise: it was, as they say, an arrangement. He tolerated them, put up with their whims and obscenities, humoured them; in return, they saw to it that he did not quite starve. But just about. In the system as it has emerged, hangers-on are kept on short leash. Buddhadeva Bose was aware that he was racing against time. The first part of the tract on the Mahabharata was ready. He had collected the notes and references for the second part, which, he had no doubt, would be his proudest contribution to Bengali letters. He needed an uninterrupted spell of a couple of years for this round of writing. He must, therefore, make adequate financial provision for that period; the wolf must be kept at bay while the personages from the Mahabharata—with their grandeur and their pettifogging, their majesty and their meanness—were being assembled and analysed.

A man with more than one hundred and fifty not altogether inconsequential volumes to his credit, a man whose commitment and integrity were beyond question, should not, one would have thought, have to worry, in the twilight of his career, about money matters. That was not to be. The government was not moved. The newspaper combines, currently the supreme arbiters of literary judgment, paid him what can only be described as bare sustenance. Therefore the man, till his very last day, kept churning out what he described as potboilers, even for disreputable cinema magazines, in the hope that he could chalk up some savings on which to subsist during the writing of the final part of the Mahabharata commentary. The home stretch eluded him. He collapsed and died before the money could be in.

This, in a way, epitomises the objective reality of the times. Illiterate politicians of assorted hues, and those who hover in their proximity, make pots of money. Through their shady deals, they collect in the course of a single month perhaps as much as Buddhadeva Bose could earn in ten years. Journalists, who cannot get the syntax right for even a single sentence, belong to this side of the establishment; there is no dearth of the appurtenances of good living for them. Characters belonging to the underworld, whose only creative talent is the throwing of the knife, nonchalantly splash crisp hundred rupee notes; don't ask how they come to their funds. But Buddhadeva Bose was unable to put together some puny savings which could last him while the tract on the Mahabharata was being completed.

A matter of some irony, Buddhadeva Bose did not realise, and therefore failed to grapple with, the fate which overtook him. For the past thirty years or thereabouts, he was a great one for 'cultural' freedom. A gullible person, given to instant emotions, he fell into the trap set for him by professional communist-baiters. The alleged inequities rendered toward writers and artists in the socialist countries would enrage him. He would work up a passion, write indignant articles, snap links with friends who were across the barricade. The tribulations of a Boris Pasternak or an Aleksandr Solzhenitsyn would exercise him for days on end. There was this curious myopia, he would miss the larger significance of more proximate things. In the society where he lived and worked, opportunities were scandalously unevenly distributed, including those which came the way of writers and artists. He himself had to be deferential to eleventh-rate journalists, who belonged to newspaper combines, who controlled the assets and could ordain some extra income for him. While he got excited over the abstract concept of freedom, he went on missing the relevant clue: freedom is not an independent variable, it is a function of the distribution of wealth. A man, be he a poet or a novelist, who is unable to provide for himself and his family, is not free. He is not free to write what he wants to write. A substantial part of his time has to be set aside to write potboilers or to humour the agents of finance-capital, and his great ambitions have to be postponed. This was so with Buddhadeva Bose, and will be so with other writers: because, irrespective of the label by which you describe your milieu, till as long as it does not ensure your food and clothing, there can be no free writing on your part.

Since Tagore, perhaps, there has been no greater talent in Bengali literature. Others, such as Jibanananda Das, have written better, deeper poetry. Manik Bandyopadhyay was a nobler writer of fiction, a natural genius, who composed what is perhaps the greatest novel in the language. Yet others have written essays which, in content and purposiveness, possibly surpass most of Buddhadeva Bose's efforts. There are others too, whose incisiveness in literary criticism may have outstripped Buddhadeva Bose's. And certainly, in this neighbourhood, there have been more competent playwrights. If you consider all aspects together, however, and also take into account his magnificent role as editor and catalyst of literary urges, his position is non pareil. Nevertheless, in the system of which we are all prisoners, he was denied decent minimum wages. He would not have agreed that the answer to the predicament lies in the writers joining the barricade. Man is free, the writer too is free, free to choose. Buddhadeva Bose chose. He chose to cast his vote against those who were for a social revolution; in his later years he railed against them, and with gusto.

The manner of his dying proved, if any proof was ever needed, that he had picked on the wrong target. Now that he is safely dead, even his death has become an occasion for brazen commercial exploitation by capitalist-publishers who monopolise the Bengali literary trade. This is outrageous, for it is they who killed Buddhadeva Bose. By their perversity and self-aggrandisement, they have pushed literary standards down to a filthy nadir, so much so that writers like him had no chance of an assured market—and were, therefore, reduced to scrounging for food. Assassins all, they have now the cheek to appropriate for themselves the mantle of principal mourners. Even as others still rage against the dying of the day.

1974

Section Two

26 The Two-Sector Model

For the past several months, a leading textile manufacturing unit in the country has been splashing a particular kind of advertisement in the newspapers. The advertisement has a certain persistence, if not charm. In a series of compositions, it narrates how a once-dowdy-looking, dowdily-dressed couple have changed, and changed a lot, in recent years. A revolution in sartorial style has overtaken them: they have stepped out of the quaint, stuffy world of the eighteenth, or nineteenth, century bagginess and, with a fierce suddenness, embraced the mad, mod world of the 1970s. It is elegance all over, supra-modernity all over. The couple have changed a lot lately; along with the couple, that textile unit too, the message continues with a nagging hum, has changed a great deal: it is as if, without the careful chaperoning of this firm, the couple would have discovered themselves lost in the bewildering world of today, this world of high living and luxury consumption, this world where it is all happiness and pop music, glamour and fancy apparel, this world where the theme of poverty and squalor and malnutrition and pestilence are unheard-of, unspoken-of categories.

It is little use blaming the individual firm. In this competitive environment, it has to chalk up profit and must expand its sales. It therefore has to plan for product differentiation, as well as for saturation advertisement. It has to take as datum the market for luxury consumption and enlarge its share of this market. And it has to proceed beyond: it has to try to germinate in those, who have not yet fallen into the trap of high consumption, the temptation for more and more luxury goods. The firm, after all, has been permitted by the Government to set up capacity for processing synthetic fibres. It has been allocated foreign exchange to import the necessary equipment and also a certain quantum of the raw materials on a continuous basis. It, and others of its genus, have been allowed by the authorities, sometimes absent-mindedly, sometimes surreptitiously, to enlarge the scale of operations over the years, so that, in many cases, the actual capacity is twice or thrice the capacity indicated in the original licence. Much of the current controversy is over the stale issue whether the capacity surreptitiously developed should be formally recognised or not. But does it really matter whether this recognition is ordained or not, whether the luxury items are produced over the counter or under? Whatever the supposed content of policy, the sum-total of the various official measures has been a furious pace of production of luxury consumer goods during the last twenty years. Equipment and *materiel* have been allowed to be imported to foster this fast-growing sector, the ready availability of foreign credit always providing the alibi. Where imports would have appeared as indiscreet, the allocation of precious domestic resources has been ensured for the indigenous surrogates. If today private manufacturing units spend hundreds of thousands of rupees on advertising gimmicks so as to provoke a higher order of consumption, the Government can hardly dare to cavil at such misdemeanours. Nor can it, with a clear conscience, deny these units their demand for additional foreign exchange so that latent capacity could be made full use of. Like the rat in Nikita Krushchev's parable, the luxury consumption sector is now stuck in the Government's throat: it can neither be swallowed nor spat out.

Which is what makes official pronouncements concerning curbs on consumption and the need for simplicity and abstinence such gross examples of hypocrisy. A puritan is one who does all the things which ordinary mortals do, but who refuses to derive any pleasure from them; a hypocrite also does all the things which ordinary mortals do, but he pretends to do so only on sufferance. All the while, politicians dilate on the imperativeness of restraining consumption: charity, however, never begins at home. All the while, the ears are constantly assailed by declamations on the desirability of promoting savings so that economic growth can be hastened and the crisis enveloping the economy effectively countered. Blood is, however, thicker than water, and the flesh is weaker than the spirit. Let there be abstinence all around, but your own children, your own friends and relations, would like to have some finery, some high quality music, some exquisite food. Abstinence is, therefore, always for one's next door neighbours. It is a split-level existence. For the masses, exhortations will go out that the rate of savings needs to be hiked, there has to be a tightening of belts, a cutting out of frills, a return to the theme of severest plain living. Having delivered the admonition, the politicians will disappear into the thraldom of the five-star hotel. Much worse, they will somehow be able to persuade themselves that the luxury they are soaking themselves in is not for personal aggrandisement, it is all for the sake of the nation. India, despite being poor, has a certain dignity and nobility to uphold; that dignity will be adversely affected if ministers do not live in a certain style, if their bungalows are not equipped with appurtenances and accessories, if banquets are not arranged with proper eclat; it is as if in case, for the select few at the top, the paraphernalia are not properly delineated, we will lose face to the foreigners, as if in this fiercely competitive world, where comparing notes is the principal avocation, in order to survive, we must develop certain pockets of affluence.

This tepid apologia fails to wash away the dissimulation. The same minister who, during the day, talks approvingly of wholesale prohibition, will, at sundown, be found downing gallons of whisky. The same minister, who has taken a pledge to be a habitual wearer of khadi, will, after hours, be seen sporting the smartest silk and synthetics. Pledges have nothing to do with one's personal code of behaviour. Certain commandments are set down for the masses, and certain other realities are reserved for the superstructure. Precepts and examples knock against one another in unbounded non-linearity.

It is not a question of ethics, nor even of aesthetics; this two-sector model cannot work for a more straightforward reason. It cannot work, for it cuts athwart economic laws. Since the policy-makers have set a particularly high standard of living for themselves, and the marketplace still remains supreme in the country, a whole array of luxury consumer industries have to come up to satisfy the wide-ranging, sophisticated, minute demands of the elite. These industries suck away a disproportionately large chunk of investment funds so that, for sustaining the momentum of growth in the more basic sectors, provision has to be made for additional capital, which can emerge only if the general level of consumption is held back, thus forcing up the rate of savings. But there can be no higher rate of savings if it is invariably not myself, but my neighbour, who has to do the abstaining. The inert masses follow the leadership; they ignore the exhortations of frugality and follow the practical example set by the leaders; the holy pursuit is toward attaining higher and higher plateaus of consumption. For the majority of the community, even this statement is a libel; wobbling as they do at sub-marginal existence, a fractional rise in their consumption would still not make a difference to the overall level of national savings. If one were to believe some of the statistical findings, their consumption standard has actually fallen in the more recent period. This, however, is not the case for a fairly sizeable stratum of the middle class, whose level of real earnings has risen quite a bit over the past twenty years and who, in other circumstances, could have been induced to save somewhat more. But they know what cue to follow. They ignore what the leaders say, and do as the leaders do.

At the cost of reportedly around six lakhs of rupees, a magnificent structure has been made ready for the Prime Minister to stay during the four days of the Congress session in Calcutta next week. The newspapers have carried detailed descriptions of the structure, of all of its four thousand square feet of indoor luxury. But one must pay obeisance to hypocrisy. Topping the four thousand square feet of opulence will be a thatched roof, rural Bengal style. The foundation will be solid luxury, the top will propagate the agony of mute poverty. The reality of India is the other way round. It is nineteen-twentieths undiluted poverty, with only the tip at the top exuding rarefied affluence. This was also what defined Plato's Republic.

1972

27 One Dream Which Did Not Come True

Despite the hopelessness in the air, to dream remains an inalienable human right, permitted even to a citizen of this bedevilled nation. The plight of the economy could not be worse, inflation rages unfettered and uninhibited, the distress of the masses mounts from week to week and month to month, the central objectives of the nation appear to be stuck deep in a morass. Yet dreamers there will be, who will continue to dream. They will keep hoping that, come the next corner, a new vista is bound to be revealed. They will keep dreaming that once this Saturday's particular unsavoury episode passes into history, the subsequent events will be wholesome and honest, and gloriously straightforward. They will keep imagining that, once the present series of official and quasi-official unscrupulousness runs its course, in the coming days everyone will turn Simon Pure. One can contemplate what the model of such a dream could be, the dream that will be at the top of the heap, that will put into shade all other bold and wonderful dreams that one could think of.

For one individual, the fondest dream runs as follows: Come the Sunday morning following the Saturday night, as he rolls out of bed and goes to the door to collect the paper, a most magnificent news item hits his eyes. A statement has been issued by the Prime Minister's secretariat. The Prime Minister, it informs him, has decided that the nation's predicament has matured enough, there has to be a turning back, this far and no further. The Prime Minister, the statement says, is going to revoke a particular decision announced by the Ministry of Industrial Development on its own and on which she was only perfunctorily consulted in the past. She, the statement goes on to elaborate, is aghast at the gumption of the Ministry in issuing an industrial licence to Maruti Private Limited. Even when a letter of intent was first issued to Maruti, she had very strong doubts and reservations. After all, the Planning Commission had long ago decided that projects for the manufacture of a small car, whether in the private or in the public sector, would not harmonise with national priorities: at the present juncture, it was not at all necessary—nor desirable—to expand the capacity for passenger-car production. Even though it was being claimed that the cost of production of the Maruti car would be considerably less than that of the makes currently available in the country, the clientele for this car will continue to belong to the affluent sections of the community. Things have, in fact, deteriorated a great deal, the Prime Minister feels, since the Planning Commission sat in judgment on the so-called small-car project. Given the grave economic crisis that has overtaken the nation, there is absolutely no reason for setting aside precious resources for the further production of passenger cars, big or small. It was already sheer folly to waste so much of the nation's assets on the three existing car units; let there be no extension of that folly. The plea that Maruti is in the private sector and, therefore, will not cause any draft on the Government's resources, the statement goes on to point out, is altogether specious; for, it is still the stock of scarce resources at the nation's command which the company will erode, and this, the Prime Minister has not the least doubt, cannot be permitted. The other argument too—namely, that Maruti cars will be manufactured with indigenous materials and without foreign collaboration—is considered by the Prime Minister to be equally fallacious; for, the indirect import costs—which will be diffused all over—are in any case going to be heavy. In view of the acute foreign exchange scarcity, the Maruti proposal has to be regarded as a luxury—and hence cut back. From now on, the emphasis in the field of transport, the press note suggests, should be exclusively on expanding the capacity of public transport. The production of trucks must, of course, continue to receive the major attention. In addition, whatever resources are worth being deployed marginally for producing mass transport vehicles—such as double-decker buses—would be considered for allocation. But, according to the Prime Minister, it would be criminal wastage of resources to allow the manufacture of Maruti.

But what about the outlay already incurred by the sponsors of Maruti Private Limited in setting up the pilot plant, and what to do with the capital already raised for the venture from various sources? The sponsors have perhaps raised as much as Rs 30 crores from private industrialists for setting up the company; they have also borrowed funds from public financial institutions, including commercial banks. Land has been acquired; steel and other scarce materials have been used up to a considerable extent. In view of all this, if Maruti is not permitted to proceed further, the Prime Minister realises that there could be a lot of heart-burning here and there. But—the press note from the Prime Minister's secretariat goes on to explain—while admittedly some diversion of national resources has already taken place on account of Maruti, that cannot be used as an alibi for a further—and greater—diversion of resources.

The statement, at this stage, refers to the government's recent decision to cancel the plan for an international trade fair in New

Delhi in view of the economic difficulties. Several crores of rupees had been spent, meanwhile, by the Union government, the state governments, and a large number of public and private undertakings, to set up pavilions and to make auxiliary and ancillary arrangements in connection with the fair. Since the authorities were of the view that, such initial expenditures notwithstanding, it would be most improvident to hold the fair, they took the decision to abandon it. The government decided to cut its losses and scrap the fair; so be it with Maruti. The plant set up by the latter, it is explained, is proposed to be taken over at cost and utilised for assembling trucks and other public vehicles.

The press note is candid all the way. The government, it mentions in passing, is fully aware that land belonging to the Ministry of Defence was appropriated for Maruti; that the public steel plants issued special quotas so that Maruti could lift the necessary steel; that cement and other precious materials were allotted for Maruti, which could jump the queue. The press note admits that those industrialists who helped to raise the bulk of the share capital of Maruti were accorded import quotas and other special entitlements as reward for their co-operation with the venture; this was scandalous, and an enquiry into how this came about and where the culpability lies in each case is being instituted. The statement from the Prime Minister's secretariat goes on to admit that prospective dealers have been made to transfer, in the name of advance dealership fees, close to Rs 2 crores to Maruti Private Limited; the Department of Company Affairs is being asked to find out whether there was any infringement of law in the way these funds were collected.

The Prime Minister, the statement says, realises that there are broader issues involved in Maruti. It is not just a car project initiated by an individual. It is not even a bland symbol of so much first-order and second-order nepotism: that is only a minor aspect of the matter. It has a much broader, greater import, namely, whether or not this nation ought to take at face value the exhortation to economise and conserve resources. Everybody from the Prime Minister down talks of the crisis the country is passing through. Each official statement dilates on the theme of abstinence, and on the need to push up the national rate of savings. What you consume, you do not save. If you consume in the way of having more of private passenger cars, to that extent you deviate from the goal of augmenting national savings. Thus Maruti could not only use up precious resources which might be used for higher national priorities: if permitted to go ahead, it would also release the flood-water of indulgence; once you permit Maruti, you will have no moral grounds to prevent other similar projects from going ahead. The Prime Minister, the press note says, recognises only too well that ultimately her call for sacrifice on the part of each and every member of the nation must be backed up by firm practice; she has decided that she must really set the example for others by taking this personal decision to ban Maruti. She is full of admiration for the energy, initiative and imagination demonstrated by those who set up the prototype of the car. If these persons were born in any private enterprise economy, there is no question that they would have gone very far; but, as it happens, they were born in India, a poor country whose resources must be conserved for ameliorating the conditions of the most wretched ones and, accordingly, savings must be encouraged at all levels. Therefore, these people have to be called upon to make the supreme sacrifice: she, as Prime Minister, has decided to step in and cancel the industrial licence accorded to them. Steps are being taken on the consequential arrangements she has elaborated. She hopes that this example will inspire others to make similar gestures.

So goes the dream. This is somebody's favourite dream not because this person is by nature crooked or holds a jaundiced view of things. He believes in the old-fashioned virtues which once upon a time ruled the world. He believes that the Prime Minister has the nobility and the sagacity to see the inter-connection of things. The Prime Minister, he is aware, is Chairman of the Planning Commission, the body which determines where the national priorities lie. She is, at the same time, head of the government, and knows more than anybody else the gravity of the present crisis. He has every hope that she will ensure that his dream comes true. It is, after all, such dreams which sustain a nation and whose fruition constitutes its pride. And the person who dreams this dream is firm in his conviction that once his dream comes true, the emotions that will be released round the country will be a thousand times more potent than those that were let loose in July 1969.

1974

28 The New Obfuscators

Pray, will insertions in newspapers help? Of late, has anybody seen the country's economists anywhere? With each week, the country sinks into a deeper morass. Charlatans, in Government as well as outside, are on the loose and do havoc to this or that sector of economic activity. Astoundingly ridiculous explanations are furnished about why prices are rising and why procurement is not proceeding according to expectations and why income inequalities are getting aggravated. The credulity of the people has been exploited beyond endurance. Even so, in the short run, the political alternatives are few and far between. This being the case, the fools and the rogues are being put up with.

One can nonetheless persist with the query: where are the country's economists? Have you seen any of them in the neighbourhood? What precisely are their preoccupations? What do they think of the present state of the economy? Have they any comments to offer on the quasi-stagnation of output, on the Government's inability to maintain the procurement and distribution system, on the waywardness of the fiscal and monetary mechanisms, on the consequences of unbridled price inflation, and all that? On any crucial issue affecting contemporary realities, has one heard even one economist make a single significant statement in recent weeks? Banalities of course continue to be uttered in plenty; for example, that a reduction in the inequalities in consumption expenditure would lead to a reduction in the aggregate demand for imports, or that in order that indirect taxation may not affect the absolute level of prices, measures have to be taken to reduce the unit cost of production. Beyond the parading of such transparent innocences, it is almost impossible to track down the minds of economists. Where are they?

They are either abroad, or possibly busy developing esoteric models of growth in some abstracted economy under some weird assumption or other about the nature of the production function, the time-path of growth, and people's time-preference. We have to pay the price of being part of a generally equilibrated world. And in the generally equilibrated world, our economists do what economists in the cosy Western countries do: the science of economics has become a plaything, and our good economists, along with those elsewhere, love to while away their time in playing at models which are purely abstract entities, and whose resemblance to the realities of life could never be even approximately established by even the most astute of prosecutors. At a certain point of recent history, economics ceased to be political economy. From the fact that analytical coherence in the elaboration of economic principles could gain from mathematical rigour, consequences followed. Gradually, the core and the periphery changed places. Frustrated mathematicians discovered that nothing has been lost, they could still make a career out of economics; economics in due course was made the peg on which to hang their mathematical abstractions. Establishing or refuting economic laws became the feeble apologia: skill-fetishism took over. In any decadent society, the involvement with live, real issues is supplanted by the exhibition of empty skills as the major activity of an artist or a technologist. In this exercise of decadence, the United States inevitably assumes the role of the pace-setter. At a level of per capita income of $5,000 annually, you can afford to allow economists to indulge in idle games. Of each additional dollar of national income produced in that country, sixty-seven cents, or two-thirds, consist of income from services. It does not really matter whether a part of the service income takes the form of remunerations offered to a decadent group of economists lolling on mathematical fantasies, or earnings from, say, the exploitation of the sexual proclivities of the idle rich. Between what gets branded as mathematical model-building in economics and what finds its way onto the pages of *Playboy* magazine, one need not make any distinction, at all.Both are illustrations of indulgences: in one case, indulgence of the flesh, in the other, indulgence of the abstract intellect. Neither leads to an increase in material output, not even indirectly. For the United States, this fact could hardly matter: that country has enough assets and incomes to play around with. Of course, the bottom deciles of the population even in that lush land may perhaps hold a slightly different view, but neither model-building economists nor *Playboy* could care less.

The problem is, however, transformed in hapless countries such as India, which spend a disproportionate share of their resources in rearing economists, pampering them and offering them all the facilities in the way of computers, equipment and suchlike, in the hope that they, in their turn, would teach the nation the secrets of economic growth. The economists in no time belie the hope. Perfect mobility is perfect mobility; our economists become aware in no time that the country's basic problems can wait, it is hypothesis-mongering which must receive priority. Besides, model-building exercises are not terribly satisfying unless conducted in the open forum of an international clientele. It is perhaps not merely the steady demand emanating from foreign markets, there is the latent inferiority complex, too, in our economists—as in others—who would like to be applauded by a non-native crowd. Their native land merely offers them some sets of raw data on which they apply their sophisticated skills for abstraction. The models that are formulated and the equations that are fitted in due course usually fall into two patterns. They are either on the basis of assumptions which are so remote that the conclusions following from them have not the least relevance to the country's problems; alternatively, after much huffing and puffing, after much dropping of obscure mathematical conditions and application of far-fetched statistical tests, the conclusions arrived at are about as trivial as the observations on the weather made by your charwoman. Economists say either totally abstract things which have no relevance for contemporary or even long-range issues, or the most obvious things through a modality of obfuscations one could as well dispense with. Meanwhile, though, prices rise, income continues to be distributed more and more unevenly, the rate of growth slides down to zero, agricultural output marks time, the industrial structure is reduced to an absurdity, politicians trot out alibis for economic failures which would not meet the test of even fifth-rate intellects, and which would never be dared to be trotted out if only economists were around. But economists are not around; they are either permanently immersed in their models, or they have gone out for their summer junketing. And those who are left behind in the country will not come out in the open.

They will not, for a variety of reasons. Even those of the

economists who stay back—and they of course constitute the majority—have done reasonably well by the system. Among all so-called social scientists, economists as a tribe have registered the most material advance since Independence, for somehow politicians found them to be the most useful of the lot. Economists became the talisman of the prosperity that was a-coming, and they have exploited this role to the hilt. But a crisis was bound to overtake them sooner or later. An economist of even moderate competence will need little time to reach the conclusion that the factors underlying India's economic stagnation are almost entirely institutional; given the conglomeration of class forces, it is inevitable that inequalities are aggravated and growth is negligible. If savings fail to pick up, if a disproportionate part of aggregate investment is diverted to unproductive channels, if procurement is frustrated, if regional inequalities are intensified, if direct taxes on agriculture cannot be raised, if the unit cost of industrial output cannot be lowered, the reason in each case is extra-economic; if prices rise and the Government seemingly does not succeed in lowering them, it is because the Government wants the prices to rise, and abet in the process. A perceptive economist has to admit that he has little residual role left in the circumstances and that his profession has been played out. As a group, economists will not, however, prefer to utter such home truths; to do so would imply that they are going against the system which has propped them up; it may involve their bread and butter; it may involve a certain drying up of funds which provide the accoutrements of comfortable living.

No, the economists know on which side their bread is buttered. If the emperor has no clothes, they will be the last persons to proclaim that fact. They love their present role, which in many respects is parallel to that played by the Brahmins in ancient and medieval Hindu society. The Brahmins were the traditional obfuscators; they were the buffers between the masses and the Hindu kings. They would manufacture alibis explaining why the kingdom was not prospering and why the poor must remain condemned to their state of servitude. In the structure assiduously built in this country over the past two and a half decades, economists have blossomed forth as the new obfuscators. Politicians could not do without them; there is no dearth of opportunity for them; there is saturation money for this or that project and for these meaningless model-building exercises. The masses must be provided with ample diversions so that they would not come to know the essential facts about their current plight; economists are providing these diversions, that is, those amongst them who have condescended to remain behind in this poor, hot country.

1973

29 A Ritual a Day . . .

The item below was carried by what is considered to be Calcutta's leading Bengali newspaper in its issues of 14 July 1974:

> Following the decision that on July 16 the Prime Minister, Shrimati Gandhi, will cross the Hooghly river not by the Howrah bridge, but by motor launch, detailed studies are being made of tidal movements and the water level of the river at different hours of the day. Apart from soliciting the views of experts and specialists, senior officers belonging to the Calcutta and the Howrah police and the Department of Marine are travelling up and down the river by motor boat to study the drift of current in the river. In addition, the State Inspector-General of Police, Ranjit Gupta, and the General Manager of the South-Eastern Railways visited on Saturday the Howrah Maidan Station and the Ramkrishnapur Ghat to check on the arrangements.

On Tuesday, the day of the Prime Minister's visit, the ferry service between Chandpal Ghat and Ramkrishnapur Ghat will be closed from three p.m. till six p.m. The Howrah *hat* (market) will be closed at twelve noon: no business will be permitted after that hour. Brisk repairs are going on of the roads around Ramkrishnapur Ghat. Two thousand and five hundred policemen have been assigned for duty in the area; they will be under the supervision of DIG (Armed Police), Partha Basu Roy Chowdhury.

Pray, what was the gala event giving rise to all this commotion? Indira Gandhi briefly visited Calcutta on July 16. She was to go across the river to Howrah, to address a meeting in connection with the inauguration of work for laying a broad-gauge railway track. The Howrah bridge, which connects Calcutta with the other side of the Hooghly river, is a little more than a quarter of a mile long; provided there is no jam, a car can cross the bridge in a couple of minutes or less. But traffic on the bridge is occasionally heavy. When this happens, cars have to slow down. The Prime Minister could not, however, waste her time. Hence the decision was taken that she should cross the Hooghly not by the bridge, but by motor launch. Coming and going added together, her journey across the river could not have taken more than six minutes. But the ferry service for the public was nonetheless closed for a full three hours. The daily market was wound up at noon, while on other days transactions continue till dusk. Experts of assorted hues were pulled out of their regular assignments to study the hydraulic details of the river. Senior officers chug-chugged, for several hours of the day, for a number of days, up and down the river, measuring its currents. Two thousand five hundred policemen were assigned duty. The roads were temporarily freshened up. Hundreds of street-dwellers, with no shelter above their heads, were forcibly removed from the route along which the Prime Minister and her entourage travelled to and from the venue of the meeting.

One can, of course, offer sad, caustic comments on how strong a spell is still cast by medievalism in this great republic of ours. Time used to come to a stop, time still comes to a stop for the rest of the nation as the sovereign fleetingly passes by their neighbourhood. The resource-wasting rituals which the above news item typifies have little to do with the normal requirements of security: they are a reflection of a near-medieval system of values which, deliberately or otherwise, has been integrated into the country's politico-cultural norm. For as long there is no sustained, organised protest, these rituals will continue, and the ordinary people will be subjected to the maximum inconvenience every time dignitaries choose to visit a particular place. Even so, the matter deserves to be discussed in some detail. One wishes that a ritual was merely a ritual. Unfortunately, it is not. The enactment of a ritual has an economic implication; it involves what is known as an opportunity cost. The economic implications of the charade which marked the Prime Minister's visit to Howrah on July 16 are there for all to see. The ferry service across the river between two extremely busy focal points was completely suspended for three hours, all because the Prime Minister was around for a total period of six minutes. Traffic across the river between these points therefore came to a halt during those hours, and one can work out the direct and the indirect economic loss of the stoppage of the ferry service. The market was forced to close early; it worked for a period at least six hours less than normal. Two thousand five hundred policemen, dancing attendance on the Prime Minister's party, who could have been deployed elsewhere, for example, in helping with the procurement of food-grains, represented yet another facet of the opportunity cost.

Because the Prime Minister was crossing the river for a bare six minutes in one motor launch, several motor launch-hours worth of diesel, furnace oil and petrol were used up by the officers who studied for days on end the tidal bores and the water levels of the Hooghly. Hydraulic experts, who ought to have other things to do, were set busy taking the measurements of the river at the particular stretch where the Prime Minister was to cross and re-cross.

Is this making a mountain out of a molehill? Or do not these facts lay bare an aspect of Indian reality, an aspect which has considerable relevance for explaining the current economic situation? Pundits berate the slow pace of economic activities in the country. With deeply felt anguish, they draw attention to the assorted sloths affecting the system, for instance, how workers while away time on shop floors making small talk or in the name of a tea or coffee break. Bitter complaints are lodged over the poor rate of turn around of railway wagons, or how power plants cannot work effectively due to lack of coordination between the units. The private sector complains of meaningless procedures, laid down by the Government, which take up a whole lot of precious time and energy. Every day, some eminence or other inveighs against bureaucratic procrastinations and the fuddyduddyness of rules which choke all creative endeavours. Management experts lament at the erosion of work ethics; the Prime Minister condemns wastage and lethargy, and broods over the lack of motivation on the part of employees of public sector undertakings, including the nationalised banks. The economic stagnation may be mostly on account of the inadequacy of capital formation, but economists all the time also refer to the latent inefficiencies, to the miserably poor rate of utilisation of productive capacity, and so on.

Rituals and sloth, however, go together. Where a society is organised along tribal lines, taboos and totems take precedence over every other thing, including essential economic activity. Work becomes secondary, rituals get pride of place. It is impossible for ordinary mortals to differentiate between categories of social behaviour. Each time the Prime Minister visits a place, normal transactions—including vital economic transactions—are ordered to come to a stop, and rituals take over. The social norms are thus laid down, what has precedence over what, what is relevant and what is not. These norms then permeate through the various organisms of the nation. The cost of subverting crucial economic goals is obviously considered worth its while, in case the pay-off is an intensely satisfying charade of hail-to-the-leader. First things first.

It was an inaugural occasion which took the Prime Minister to Howrah. Will it be unpardonably rude to chant: a ritual a day perhaps keep the hour of reckoning away? The other day, when the Prime Minister read out a long essay on economic ethics in Bangalore, the occasion again was the laying of the foundation stone for a particular institution. She was preaching the need for all-round economy in the use of resources even as she was abetting in the act of wasting some: this is the inherent, behaviouristic contradiction from which none is seemingly keen to opt out. The amount of time which ministers spend on inaugurating seminars or laying foundation stones or pressing the button to open a factory or a fish market could have been usefully deployed for more coherent economic guidance and policy-making. There is also a second-order effect of the waste of time—and resources—thus brought about. Ministers waste their own time and of course Government resources by travelling to these inaugural shows; and since medieval tradition insists that, as their chariots pass by, the commoners too must stop work and pay them obeisance, more time and resources are brought to nought. As a direct consequence, certain other notions also get implanted into the nation's stream of consciousness, namely, that appearance is the reality, that ritual is the sustenance, that invocation is the essence of economics. Each of these may be dangerously misleading or false, but till as long as the culture of the polity is what it is, there is no escape from their tentacles.

All power to the people. If people want to set up an administration based on the adulatory principle, it is their affair, even if we happen to be situated in the twentieth century and in the dying third quarter of it. After all, quasi-monarchies are still around, including one or two absolute ones. It is, however, the combination of medievalism with tribalism which spells danger and agony, for then adulation and economic sloth tend to turn out as inseparable joint products. It will take the people quite some while to comprehend the implications of this joint supply. After that, again, it is a matter of their own decision. If they are to prefer ritual to economic progress, you or I have no business to interfere; you or I know so little about the philosophy of the death-wish.

1974

30 Toward the Ultimate Solution

Remember the American general who had to destroy that village in Vietnam in order that he could save it? Something almost similar, but on a much more ambitious scale, is happening here. The Indian people have to be saved from starvation; in order that this happy denouement may come about, the majority of the countrymen are being, and will continue to be, starved to death.

Assume an Indian has to live on grain alone, all other possible sources for the intake of calories being still costlier under existing conditions. Nutritional experts, who swear by a minimum intake of 2,250 calories per capita per day as essential for survival, would thus perhaps suggest a provision of around 245 kilos of grain per annum. The wizened ones in the United Nations assume 13 ounces of cereals as the rock bottom daily intake per person necessary to keep body and soul together; this works out to 215 kilos per annum. The Chinese, going by the evidence of Edgar Snow, are allowed, depending upon the nature of work performed, a monthly grain ration of 30 to 45 pounds. Even on the basis of the lower quota, the annual per capita grain intake in China would therefore appear to be around 165 kilos.

Forget the nutritional experts and, in good measure, also the United Nations. Merely assume that we want to provide our compatriots with an annual grain ration equal to what the average Chinese gets, and let us conveniently forget the fact that the Chinese supplement—and to a substantial extent—their grain intake by other foods. It will be less than patriotic to question the soundness of official estimates, so, to still all controversies, also take it for granted that, since the draft of the Fifth Plan says so, foodgrain output in the country in the current year will reach 114 million tonnes. Accept again the conventional practice of setting aside 12.5 per cent of the total crop for seeds, wastage, etc., which would then make available roughly 100 million tonnes for distribution among 580 million Indians. In per capita terms, this turns out to be around 170 kilos, so that, if it be a matter of figurework alone, we should be able to reach to our countrymen as much foodgrain as the leaders of China are reaching to *their* people.

Is there a snag? The grain can be reached to the people only provided the people have the income to afford it. Take the prices at which the cereals are to be distributed from the ration and fair price shops during the current season. Since hardly any sizeable quantity of the coarser cereals has been procured, one can leave them out. The commonest variety of rice is, however, unlikely to be sold at anything less than Rs 1.50 per kilo anywhere in the country. With the wheat lobby setting its sights for a procurement price of at least Rs 100 per quintal this year, the issue price of that grain too is unlikely to be set at less than Rs 1.25 for each kilo. You can work out any kind of internal composition of the different grains within the quota, the minimum outlay that will be needed to match what the Chinese receive—165 kilos—will be around Rs 220 per annum in case you get your quota exclusively through the public distribution system at the Government indicated prices. If only half of the quota is to be obtained at officially fixed issue prices and for the rest a person has to pay 50 per cent more, the outlay needed would approximate Rs 275 or thereabouts. If only a quarter of the quota is met by public distribution, and the other three-quarters are to be met, at prices 50 per cent higher, from elsewhere, the necessary expenditure would spill beyond Rs 300. Since, however, not more than 10 million tonnes of grains are channelled through the public distribution system, on the average only one-tenth of the quota is being made available at Government prices. Besides, the pattern of public distribution is highly skewed; perhaps as much as nine million tonnes of grain flow out to the top 10 per cent of the population. Never mind the polemics of the poverty line, the nation's majority are now facing a situation where, if the minimum quantity of cereals needed for bare maintenance has to be obtained, they have to arrange for an outlay which is well beyond their current income; they can forget about the rest of their daily requirements.

This is a reality which no sleight of statistics can hide. For consider what is happening in the present season. The *kharif* harvest is now in full swing. Yet, over large parts of the countryside, the price of rice in West Bengal is ruling at anywhere between Rs 3 and Rs 5. Wheat, wherever it is available, is being quoted at around Rs 2.50. To match the Chinese ration—something which, on per capita terms, is not to be ruled out, given the country's level of foodgrain output—one would then have to spend at least around Rs 450 per year. For at least three-quarters of the people in this State, such an order of expenditure is, who can dare deny, palpably impossible, for the simple reason that their level of income itself will be less than this sum. After all, while foodgrain prices have jumped by as much as between 50 to 80 per cent in the past twenty-four months, the per capita income even in money terms has remained more or less stagnant for the overwhelming majority of the people. They therefore do what is only to be expected in the circumstances: as food prices soar, they continue to cut down their consumption of cereals. The quantity of grain intake goes down and down. In many households, after a time cereals quietly disappear from the diet, and substitutes, such as roots and grass, if available, are commissioned to assuage the pangs of hunger.

What sense does talk of self-sufficiency in foodgrains make in this situation? Self-sufficiency for whom, and at what level of prices? A panicky Government has seemingly proceeded beyond the pale of reason, and the cliche of incentive prices is currently drowning all other cliches. At the level of procurement prices which have been set for rice and paddy—and are being seriously considered for wheat—many of the surplus farmers, particularly in the north-western parts of the country, would be reaping a rate of return of 70, 80 or 100 per cent—or even more. At the issue prices which will correspond to these procurement prices, the foodgrains being raised in the countryside are clearly beyond the means of the nation's majority. The Government's, call it reluctance, call it inability to expand public distribution in the countryside can be attributable to this factor rather than anything else: it is pointless to try to extend the public distribution system if the grains to be supplied through it remain beyond the reach of the millions of landless labourers and small farmers.

Therefore the assurance of the arithmetic is misleading. In per capita terms, we may have as much grain as China has. But so what, this will continue to be unevenly distributed. Foodgrains available in the country will be unevenly distributed because the incomes of the people of the country are unevenly distributed; thanks to inflation, the unevenness in income distribution has, if anything, aggravated further in recent years. Those constituting the top 10, 15 or 20 per cent of the income-brackets will continue to consume beyond their quota of 170 kilos per annum. For others, the consumption will be horrendously less. And once the means to consume foodgrains have been exhausted, the surplus stocks will perhaps be fed to the rodents, or allowed to decay. After all, destruction of crops in order to maintain their price is not such a unique phenomenon: kulaks in different climes have shown the way: if you cannot restrict output, you can always regulate supplies.

Providing adequate incentives to the farmers can be an unending process: once you have got attuned to a rate of return of 70, 80 or 100 per cent, there is no reason for your not asking for more. Thus with the Government and the kulaks continuing their love-feast, foodgrain production will perhaps pick up in the country. One of the major planks of the Five-Year Plans is to make the country self-sufficient in foodgrains. In order to make the country self-sufficient, therefore, prices will have to be raised. As prices are raised, more and more people will be unable to afford to eat the food that will be produced. This is a perfect echo of the American prescription of destroying Vietnam in order to save it: in order to enable the people not to starve, they will be made to starve. This is a mechanism which succeeds at both ends. At one end, with rising prices, the output of foodgrains will, it is hoped, increase, at the other end, with rising prices, more people will starve to death, therefore reducing the absolute requirement for food. Either way, we shall be approaching the ultimate solution.

1973

31 Two Bits of Extra Chips

A couple of years ago, Calcutta's walls used to invoke eternal glory to China's chairman who was also chairman to the young enthusiasts down the lanes and by-lanes. About this time last year, invocation to Indira Gandi became the surrogate function of the posters generously splashed all over the city. This year, it is vasectomy and tubectomy. A great big campaign to drown all past campaigns is on: hardly any space is left uncovered along the walls. Come ye, each and all, to any of the designated hospitals and health centres, be a patriot and agree to, if a man, a vasectomy, if a woman, a tubectomy: we will pay you forty rupees per operation. And that is not all. Here is the clincher, every person agreeing to be operated on will be offered, additionally, a conveyance allowance amounting to two rupees. There is no incentive to beat the monetary incentive: the campaign poster almost breaks out into raptures, who in our great and noble land would, it implies, dare to resist this marginal allure of two bits of extra chips: a roaring success in family planning ought therefore to be assured.

Twenty-five years of political freedom and patriotism have been reduced to the aborting of births, to a transaction in the marketplace. Forty-two rupees per turnover. Commodity fetishism could not go further. Is it any use trying to tell the Government that obscenity, too, could not go any further? Forty-two rupees will fetch you a vasectomy or a tubectomy. It will also fetch you a fifth of locally produced whiskey. There are cabinet ministers or industrial tycoons whose daily expenditure on cigarettes exceeds forty-two rupees. Dainty ladies who, in two's and four's, patronise colonial-style restaurants, run up bills in the course of an afternoon for tea and patisserie which amount to more than forty-two rupees. Take any major city, forty-two rupees will represent a couple of hours of taxi fare. In this India of socialism, forty-two rupees, a little more than five American dollars at the current rate of exchange, is also the opportunity cost set for an extra human being; the cost, please note, includes conveyance.

No, it is not just the sheer magnitude of social inequalities which hurts here. Nor is it the shock of realising how poor are our poor, for whom these posters and invocations are intended. No, it is the vulgarity which our ruling oligarchy displays through such posters which wears one down. The poor may each have a vote in the elections. That vote may be worth as much as the vote cast by a multimillionaire. That is an unfortunate idiosyncracy of the system. The family planning campaign at least has no doubt; the poor may have a vote like us, but they are different, they have no pride, no sensitivities. We spend forty chips to buy their vote, we will also offer them forty chips to persuade them to agree to a sterilisation. If that will not satisfy them, we will throw in an extra two quid to cover conveyance expenses. If simple-looking condoms will not do the trick, produce condoms in attractive colours. As if condoms are lollipops, and the poor people in this country—the majority of the electorate of this sovereign republic—are imbecile children. It is only where the masses are held in total contempt that one could dare to get away with the crude obscenities which these posters are.

All the time, one talks of the great cultural heritage of this nation. The grandeur of the *bharatanatyam* and the sitar is flaunted all over the world. Ministers quote from the *Vedas* and the *Upanishads*. The temple carvings are alluded to as examples of India's exquisite artistic sensitivity. How do you match these against the degrading vulgarity of the family planning campaign? It is taken to be axiomatic that if you are poor, you have also no aesthetics, nor can you have any reservoir of dignity. Nobody stops to think, it is taken for granted that the loud, rude jingle of money will make the poor acquiesce in a temporary suspension of their manhood or womanhood. The republic may be socialist: but an extra unit of the poor is only worth forty-two rupees.

Yet, look at the facts. What is material is not the cumulative barrage of propaganda but what is happening in villages, towns and cities. What matters is the crude birth rate. With all the efforts mounted by the Government, it would be indeed difficult to prove that, in the country as a whole, the crude birth rate is perceptibly any less than what it was ten or twenty years ago. Even if one were to brush aside aggregative data and enquire as to actual results obtained in areas which have been blanketed by family planning campaigns, it would again need a lot of verisimilitude to claim that any perceptible impression has been made on the crude birth rate. Here and there in isolated localities, one can indeed discern a slight lowering of the rate but statistically it would be difficult to correlate this reduction to the campaign as such.

Also, consider the incongruity of it all. Under the Fourth Plan, we were supposed to spend fewer than Rs 240 crores over the five-year period on elementary education, but the outlay on family planning was supposed to be as much as Rs 350 crores. Large groups of economists, sociologists and demographers may keep telling the Government that, in the final analysis, the only sure way to reduce the birth rate is through an initial improvement in living standards and through better education. They may also agree amongst themselves that economic development—and rise in living standards—hinges a great deal on the dissemination of education. In terms of our Constitution, too, we were supposed to provide free and compulsory education to all children of school-going age by a date which is now passed. The Government's priorities are, however, indelibly etched: family planning comes ahead of primary education.

One can scan at least three separate reasons why this should be so. Primary education may be crucial for economic growth. It may raise productivity: may improve the adaptability of people to new technological processes; may create an environment which makes it easier for the relatively worse-off to perceive the significance of family planning. At the same time, though, primary education has its risks. If you provide landless labourers and small farmers in the countryside and slum-dwellers in the cities with a modicum of education, you may also be indirectly hastening the process of social alienation. Primary education may vocalise the discontent latent amongst the poor. It may induce the poor peasantry, the army of the unskilled workers and the unemployed to organise and articulate themselves politically. Primary education may teach them not to stand still.

There is no such danger in family planning campaigns: they contain no seeds of revolution. They offer a further advantage. Family planning is a racket which entices foreigners, and foreign exchange. Foreign aid and foreign technical personnel flow in freely. Funds are received in abundance. No such easy flow of money is likely to be forthcoming if you were to launch a comprehensive programme of primary education. To spread literacy is hard, slogging work. It is not exciting. Vasectomy and tubectomy perhaps are. As the Americans would say, perhaps there is more sex appeal in family planning, none in primary education.

Finally, in a parasitic society, family planning campaigns immediately attract a large group of parasites in the form of public relations experts. There is enormous scope of leakage of liquid funds in such campaigns. You contract and sub-contract the work, and keep happy large numbers from amongst the elite groups. They really go to town; almost every day they come up with newer and newer creative ideas about how to spread the message of sterilisation. The emphasis in the campaigns is almost as much on promoting ideas as on opening clinics. There is no similar short-cut to the spread of primary education. Mere toting of ideas is scarcely enough here. You must develop a countrywide organisation which goes deep down. You must get to know each of the country's five hundred and fifty thousand villages, must penetrate into each of its urban slums. You can do all that provided you have a well-knit administrative structure, an honest political apparatus and a Government which can sort out the gimmicks from the real issues in economic development. And, who knows, perhaps you need the presence of precisely each of these even if you want *effective* family planning.

For us, there is for the present no passage to China. China too has mounted a family planning campaign, one which has possibly attained a larger order of success than ours; according to all reports, the crude birth rate there has come down appreciably in recent years. No lurid posters stare out at you in China, but, on the quiet, through persuasion, through education, through a code of moral behaviour, through a method of social discipline, politicians and administrators have been able to raise the age of marriage for both boys and girls. In China, too, they distribute pills to women and condoms to men, but this act of distribution is not shouted from the rooftops. There is that story about how an American demographer, visiting China a few months ago, had enquired of a social worker whether pills are also distributed to unmarried girls. But what will they do with such pills, was the puzzled response. That response indicated a universe of morality and social demeanour which is perhaps beyond our pale. Maybe so. But that does not still explain why we should have to tolerate the obscenity of the vasectomy posters. Even we deserve better than this.

1972

32 We Have Been Here Before

We have been here before. The ministers almost foamed at the mouth, proclaiming to the world about the record *kharif* harvest. The Chief Ministers met in New Delhi, congratulated one another, praised the Prime Minister's leadership, and raised procurement prices across-the-board by nearly thirty per cent. Instrumentalities of the State were apparently all set ready for a giant procurement operation. The politicians had learnt from the disaster of the preceding *rabi* season. They had now revised their strategy: they would no longer be led up the garden path of vacuous ideology-mongering, no more the theme of wholesale takeover of trade; instead, in this new season, the strategy would consist of dangling high procurement prices before the traders and farmers. You could almost see the smug feeling of self-contentment oozing from the pores of the ministers' faces; everything was keyed up for a record procurement from output of the *kharif* crop. Trumpets rent the air. For rice, the procurement would be five million tonnes, no less: for coarse grains, for the first time a determined effort would be made to attain a target of 1.5 million tonnes. Till as late as December, Krishi Bhavan was found to give vent to the conviction that in the case of both rice and the coarse grains, actual procurement might even exceed the targets.

But we have been here before, over and over. The effective part of the *kharif* procurement season is more than half-way through. Barely 1.8 million tonnes of rice have been procured;

the performance with the purchase of coarse grains—the feed of the poor—is even more dismal. The bulk of the procurement of rice has been in Punjab and Haryana, where the cereal is barely consumed and the crop is intended mostly for export: the farmers and traders there were also exceedingly happy with the generous increase in the procurement price, which was much higher than what the local market would have ever offered. In contrast, in the traditional rice-producing States, the substantial increase in the Government's purchase price has not made the least difference. In most of them, procurement is even lower than last year's. On an average, market prices have risen by roughly a quarter over the year, while the procurement price has risen by one-third, the relative distance between market and procurement prices has therefore narrowed. But so what? What fool of a farmer or trader is around who would voluntarily hand over his stock to a Government agency when, by holding it back and selling it to a private party, he can get a much higher rate of return, particularly since the Government itself has arranged for the credit which makes such holding back of grains a costless operation?

Thus it is that, while on paper the production of rice in the country has perhaps increased by close to forty per cent during the past decade, a magnificent constancy has attached to procurement: it has always hovered around 3 million tonnes each year, until last season when, following the nation's solemn reaffirmation of faith in the noble leadership of the Prime Minister, it suddenly dipped to a million tonnes. The record harvest notwithstanding, given the rate at which things are progressing, this year too, the procurement of rice is unlikely to exceed 2.5 million tonnes. Even in those near-famine years, 1965-66 and 1966-67—it is by now almost tiresome to point out the fact—

procurement was substantially more. And in the matter of the coarse cereals, the less said, the better: why bother at all to procure these, how does it matter if the needs of the poor are not met? The poor are dispensable.

Procurement, in other words, is impervious to both production and prices. It is all a unilateral arrangement. You sink money in expanding irrigation facilities, you spend money to bring the farmers high-yielding seeds, you dispense funds for ensuring the supply of pesticides and insecticides, you make outlays in precious foreign exchange and import scarce fertilisers, you go slow with land reforms, you turn the other way in case any committee of innocent experts suggests a slightly higher impost on agricultural holdings, or calls for the up-to-dating of land records. You fly in the face of facts concerning the actual cost of production, and fix inordinately high purchase prices for the grains. All this enables the farmers to raise production. But what for? None of the additional grain raised can be claimed for purposes of the State—for meeting the needs of the public distribution system, or for feeding the rural poor. Quite the contrary. Since you raise the level of price, an inflationary bias is introduced, market prices adjust themselves upwards; if the wages and earnings of the rural poor fail to keep pace with this rise in market prices, distress in the countryside is intensified. Besides, since foodgrain prices are the most crucial element in the cost of living in this poor country, the price inflation spreads everywhere. There is no apter instance of the classical precept of *kalakaivalyam*: the increase in output is only for the sake of the increase, the increase in procurement price too is only for its own sake, let not anybody suggest that either factor should lead to a rise in procurement, or to the furtherance of some other vulgar national goal.

We have been here before, over and over again. Thus, come next July and August, there would be another crisis in the public distribution system. With each year, as the holding power of the affluent farmers and traders goes up because of the rise in prices and the generous supplies of credit from various official sources, the market availability of foodgrains shrinks, and landless labourers and small farmers, who have to buy their requirements from the market in the lean season, totter on the verge of starvation. Come next July and August, they would begin to trek to the urban centres in search of food. Another crisis would be at hand, irrespective of the size of, or the procurement from output of, the *rabi* crop. Once more, an official delegation would therefore begin to negotiate with the Russians or the Canadians or the Australians for an emergency quota of foodgrain imports. Self-sufficiency in food would begin to be interptreted in a new manner. Per capita availability may go up, but who says this increase has to be related to a diminution in the per capita dependence on imports? Under the Indian arrangement, self-sufficiency will be distinguished from self-reliance. We shall have progressively more food produced in the country, at the same time we shall continue to rely on others for maintaining our public distribution system.

Once the food is produced in the country, irrespective of the level of price offered by the Government, it is not impossible to appropriate a modest proportion of it, such as 10 per cent or less, for purposes of the State. But, to bring this about, you need to enforce a quality of national discipline. You have to impose a levy on the producers, the traders, the millers, the hullers, and such others, and enforce this levy. You have to cordon off areas, prevent the movement of grains across the borders of *talukas* or districts, deny credit to parties known to indulge in speculation, refuse to shower favours upon your partymen where they belong to entrenched interests or to the underworld. What is the point of being polite? Each year in recent times, this discipline has petered out. Once a political system has been nurtured on the basis of, and is made to depend entirely upon, spoils, it is difficult to enforce the called-for discipline, for the government is reduced to an apparatus from which all sections—farmers and traders included—only expect favours. The moment the administration tries to extract a *quid pro quo* from those classes for whom it has been the benefactor, they revolt. The character of the Congress party, who does not know, has been transformed beyond measure in recent years. Not a trace of ideology is left in it anymore. Perhaps it was always a party of graft, but never so unashamedly so. The Government—the men and women belonging to the party, or supporting it from outside, have been given to understand—exists exclusively for their satisfaction. To talk of compulsory levy and other similar measures in such an atmosphere would be fantastic nonsense. Which is why procurement is left to its own devices: an instance of indicative planning *a la* France, the smart ones would say.

This need not be the case, others may argue. Does not the strong stance the Government adopted against the employees of the Indian Airlines belie the above proposition? The authorities have stood resolutely firm; the lockout of the airline's employees was not lifted, and the unions were not offered the slightest concession: one can now witness the extraordinary scene of the vast majority of the employees tamely going back to work. But, here again, it is the class character of the employees and those ranged against them which has been crucial in Government decision-making. The victims of the alleged sloth and inefficiency of the airline workers are made up of the upper classes—businessmen and industrialists, senior civil servants, affluent professional groups. They have fumed and fretted even as the go-slow practices of the Indian Airlines employees have delayed them for hours at the airports: their schedule of engagements has been upset, they have missed their lunch or dinner dates, their wives have waited long and hard for them to return home from trips to other cities, their children's barely month-long vacation from Doon or Woodstock or Mayo has been fouled up. Despite the impression deliberately sought to be created, there are only a handful of highly paid ones in the airlines, the bulk of the employees belong to the category of low-paid clerks, technicians and porters. By taking a firm stand against them, the authorities have gladdened beyond measure the hearts of their own class supporters. Now they will not have to wait for more than five minutes to get their bags, there will be no interminable waiting for flights to take off. Discipline above all, but, for eminent reasons, not a whiff of a similar enforcement of discipline is suggested when procurement lags way behind and the common people have to go without food. Kicks for the vassals and serfs, kisses and consideration for our class brethren. Waiting for the weekly bread ration is only normal and nothing to raise one's hackles; waiting for one's baggage to be unloaded from the plane is, however, an intolerable imposition and must be redressed immediately. First things first. Isn't the first principle of our Five-Year Plans the sorting out of priorities?

1974

33 The Species of Make-Believe

No apologies need be proffered for continuing with the theme of the season, but let there be a shift from the general to the particular, from the problem of procurement at the national level to the woes of procurement in this state. Production of rice in West Bengal in the current year is supposed to have exceeded all past records: a crop of seven million tonnes, the people have been informed with a triumphant wink. One can see how the output of rice in the state has moved up and down during the decade: it was 5.8 million tonnes in 1964-65, but came down to 4.9 million and 4.8 million respectively in the drought years of 1965-66 and 1966-67, rose to 5.2 million in 1967-68, galloped to 6.2 million in 1968-69; from then on, it has been 6.4 million in 1969-70, 6.1 million in 1970-71, 6.5 million in 1971-72 and 5.7 million in 1972-73. And now, in 1973-74, the output is supposed to have scaled the glorious height of seven million tonnes. Procurement of the grain has, however, maintained no relationship at all to the trend in production. In 1964-65, procurement was 335,000 tonnes: despite the drought, P.C. Sen in his innocence was able to push it up to 584,000 tonnes in 1965-66. Next year, procurement fell to 123,000 tonnes, but was again up to 265,000 tonnes in 1967-68. Largely because of the efforts of the United Front administration, it was once more as high as 434,000 tonnes in 1968-69 and 411,000 tonnes in 1969-70. Under President's rule, the purchase of rice slid back to 266,000 tonnes in 1970-71 and stayed at around 250,000 tonnes in the following year. In 1972-73, with political stability allegedly fully restored in the state and a Congress government reinstalled in power, procurement dropped further by as much as 100,000 tonnes compared to the previous year, and was only 150,000 tonnes. In the current year, never mind the record output, hardly 60,000 tonnes have been procured till the middle of January. The only issue that seems left to be determined is whether, as the season closes, total procurement would be even lower than what it was in 1966-67. The year with the decade's highest output could thus indeed also be the year with the decade's lowest procurement.

Before the season began, the state government had fixed a procurement target of 500,000 tonnes, about seven per cent of the estimated output. Some amongst the amateurish ones within the ruling party had then claimed that the target was too low, at least ten per cent of the production ought to be commandeered by the State. These days of *naivete* were soon dissipated. The bulk of the rice has already been harvested. The peak of the marketing season is over. Each day, newspapers are full of some fresh measures of cordoning and dehoarding proposed by the authorities. But these belong to the species of make-believe. The bird has already flown: it is now too late in the day to do anything to reach anywhere near to the procurement target.

Of the total target of 500,000 tonnes, the rice mills were supposed to deliver 360,000 tonnes; the rest was to be collected through a levy on the big producers. Till last week, the rice mills have handed over hardly 20,000 tonnes. If you go round the countryside and visit the *mandis*, you will find the mills apparently all lying idle. They have, you will be told, no custom this year; despite the sharp increase in the procurement prices of rice and paddy, the latter are still 25 to 30 per cent lower than market prices; nobody therefore chooses to deliver the paddy to the rice mills; the paddy goes to the hullers, who are innumerable, and to the thousands of husking contraptions in private households. This, however, is oniy one part of the story, for one also hears of rice mills which work, clandestinely, at night, under the benign patronage of the local political boss. There is the general environment in the countryside, too, to be considered. The agent of the Food Corporation, poor creature, will have to run for dear life if he tries any funny tricks. Since he cannot collect from the rice mills, he dares not even collect the levy from the big farmers. And those who have been called upon to pay for the levy have merely put the squeeze on the share-croppers for some extra parting with the grain. All told, it is a bizarre situation. You wanted stability, it is now there; from village after village, the trouble-makers, the leftists, have been driven out; neither the share-croppers nor the landless labourers can any longer afford to make even a squeak: the Congress party's sway is complete. Yet, none of these is of any help: procurement is perfunctory. Naturally, certain consequences have followed. It is only January, but the public distribution system is already under strain in many areas in the state: its total collapse is being feared in the lean months.

For there is a certain auto-regressive quality in what is happening. Procurement is poor, supplies from the Centre are fitful, therefore everybody is predicting the disintegration of the public distribution system in the coming months. But precisely on account of that, each and all—big farmers, small farmers, big traders, small traders, urban housewives, peasant women—are trying to stock up. In the countryside, even the most impoverished ones have started to sell trinkets and utensils in order to have cash with which to buy some cereals for the dire days that are a-coming. Petty clerks in towns are borrowing from their provident funds for the same purpose; stock up, stock up, food will be still scarcer in the lean season, the government will not be able to help, so do stock up now whatever little you can. Since nearly everybody is gripped by this psychosis, the price shoots up even more in the market, and so much less is available for procurement; what starts as a scare soon turns into a panic, and the panic soon assumes the corpus of an inevitable doom.

In all this, one can hardly ignore the class composition of the Congress party in the countryside. The rich farmers and traders continue to form the solid, enduring core of the party; they have lived through the nightmare of the leftist jackals: now that a dazzling day has followed that grim interregnum, let them, for a while, breathe the free, non-claustrophobic air. It is sheer ingratitude to ask them to disgorge their stocks. True, procurement prices have been raised, but market prices have also jumped. True, traders and farmers cannot claim the entire credit for the rise in market prices: the government, through its various policies, has also helped a great deal. But, after all, it is their government, it is its bounden duty to keep prices high so that they could widen their rate of return. Is it natural justice, they would ask, for their *own* government to press them to sell the grain to the Food Corporation at a laughably low price when it can fetch at least forty to fifty per cent more in the open market ? To bully them to do so would be an un-Congresslike act. The Congress is there to support and protect the affluent: the whimsies of those talking in leftist jargon must not be allowed to harm the interests of the party's original, essential class base.

But this is by now a commonplace: about everybody knows

that it is difficult for the ruling party to alienate the rich farmers and traders. There is, however, something else too happening in the countryside and which makes it altogether impossible to enforce a rigorous programme of procurement. The young, unemployed ones on whose strength the Congress has returned to power in this state are not to be scoffed at. It is they who, with the active connivance of the forces of law and order, combined most effectively with the elements of the underworld and squeezed out the leftists from their traditional bases. Two seasons ago, they were promised a lot: once the Congress rule was restored and stability returned to the state, milk and honey would start flowing, industries would revive, agriculture would flourish, opportunities would multiply, banks would offer saturation credit to the self-employed, there would be a thousand new schemes for the expansion of jobs and incomes, it would be a golden Bengal. The performance of the Congress ministry, installed in March 1972 following the decimation of the leftists, has been anti-climactic beyond measure.

The young ones who were promised work and prosperity find that things are now much worse. A handful, who are either close to ministers or have come to handle the party's funds, have managed to flourish. But the vast majority are left out. Envy has sprouted, and the youth wing of the Congress is now riven by wide, sharp divisions. The guns and bombs are out: almost every day there is internecine warfare, accompanied by one or two murders. Attempts to patch up the differences have failed. The party's leaders are finding it extremely difficult to cope with the wrath of the disillusioned cadres.

A large number from amongst them have decided to fend for themselves. Procurement can never succeed in the state because the young ones—mostly from middle-class and lower middle-class homes—who now constitute the Congress party's storm-troopers are also those who run the statewide operations in smuggled rice. From the lush villages to the not-so-lush ones, from the surplus districts to the deficit ones, from the countryside into the areas covered by statutory rationing, from across the state border into the isolated high-price belts in Bihar such as Jamshedpur, Sindri and Barauni, lies the rice route, completely taken over by the Congress rank and file, either on their own or on commission from the more exalted ones. Some months ago, there was much high-falutin' talk of fifty thousand young Congress workers who would help the official agents in the procurement operations. On a rough reckoning, fifty thousand Congress workers are in fact at the moment blanketing the West Bengal countryside: they are, however, on the other side of the operations. Each such person is perhaps either directly engaged in smuggling, or has entered into an arrangement with a trader to ensure the safe movement of smuggled rice within a particular police station. The terms, apparently, are arranged in advance. For permitting untrammelled movement over a distance of ten miles, the levy to be paid per quintal of rice is maybe seven rupees for a Congress worker and three rupees for the minions of the police. This is all part of a secret network, but it has its own logistics, decentralised operational commands and signalling arrangements. The overheads and the operational costs are neatly spread across the total turnover. If, to reach the cordoned area of Calcutta, a quintal of rice has to be transported over a distance of forty miles, obviously forty rupees will now be added to the price over and above what is quoted in the village market from where the rice originates.

This relay system of smuggling is maintained through headloads, and through movements by cycles, boats, trains, occasionally even trucks. It is a regular, full-fledged operation and, in some senses, more efficient than the officially maintained public distribution. In areas notionally covered by statutory rationing, such as Calcutta and Durgapur, the actual delivery of rice through this network in some weeks even exceeds what the consumers are able to get from the ration shops. They of course have to pay two and a half to three times the price charged in the ration shop, but given both the current shortage and the spectre of famine five or six months hence, there is no lack of demand. In the so-called 'fringe' areas not served by statutory rationing, where the supply through the fair price shops has almost totally collapsed, it is in fact the bounty of the smugglers which is providing the daily bread to a large majority of the people.

This is a precarious equilibrium which you cannot afford to disturb. Something, somewhere has got to give: political stability of a kind has been thrust back on West Bengal, the leftists have been hounded out: a price, however, has to be paid. Since, in the absence of jobs, the young ones who, with their guns and bombs, enabled the Congress to come back to power have to be kept happy, they must be given an extra cut by traders, farmers—and the authorities. The urban and semi-urban consumers should not complain either: at least a surrogate has filled in for a government which has stopped functioning. And those unable to buy the cereals at the price quoted by smugglers have the freedom to starve: it is, after all, not such a new phenomenon in this country.

1974

34 He Who Escapes . . .

He who escapes, lives: so goes that adage in Sanskrit. Young people from middle-class homes evidently are sold on it. The travel regulations are pretty rigorous, to arrange a passport can take months, foreign countries—even those who were generally hospitable in the past—have gradually clammed up, most of the time an uncertain future awaits the young men and women who migrate. They are still not deterred. It is not so much the pull of distant lands: the reason for their eagerness to take the plunge is more humdrum. They want to escape from their native place, from its hopelessness and claustrophobia. These youngsters are a near-desperate lot, bonds of emotion do not detain them, they want to forsake their heritage. Every day, you can see them crowding at the foreign consulates, swallowing the insults and ignoring the brush-offs from lowly-placed officials.

One can rail against them. One can berate their lack of dignity, castigate them for their selfishness, be aghast at the poverty of their ideals. To sit in judgment over the conduct of others is, however, a hazardous occupation in all seasons. Moral issues are hardly ever resolved through polemics or through a show of hands either. More often than not, patriotism provides instances of I-have-loved-thee-Seneca-in-my-fashion. Some of the young people would even argue that, by leaving the country, they are in fact lessening the burden of the economic problem for the rest of the nation, the authorities will now be saved the bother of worrying about *them*. Pitted against this is the by-now-stylised argument: the nation has invested so much of its scarce resources over so many number of years to feed and train these young men and women, the latter therefore have no business to depart, along with the capital embodied in them, for foreign shores. A cost is involved in rearing and educating them: to allow them to leave is akin to a total write-off of a certain volume of invested funds, which this poor country can ill afford. The arguments on either side will rage fiercely. A would-be emigrant, slightly disturbed by the moral aspects of his decision to get away, will perhaps commit himself to remitting from abroad the equivalent of the estimated approximate sum till then spent upon him by society. Or perhaps he will turn round and counter-attack: accident of birth is accident of birth, his commitment is not to his native land, but to science and technology, and he will be in a better position to contribute to both if he is permitted to work, under immensely more congenial conditions, in a foreign laboratory or plant than at a dreary place at home. He might even decide to be viciously belligerent: if the nation were interested in him, well, it should have provided him with wages and facilities commensurate with his talent, and in accordance with international standards. The majority will, however, stay away from controversies. They will not even try to rationalise their decision, or to provide it with a moral cloak. They escape for bread-and-butter reasons, because, with all its uncertainties, life is still much easier in a foreign country, corruption is less rampant, bureaucracy is a shade less hide-bound, and jobs are still relatively a-plenty. It could be that the existence over there will be drab and anonymous, maybe one will miss the challenges and excitements one faces at home, but maybe one will also avoid the tensions and frustrations, the pettinesses and the lack of opportunities of advance. There is, after all, only one life to live; make the most of it while you can, if necessary even at the cost of alienating the large, large numbers of your own people who are not as lucky as you are, who cannot escape.

There is a certain heartlessness in the phenomenon. Given the structure of distribution of assets and incomes in the country, some people suffer more than others from the stagnation of social and economic growth. Those with the advantage of good education and of a disproportionately larger share of the capital stock are able to get something out of even a decaying system. And as they succeed in extracting more despite there being no growth, the availability of goods and services, and therefore the standard of living, are pari passu reduced for others, who experience an erosion of their real income. If you want to stay alive, escape, says the adage. But the bulk of the impoverished ones do not, cannot escape to foreign lands. Even to escape, you need assets. It is only those who have assets—and 'connections'—who manage to fly away.

Should one roar against them? Lack of idealism is, however, hardly a culpable offence. And making the most of the opportunity of free mobility is one of the proclaimed virtues of the system of *laissez-faire*. Before firing an ideological salvo, one must be sure of one's own moral foundations. Patriotism cannot be forced into an individual's metabolism: either he has it, or he has not. There can be no cram course where you pay the fee and pick up lessons on how to love the country. One comes to patriotism through one's sense of pride in one's own native land. That pride is a gradually disappearing category for a not-altogether-insignificant number in this country. This was not always so. Recent events have ushered in a kind of non-philosophical anarchism. There is a loss of pride in the nation's achievements, perhaps because these have been so few and far between. From loss of pride follows the loss of a sense of involvement. The young people try to escape: they suffer from no ethical bond. Life is not worth living here, escape, join the rush to Canada, try hard for an immigration visa for the United States, wangle a work-permit-cum-entry certificate from the British High Commission. Arrange something and go, go, go. Let the nation be left to its own devices. To stay on in India is to condemn oneself to the daily grind of despair, escape while there is still time, while the visas and the entry permits are still relatively easily grabbable.

Stop the world, we want to get off: say these youngsters from middle-class homes. Another lot of them, equally sick with the state of affairs in the country, choose another course. Those amongst them who do not get killed, are locked away. Does one venture to sit on judgment on either—or both? Must not those who stay behind and continue to fight for principles be preferred to those whose thoughts turn toward escape, most of the time comfortable escape? But that too would be an exercise in choosing between systems of value. This is a hazy world, ruled by indeterminacy. That the rate of economic development has been brought down to the level of near-zero is a statement which does not involve any moral dictum: it is a fact. That opportunities for gainful work have almost totally dried up is another fact. That corruption has proliferated, both inside the citadels of power and outside, is an equally valid datum. That the credibility of the Government has been so much eroded that many will not trust it even with the time of the day cannot be denied either. But, beyond such assurances, what else can one cling on to? Gloom and loss of faith; a feeling that nothing matters any more; the blurring of distinction between idealism and the lack of it: these are the staples of the day. There was perhaps, at one point of time, an excess of identification between the processes of the Government and the nation's aspirations. This, the cynic would say, was the leftover gift of socialist pretensions. Now that the Government has been seen plain, the crumbling of faith has dragged each and every thing down. The nation is infested by hypocrites: the proposition passes by a unanimous show of hands. The nation has been captured, and is being led, by a claque of crooks: motion approved again. The nation lacks altogether moral principles, this is what the leaders have reduced it to: again, the proposition wins, hands down. The nation does not any longer grip you, it cannot therefore command your allegiance. The amorality at the aggregative level is matched by a frightening array of individual amoralities. Call it brain drain, call it the apotheosis of talent, the rush to forsake the native soil therefore continues, and you are admonished to withhold your moral judgment. The stringency in 'P' form regulations cannot stem the tide. People find devious ways to give the nation the slip. They manage to get away from it all.

Those who make the getaway do not stop to consider the plight of the millions who cannot escape, who will have to remain behind, grist to the mill of the ruling class. Now is for now, and each is for himself or herself. Those who can, escape, for they have learned that those who escape, live. Whether those others that are left behind deserve an equal opportunity to live is a thought which does not detain them: this callousness they have picked from the environment which is currently the nation. This cynicism, in a manner of speaking, synthesises within itself the saga of the Indian tragedy. Shut your heart against the past and the future: now is for now. What is even worse, right is wrong and wrong is right, and none could tell it all by sight. The consequences can be seen whichever direction one turns to. Words have been beaten to pulp so that their original meanings have been rendered pallid. Crass authoritarianism can now pass for humanism; fascistic behaviour can parade as socialism; putting the squeeze upon the poor can be trumpeted as another milestone on the road to egalitarianism. Crooks are rewarded with national honours; opportunism is elevated to the status of a national code; debauching the modalities of justice, so as to serve a sectarian cause, is applauded from official forum; bending the administrative processes to further a narrow, partisan objective is asserted as a fundamental right; the country's economic future is bartered away through heavy borrowings abroad and the operation is described as a decisive step towards self-reliance. The pride is gone, but not because this is a poor nation, not even because the nation has little to show by way of achievement in any sphere, but simply because it—rather, its self-styled leaders—have promoted the lack of integrity as the centrepiece of the new morality. The listlessness one senses is the listlessness which follows from an abdication of faith. One particular code of faith, on which one was wont to lean, has been sabotaged, and no substitute seems to be around. Nobody knows for certain how long the interregnum is going to be, or whether this tunnel, where one waits, itself constitutes the remainder of one's existence. Since no specific co-ordinates of social behaviour are any longer considered viable, people make their own rules. Some of the stragglers, really the old-fashioned ones, still join processions, dream dreams, and crowd into prisons. Others, who have liberated themselves, either make their pile in the black market, bribe ministers and buy governments—or quit the land. In the absence of a community preference map, who is to judge who are the saints and who are the sinners? The climacteric of the Indian drama is at hand: right is wrong and wrong is right, and who can tell it all by sight.

1974

35 Let Facts Speak . . .

Abjure adjectives, let facts speak for themselves. Certainly. There is little doubt that, once the grim season passes, some kind of a Famine Enquiry Commission will be launched, and it will duly present a report analysing the factors which caused this year's tragedy. Perhaps, a few months hence, the National Sample Survey Organisation will undertake a sample study on the incidence of starvation deaths which would occur, district-wise, *taluka*-wise, village-wise. There will be impressive-looking schedules attached to the questionnaire: description of the household—whether it was a cultivating or non-cultivating one; whether owning or not owning land; if owning land, the size of the holding; the quantity of cereal consumption per capita during the preceding month or the preceding quarter; what consumer durables the household possesses; whether the household disposed of any such durables in the course of the preceding week or the preceding fortnight or the preceding quarter; if it did, what was the realisation in cash or in kind; did any deaths from starvation take place during the preceding week, the preceding month, the preceding quarter: were any of these deaths certified by a physician; if not, the reasons for non-obtaining of certificate; if the deaths were certified by a physician, was the latter a degree-holder, or a licentiate, an allopath or a homeopath; were the deaths because of (a) lack of food, (b) lack of nutritive balance of intake, or (c) indeterminable factors; were doles available in the village, or in the *taluka*: if not, were they available within 10 miles of the homestead, 15 miles, 20 miles: were gruel kitchens operating in the village, or in the *taluka*; if not, within 10 miles of the homestead, 15 miles, 20 miles; what was the price of rice, variety-wise, in the village and in the *taluka* during the preceding week, the preceding month, the preceding quarter; was work available in the village or in the *taluka* during the preceding week, the preceding month, the preceding quarter; if the answer to the last question is in the affirmative, what was the wage rate, in cash or in kind, in the village and in the *taluka*.

Facts are sacred. They have to be gathered. We have one of the best statistical systems in the world; the facts will be gathered. Meanwhile, there is the stench of death all around. There is no food for the poor, who are dying in their hundreds. In due course, the relevant statistics will be brought together, statistics that will be faultily faultless, icily regular, splendidly null, dead perfect.

Dead perfect, but no more. For, meanwhile, anticipating the investigation to be launched by the National Sample Survey Organisation, Haripada Dolui, village Garalgacha, police station Dankuni, district Hooghly, throws his five-year old child into a pond; the boy drowns: he had been pestering his father for a morsel of food which he did not get for the preceding 72 hours. In the same district, police station Arambagh, village Haraditya, Binod Barui, day labourer, having a household of five members, bashes the head of Nityananda Majhi, day labourer, having a household of six members: their families were starving for one full week, they were collecting artichokes from the same bush, not enough artichokes to go round: they therefore fought, fought like dogs, snarling animals determined to survive. In District Cooch Behar, sub-division Dinhata, village Kharubhoj,

Chunibala Dasi, age thirty-two, thrusts the half-boiled stem of a wild oat down the throat of her whining two-year old daughter; Chunibala, whose husband dropped dead last week, had her last taste of rice three months ago, when the *anchal pradhan* of the next village organised a feast and she rummaged through the leavings thrown outside. Harish Chandra Roy Burman, Congress boss of Sahibganj *taluka*, of same district, does not cook any meals at home; there are too many beggars around who flock to his house at the smell of cooked food, so he eats, stealthily, in a restaurant. In village Chinigram, police station Islampur, district West Dinajpur, Kamalrani Chakraborty, widow of a Brahmin *pundit*, is busy dismantling the corrugated sheets from the roof of her corner hut, she will sell the sheets in the market and get Rs 40 which will buy 10 kg of rice. In district Purulia, village Birshah, Tudu Soren, *adivasi* labourer, offers wife, Rangia Soren, for sale, at a price of Rs 35 cash down which will fetch eight kg of food. In township Krishnagar, district Nadia, a huge crowd of starving men, women and children collect outside the civil hospital: please admit us in the free ward, we can then claim one meal a day; if not, please, give us some vitamins; even the latter are, however, available in limited stocks and have to be rationed. In district Twenty-Four Parganas, subdivision Kakdwip, police station Gobardhan, there were 12 deaths yesterday, day before yesterday, nine; today, till one o'clock in the afternoon, seven, but further reports will come in before dusk, the *chowkidars* are out on the beat. In district Bankura, police station Ranibandh, village Salhati, Prakash Malo starts out for Bishnupur town where there is a gruel kitchen running, accompanied by wife, three children, and two dogs: only he, one child, and the dogs make it; the rest die *en route*. Corpses to the left of you, corpses to the right of you, corpses in front of you. True, some of the corpses are still technically living, bodies on legs, dragging themselves, crawling, or being dragged toward where there could be some food. Do not worry unnecessarily: by nightfall, they will be dead.

Abjure adjectives. What, however, is the surrogate function? What would you expect a member of the literati to do instead? He can, of course, narrate, for your edification, more names, names of those who are dead and of those who will, assuredly, die of starvation before the middle of the week. But names, especially names of the poor and the wretched, have a certain air of anonymity. By themselves, they are not interesting. By themselves, they are indistinguishable from one another. It is not really essential to multiply the list of the dead. In a manner of speaking, the story is pretty straightforward. The poor do not have the income to buy the costly food which this nation produces: therefore, they have to go without food; since they go without food, they are smitten by hunger; when they are smitten by hunger, they begin to consume non-edible stuff; lack of food and consumption of non-edible stuff soon lead to complications: soon they are dead.

What do you expect a member of the literati to do? Should he attempt to salvage his so-called social conscience, or should he fend for himself? On the individual plane, he could attempt to share his income and food with the starving people. Many of his friends and colleagues are quietly doing so, their names do not catch the newspaper headlines: he could join them. But, clearly, there are limits beyond which such personal gestures cannot proceed. Besides, even amongst the literati, many of the lesser mortals will worry, in the first place, about their own households: already, with inflation roaring, there is a rapid erosion of living standards; a considerable number amongst the literati do not feel bounden to consider themselves keepers of the government's conscience; let the authorities look after the hungry and dying, the literati will take care of their own kith and kin. Many of them—it will be pointless to question their integrity—will have worked out the arithmetic: their draft on the total food available in the country is of negligible proportions, so what is the point of asking them to eat and spend less?

Should the members of the literati then simply read the writings of a former Prime Minister of India, who was amazed that, in 1943, the people of Bengal starved and died in silence, without protest, and did not raid the *godowns* stacked with grains? Should the literati take, literally, this admonition from the greatest Prime Minister this nation has till now produced and join the barricades? But will not such a gesture be totally futile also? Will not the regimens of law and order pick them up in no time, while those who are dying would continue to die? Few of the latter will have the physical or mental strength to follow the literati to prison. Moreover, as some worthy members of the literati will point out, any act which embarrasses the government in New Delhi plays into the hands of elements—internal and external—who are conspiring to bring our socialism down. So even if they had the capability—which, mercifully, they do not have—the opposition parties, while agitating for food for the poor, must take care not to act irresponsibly. Abjure emotions. Analyse facts. The current crisis, it is obvious, is a culmination of the imbalances developing in the economy ever since the devaluation of 1966 and the recession which followed immediately after. The distortions which then got introduced in the investment pattern need to be corrected, therefore, which makes it imperative that the core of the Fifth Plan be saved. This is the agenda for today. Eschew invective: Left adventurism too must be tackled along with rampant manifestations of Right reaction. Objectively considered, 1974 is not 1943. It is a pity that the poor have begun to die; we must demand the opening of more gruel kitchens under each police station . . .

There is a snag here, however. The current famine is not on account of any distortions as such in the investment pattern. It has not been caused by any lack of availability of food. The famine has come about because a few greedy ones, who are in control of political power, have decided to corner stocks, manipulate prices and enrich themselves. In a regime of *laissez-faire*, no opportunity to enrich oneself is to be missed; that would be against religion. Come to think of it, there are possibilities of self-aggrandisement even in the opening of gruel kitchens. My faction of the party must move in and run these kitchens; we could dilute the gruel, cheat on quantity, and so make a neat pile. The opposing faction of the party, too, has a similar gleam in the eye. Both factions are near and dear to the government, and equally so. There is an impasse. Many of the proposed gruel kitchens cannot even be opened, therefore. Which means that some of the starving will die.

The members of the literati, the toothless ones, must behave in a responsible manner; they must abjure adjectives. But what *should* they do even as corpses collapse by the wayside and the wail of the dying rents the air? Should they listen to Mozart's Symphony Number 25 in G Minor, or revert to reading the beautiful prose of the dead Prime Minister?

1974

36 The Jesting Pilates

The winter is ended, the season of discontent has, however, only begun. Nearly everyone, it seems, is walking away from his job and is out in the streets, agitating for higher wages: railway guards, power men, engineers, doctors, teachers, municipal employees. The inert middle class has suddenly discovered the need for organised action to protect their living standards. The once-snooty attitude toward the wretched labouring sections who resort to strikes every now and then is gone. Inflation, evidently, is a great leveller.

The point can no doubt be made—and is being made—that what is happening is absolutely scandalous. The poor in the countryside and the unorganised urban proletariat are suffering a great deal more from rising prices and the growing shortage of essential articles than the middle class. But so what? If those who have been hit the hardest by the inflation have not mounted a protest, or have mounted one which does not match in intensity the agitation launched by such tribes as doctors and engineers, that is not because the very poor love the phenomenon of spiralling prices: the feebleness of their protest is because of their lack of organisational strength. Those who have the strength will try to protect their interests. Besides, it is basic human nature to compare one's own state of affairs not with the plight of those who subsist below; comparisons are always turned the other direction. Even were the threat of absolute penury not there, those earning ten to fifteen thousand rupees a year would still judge how they are faring on a relative scale. They find out how, for example, those who were making thirty to forty thousand a year a while ago are doing now; the latter in their turn worry whether they have further slipped away in the relative scale vis-à-vis those whose annual earnings were a hundred thousand rupees a while ago. And so it goes. In such an atmosphere, moral exhortations lose their currency. Enrich thyself, spake N. Bukharin to the Russian kulaks in the 1920s. Enrich thyselves, so too seems to have been the message transmitted by the regime of the land here to the surplus-raising farmers, traders and industrialists. If it is permissible for these classes to enrich themselves by taking advantage of the inflation—and, in the process, by stoking the inflation further—the emaciated middle class experiences no moral scruples at all in taking to the streets in defence of their own standard of living. Everything is fair in love and war; inflation is war, no less. Everyone is therefore for himself or herself.

This is the major danger the country is going to face as food supplies further shrivel up in the coming months. Inflation is bad, the economists say, because it fouls up the investment signals, and those with money to invest feel tempted to go for speculation rather than for increased production: thereby the shortage of goods is aggravated and the pitch of the income velocity of money is further queered. Still, these economic effects are only a veil and a symptom; the social and political implications of the process could be more lethal. Those who run the wheels of production, those who keep the nation's economic infrastructure going, those who switch on the power plants or regulate the flow of water from the irrigation dams, begin to walk away from their jobs as the scourge of inflation spreads and their money earnings fail to cope with the rise in prices. Where they do not exactly walk away, they perform listlessly, grumbling all the while: they could not care less whether output grows at a satisfactory rate, or whether the equipment is being maintained properly. India is not *sui generis*, the kind of wholesale disruption of productive activity currently being witnessed here has happened elsewhere too whenever wages have been unable to keep pace with prices. To appeal to one's sense of patriotism is altogether pointless at this stage. A practising doctor or engineer or railway guard loves the country in his own fashion, he does so despite the fact that he does not hit the newspaper headlines. Talk to him, he might even come to admit that his demand for more adequate compensation against the price rise could set the regime additional problems. But he has reached a stage where he could not care less. A government can demand, and receive, some consideration from its citizens provided the latter are convinced that, despite their limited options, those in authority are making an honest effort to control prices, or at least are even-handed in their distribution of the hardships caused by the inflation as between different classes and groups. Once this basic faith has evaporated, the situation is beyond redemption.

As one looks around, it is difficult to get away from the feeling that the Government has as good as caved in, and invited the devil to take the hindmost. It needs a particular talent to ride inflation. By now an average Latin American country knows how to cope with an annual order of price increase of 30 to 40 per cent or more, for it has been at the job for umpteen years: the country's agrarian structure is insulated from the inflation, and periodic adjustments in the exchange rate and injection of resources from abroad take care of some of the residual problems. Even the

Latin Americans, though, are having second thoughts: the rate of inflation in Brazil, for instance, has come down from around one hundred per cent in the middle 1960s to just about 12 per cent at present. For us, it is an immensely stickier wicket. At one end, the specific skills which go with the management of inflation, skills which are a function as much of attitudes as of practice, are still missing. In per capita terms, the annual injection of foreign resources in the country is not even 5 per cent of what it is for a Latin American nation. Hardly any step has also been taken to isolate the country's agrarian base from the impact of spiralling prices. Public distribution of foodgrains at reasonable prices is supposed to cater for the vulnerable sections: one, however, doubts whether the rural poor, despite constituting as much as 40 per cent of the nation, receive, through the public distribution system, even I million out of the total domestic output of 100 million tonnes of foodgrains.

One thus comes back to the basic issue. In this poor land, if you want to control prices, you must begin with controlling food prices. Something must have gone hopelessly wrong with an economy if the per capita national income can fetch only 4 quintals of foodgrains per annum, or if the average earnings of at least half the population are not sufficient to buy even 2 quintals of grain over the year. The chief ministers meet and decide to raise further the prices of grains; since they do not do anything to raise the earnings of the poor by their decision, they only manage to push, at one stroke, a few more millions below the poverty line. Many others, too, have their living standards brought a few notches down. Some of them, who are organised and have staying power, refuse to accept without demur this erosion of their level of living. From then on, it is a free-for-all.

Traders and farmers, who have the holding power, keep back the stocks of grain, which enable them to push up prices still higher. The rural poor, who have neither the stocks of grain nor staying power, suffer and suffer quietly. Doctors and engineers and locomen and municipal workers and all the rest, who have some staying power, agitate, go on strike, interrupt output, and thus become partly responsible for a limited rise in prices. A government which will not lift its little finger against the farmers and traders—on the contrary, will coddle them further—can, however, have little moral authority to rail against the agitators.

It is only March, the lean months are yet to come. Calcutta's dilapidated streets are nonetheless every day getting crowded by mid-afternoon. They march, teachers, industrial workers, housewives, engineers, doctors, municipal employees; slogans rend the air; each group demands compensatory adjustment in wages or a lowering of prices. They need to be provided with some relief. There is no dearth of Jesting Pilates, though. While refusing all other kinds of relief to the public, the Railway Minister has decided to restore the concession for travel to hill stations. It you cannot have bread, you can travel to the hills and cool off.

1974

37 A Gleam in the Establishment Eye

This could have been predicted. Now that the saints have come marching in, and private enterprise has worked its way back into the Government of India, where else to look for guidance and light than Brazil—the Brazil which treats the entire toiling population, whether mulatto, negro, or Indian, as so many millions of serfs? This gushing Brazilophilia, so evident from the newspapers, must represent a genre of neocolonialism. If the American journals and newspapers are full of the Delfim Netti device of 'indexation', and Milton Friedman and the Chicago School have been talking gloatingly about it, why not we?

Inflation, particularly runaway inflation, is in any case manna from heaven for the rich ones in society—the industrialists, the traders, and those who have succeeded in developing agriculture along capitalist lines. While the rich prosper during an inflation, the fixed income groups are squeezed, the subsistence farmer and the landless labourer who hires himself out for daily wages are in great difficulty, the organised working class too can protect its real earnings only after prolonged struggles. Inflation is a conscious act of income redistribution on the part of the powers that be: its purpose is to erode the share in national income of the lower deciles of the population and to transfer a larger part to the rich. The avarice of the luckier sections in all societies is, however, truly extraordinary: the more they have, the more they want to have. This is perhaps the principal reason for revolutions, the successful ones as well as the flops. Those who prosper by exploiting others often tend to forget that, as with other things in life, it is disastrous to carry the act of exploitation beyond certain limits of tolerance.

As inflation marches on, and strong-arm methods are used to put down workers, there is a gleam in establishment eyes. The attention of the affluent ones is riveted on the Brazilian example. Inflation is good, it swells their pockets, it enables them to rob the poor; but inflation, accompanied by the stratagem of 'monetary correction', is even better. Eating the cake is great, but eating the cake and having it too is absolutely heavenly. For this is what the Brazilian artifice of indexation is all about. Because of the runaway inflation, the rate of return enjoyed by the tycoon on his invested capital has perhaps jumped from 8 to 80 per cent in the course of a single year. That obviously is not enough. Over the year, the general price index has moved up, say, by 40 per cent. For tax purposes, therefore, the tycoon's earnings must be recorded with a downward adjustment—that is, 'indexated' inversely to the rise in prices: a rebate must be shown due to him. The exchequer will thus receive as revenue much less than is nominally its due. Similarly, if the tycoon's wife has purchased some fixed interest-bearing Government securities, the yield from these must be subject to 'monetary correction', so that there will be no danger of the holder of these bonds being made the victim of untoward bearish sentiments in the market. And, if the tycoon has some footloose cash which he wants to keep as bank deposits, the interest the banks offer against the deposits must also be adjusted so as to compensate fully for the erosion of the money value of the deposit rate. This, then, is a foolproof system, innovated by the rich for the rich, under which, in an inflation, they will never suffer. They will appropriate the gains from inflation, such as a widening of profit margins, a fantastic increase in the return from speculative activities, and so on. They will also have the completest insurance against the common inconveniences which stem from a spiralling of prices, such as a drop in the real rate of interest. Blessed are the rich, for they shall inherit the earth via indexation.

But, even under indexation, somewhere a line has to be drawn. Your enthusiasm for the new device must not be permitted to carry you away. There are such things as broader social responsibilities. Indexation is all right for the rich and the privileged, it is not all right for the working class. Most of the present turbulence in the country in the field of industrial relations is on account of the plea of the organised sections of the working class that they must have a hedge against inflation, that their wages must be adjusted against the rise in prices. This, to be precise, is an echo of the demand for 'monetary correction' *a la* Brazil. Yet, as in Brazil, so here, the authorities and their hangers-on will be aghast at the idea of their precious formula being also applied for the earnings of the wretched workers. One must not press the point of symmetry to absurd lengths. So, while for rentiers and capitalists there shall be the boon of monetary correction, for the labourers the principle to be followed shall be that of wage adjustments *pari passu* with rise in productivity. Nobody shall be permitted to be officious enough to ask how the productivity of a rentier is to be measured, or what is the contribution made to the national output by a speculator. In the case of the rich, questions concerning productivity are *lese-majeste*; they become relevant only if the working class is involved. When the crunch comes, the trade unions will be able to trot out statistics which indicate that, in the 20 years since 1953-54, adjustments in money wage rates in this country for a whole range of industries, old and new, have lagged far behind not only the rise in prices, but also the advances in productivity. But such awkward facts do not deserve a free airing, the newspapers will be asked to play such facts down, or to have them completely censored.

It is a nasty wind which is currently blowing. What causes greater worry, however, is the slow deadening of even elementary social conscience. The character of a polity is determined by the structure of its classes. One should not, therefore, feign surprise at the asymmetrical attitude of the powers that be towards the relative merits of compensating the rich and the poor against inflation. But, whereas a few years ago there would have been a certain shamefacedness about the way the subject is broached, today the deference with which proponents of the Brazilian solution are being treated is indeed breathtaking. Formerly, the attitude would have been, yes, the matter is engaging our attention, the share of wages in national incomes has declined, something ought to be done about it, we are trying to curb the excesses of the rich, but, you know, it will take a while, they are politically so powerful. Anyone suggesting that it is the affluent ones who deserve official protection against inflation would have been ignored, and even held up for ridicule; now, such a person will receive a respectable press coverage, official circles will promise to have his point of view 'examined', perhaps even the Prime Minister will give him audience and listen to his prescriptions: that wages of workers must occasionally be adjusted for the rise in prices will be read the Riot Act, he will be apprised of the Defence of India Rules and the Maintenance of the Internal Security Act. The taxpayers' money will be invested in a lavish bid to inform the countrymen that one propagating such dangerous ideas represents 'the enemy within', what our external foes could not do in 1965 or in 1971, this person is currently bent upon doing. All this and more, because the person has asked for 'indexation'—but not of the profits of capitalists or of the interest accruing to *rentiers*; he has asked for indexation of the wages of labour, oh horror, horror, foul, foul, foul.

There it is. The fangs are out when railwaymen strike. But when traders refuse to part with their stocks of grain, the response is a gentlemanly whimper. It is not the Territorial Army and the Border Security Force whose services are commandeered in the face of this emergency, it is the President of the Federation of Indian Chambers of Commerce and Industry who is invited to accompany the minister to the Punjab *mandis* to plead the Government's cause with the traders and hoarders. At such moments, history is made. The only apt parallel could be Al Capone's accompanying the law enforcement officers to the speakeasies and beseeching the bootleggers to behave: Al Capone would have regarded the idea as a huge joke. There is no reason to believe that the FICCI President felt any differently about his weekend motorcade around the *mandis*.

Where do we go from here? It is an unquiet land, almost exclusively because prices have not been kept on leash. Neither the railwaymen, nor any other set of workers, not even those wretched junior employees of the Indian Airlines, who seem to be everybody's whipping boy, are responsible for the unbridled price increase. The inflation cannot even be laid at the door of stagnant output: a record *kharif* crop, after all, has been accompanied by a record rise in prices during the so-called busy season. Prices, let us face it, have risen because in several cases the Government wanted them to rise; it either connived in the price increase, or benignly crcated conditions—for instance, through liberalised bank credit—such that price spiralling became inevitable. The guilty men are in the Government and on its fringes. The responsibility for undoing the inflation therefore also rests with the Government. In such matters, it is often difficult to sort out the wheat of folly from the chaff of knavery.

Instant solutions to the scourge of inflation are being peddled every day: there is a beeline for meeting the Prime Minister: you can spot in the queue nearly all the well-known quacks and charlatans out to make a fast buck. One can take a little wager; most of the cures currently suggested will only aggravate the malady. The Government, however, appears to be lapping it all up; its love for the charlatans could not be more transparent. As for its hate, that is reserved for the hapless working class.

At this rate, though, very soon, will it not be time to chirp, who deserves greatness deserves your hate?

1974

38 The Champion Pan-Handlers

The glory lies in the size of the grab. And there is a certain catholicity in taste: discrimination of any sort is frowned upon, our leaders cringe for money from each and all, from big and small countries alike. The hoity-toity days of the late 1950s are gone. Then, it was only the Americans who mattered. There has been a secular growth of learning since. Beggars are not supposed to be choosers; our leaders cannot any longer be accused of choosing. In other seasons—or in the same season, given a different forum—these same persons would preach the morality of self-reliance. Chameleons are not bred, they are born. At this specific moment, the leaders are engaged otherwise, cringing for funds. Just watch how newspapers display the proud headline: our begging missions are increasingly gathering fruit; the Japanese are going to assist at Bhatinda; God bless the thousand-year rule of the Palevis, the Shah of Iran has promised continuing help for the refinery at Madras; Iraq has taken kindly to us; for the first time Ireland has made budgetary provisions to offer us aid. There is no mistaking the smirk of satisfaction: we have emerged as the champion touch artists in the world, there could be no greater salvation for the great Indian people.

Indignity, where is thy sting. A certain imperviousness has spread its domain. That to beg, in this manner, could be demeaning beyond words, hardly occurs to the operators in New Delhi. Till the other day, the Government of India used to maintain a patronising, sneeringly superior attitude toward the Arab shiekhdoms. All that is gone. There could have been no greater cultural revolution. We now stoop to beg from each and all. Whoever has a buck to spare will be pursued by India. The individual and collective images are on the point of getting merged. A sight fairly common, in Europe as much as in North America, is that of hordes of slightly seedy-looking compatriots clustering together at a travel agent's or at a discount shop, avarice writ large across their faces, higgle-haggling for an extra bit of concession or for another five per cent cut in the price, for the goodies they are wanting to buy. The official image of the country is by now scarcely any different. The Government of India's shifty-looking emissaries are all over, buttonholing the rich, the reputed-to-be-rich and the not-so-rich with equal fervour; make no mistake, whoever can be embarrassed into giving us a few morsels of extra aid will be embarrassed. Our embassies will cringe before them, pester them, bully them, cajole them. But the sanctimony will still be there. A virtue will still be made of the act of begging: as if the foreign governments should actually be beholden to us, as if it is they who should be proud of the fact of having been presented with the chance to offer assistance to India, the great India, the country of such noble culture and tradition.

The country of such noble culture and tradition will stretch its palm and seek money from practically everybody. If Chad has money to offer, India will take it. If Fiji has, ditto. If perchance Zulfiqar Ali Bhutto, in a fit of malicious generosity, will offer New Delhi a couple of million dollars of aid, trust our politicians to accept that too: some subterfuges will be worked out to call the proffered aid by another name, but that will merely prove the point of a strong positive correlation between the art of panhandling and that of hypocrisy.

One has a thousand complaints against the administration ensconced in New Delhi. Some of them are substantial, some are lightweight, some are superficial, some are sentimental. But the most serious that can be brought home, putting to shade all the rest, is this one, namely, stripping the nation of its pride. The British were here, ruling over the land, more or less with an iron hand, for more than a century and a half. It was alien rule, there was that ignominy of total disenfranchisement. Not even the feudal overlords, nor the small group of industrialists or commercial pretenders, could claim to be their own decision-makers. A brat of an English or Irish or Scottish boy would descend on four thousand square miles of a district, perhaps inhabited by as many as a crore of people, and administer it in the manner of an absolute oligarch. This went on for decades, this was a subjugated, emaciated, downtrodden nation. But, by and large, we retained our composure. Scars of deprivation were writ large across the countenance of countless poor men. The wounds of not being free were invisible to the eye, the indelible marks of that state of being were nonetheless written across the heart. Yet, there was no surrender of dignity. The people were not dispossessed of their pride. Inevitably, there was a handful of cringers. But the nation, considered as a whole, did not give in. It accepted the fact of its misfortune: it accepted the fact that subjugation by an alien power calls for a particular restraint in manners. Indian society had its cruelty and heartlessness; it had its built-in inequities and absurdities. The residual attributes, however, formed a substantial core. Poverty, the nation taught itself, was reconcilable with dignity—but only as long as you were prepared to live within your means.

It is soon going to be twenty-seven years since 15 August 1947, and look where we have arrived: the champion pan-handlers, running after whoever has the cash, our eyes lighting up as the stray passer-by, impatient to get away, drops a careless penny into the pan. We have begun to scrounge before the Iraqis and the Yemenis; very soon, it might be the turn to beg a line of accommodation from even the Nepalese and the Burmese, who are hardly better off than us. The pattern of behaviour will also be completely reversible: those who will have no cash to spare, we will treat them with appropriate disdain. Ethics will come to have a new set of parameters attached to it.

And this after all the torrent of frothy, wearisome talk on self-reliance. Self-reliance is pre-conditioned upon an internal system of discipline. You resolve that you are going to manage within your means. Having made the resolution, you go about it remorselessly, re-arrange the distribution of the goods and resources that you have strictly on the basis of nationally determined priorities, and there the matter ends. Remorselessness in this instance represents the highest form of empathy and pride, for it allows you to stay away from the indignity of cringing before others.

The arithmetic is actually simple. You can do without foreign food and yet have no famine, if only you arrange to collect the food from where it is plentiful in the country, and distribute it, equitably, in those areas where it is relatively short. You can do without foreign petroleum products—or at least cut down drastically the order of your dependence on them—if you can enforce a strict system of rationing, realign the pattern of your energy utilisation and get the maximum out of your internal capacity. You can severely reduce your requirements of foreign equipment, spares and raw materials if you agree to enforce a moratorium on a whole range of consumer goods industries whose output caters exclusively to the demands of the top fractile of the community. You can get more production out of your existing industrial system if you rationalise your power grids, be ruthless with those elements who deliberately restrict output for boosting their rate of profit, and take a few honest steps to check the spiralling of prices so that your labour feels somewhat less grumpy. You can discipline your balance of payments and yet ensure a satisfactory rate of growth if exports are forced up through, once more, an internal disciplining of prices. If only your foreign policy is not deliberately pushed along the wrong rails, external trade relationships may perhaps be developed along lines which could provide for a more balanced exchange of goods with countries which are in a position to offer you, for example, fertiliser and oil. If, again, hysteria were eliminated as an important adjunct of foreign policy, the nation could stop the insensate diversion of precious resources into the cul-de-sac of mounting defence expenditure and the money thus saved used for purposes of rapid economic development. If only sixty crores of rupees were not to be offered as tax concession to the rich, you would be spared the indignity of begging for an extra sixty crores of rupees worth of foreign aid.

But all this is folly to the Government. Decisions are taken on the basis of what is preferred and not preferred by that thin section of the population at the top. This fraction have evidently chosen national indignity in preference to national discipline. Measures toward disciplining the economy would mean depriving them of a large chunk of their current command over goods and services, which, if redistributed, could have allowed the nation to do without dependence on foreign resources. But material comforts count above all; this section of the population does not mind cringing before others, they do not mind filling the role of looked-down-upon pan-handlers for as long as that ensures their own standards of life. They constitute a gross, vulgar sample: their immediate wordly well-being comes ahead of everything else. While the masses are made to share this national ignominy of begging from others, they receive no part of the consequential dispensation. Whether or not one subscribes to the theorem that there has been an absolute immiserisation of the majority of the population since Independence, it would be difficult to controvert a simpler proposition, namely, that whatever improvement in the per capita level of living has taken place in the case of the majority of the nation could have taken place even without foreign aid, and therefore without the massive surrender of dignity which has taken place under the auspices of the ruling elite.

Newspapers meanwhile, though, talk of another breakthrough: is it Cyprus now which has kindly agreed to offer assistance to us?

1974

39 A Diary from Nowhere

Nobody is anybody's keeper. You go your way, I go mine, we embrace each other only when there is a certain area of convergence in our interests, such as when these interests can be advanced by a common set of politics and stratagems. We glare at each other and begin exchanging epithets as soon as our interests emerge as aspects of a fearful asymmetry. Once the special situations are excluded, nations behave more in the manner of tenants residing in high-rise apartment buildings: it is not an instance of none daring to care about what is happening to his neighbours, none in fact bothers to care.

As one switches planes, mislays one's baggage, is hustled by ground stewardesses from one landing area to the next, and is hurtled by jets across nondescript sets of alien borders, the realisation sinks in. India's near-six hundred millions are a near-irrelevance, a speck of uninteresting statistics. Calamities—natural or engineered by men—still hit the headlines: a passenger-loaded bus falling into a canyon, a tornado sweeping the coast of a distant land, the carnage of some insensate war the Americans seem always to be fighting ten or fifteen thousand miles away from home. Or oddities and spectacles: a train hits a cow, the train stalls, the enraged passengers catch the cow, arrange a barbecue, and eat it up; a King Birendra goes through the tomfoolery of a coronation beyond the high Himalayas; a Jacqueline Bouvier Kennedy Onassis embarks on a search for the third consecutive husband, this time perhaps an Arab sheikh.

It is as simple as that. When a few thousands die of starvation in India, that too is a spectacle, we are in the news. When India's ruling class detonates a nuclear device, it is again news, as an illustration of the point that a nation which is unable to feed itself might still be so possessed by ego and effrontery as to go for a nuclear bomb. But these encounters with India are altogether brief. There are other nations, other voices, other happenings of direct concern. So you better get lost. Brother, nobody is anybody's keeper.

Besides, this is the decade of the Arabs. And, of petromoney. One hundred and twenty million Arabs do not quite constitute even three per cent of the human population. But no matter. They have finally got the rest of the world where they wanted. Accounts are now going to be settled. Nothing has been forgotten: the indignities heaped by the marauding Europeans beginning with Napoleon Bonaparte, the snide references to alleged sexual perversities in Western lexicon, the American movies in which the shifty-eyed one is always the Arab oligarch and the Arab girls are made to expose their naked bellies and hips to the filthy glare of dirty-minded heathens. The day of reckoning has arrived. As a harried Henry Kissinger shuffles from one Arab capital to the next, the monocentricity of the news is striking. All of a sudden, this world is for sale—to the Arabs who have the oil and therefore the money. Perhaps the world was always for sale to those who could bid for it. But for the Arabs, it is sweet retribution: they have got the heathens where they wanted.

India does not belong to this scenario: nobody seemingly has even heard of it. This cannot be just on account of lack of oil, however. Plenty of other nations get along without oil, and obtain a hearing in the international concourse. The vacuum of oil-lessness is filled up by other attributes, such as spectacular economic performance, or high-minded devotion to ideology, or maybe plain good manners. Twenty or twenty-five years ago, India's capital stock was about as much depleted as it is today, but it had one great asset: it provided a confessional to each and all. Once Krishna Menon was eased out, that profession slipped beyond India's reach. A zero rate of economic growth is a poor base on which to build a second international career. The nuclear clout ought to have fostered at least a grudging respect; those who detonated the device must have banked heavily upon this expectation. Instead, it has only evoked derision: a combination of splitting the atom and permitting thousands of the nation's millions to die of starvation is—it has apparently been decided—the ultimate in tastelessness.

If you cannot beat them, join them. Nearly everyone—Israel's stoutest supporters from yesterday not excluding—are jumping onto the Arab bandwagon, and making sure of their bread tickets. We too have been trying hard; New Delhi's ministers have been coming and going, and in turn inviting the Sheikhs, in the manner of Melina Mercouri, to be their guest in New Delhi. This, however, is turning out to be an instance of Ramu-come-lately. You do not need an elephantine memory to recollect the spectacle, till only a few years ago, of the hundred insults, with the Arabs at the receiving end and the hoity-toity Indians at the dispensing one. It was a magnificent demonstration of proper, neo-colonial disdain. Ah, Abu Dhabi, Bahrain, those are the spots the wretched smugglers come from, smugglers, gold-runners, card-sharpers, run-of-the-mill cheats; we could not possibly associate with them and do harm to our reputation. The Arabs were for slighting. The Arabs embarked upon a plan to break the international cartel run by the Western airlines by offering substantial discounts on the fares charged by the International Air Transport Association; the noble Indians were horrified; they could not possibly connive at such dirty practices; cartels were forever, and Air-India would stick it out with the whiteys of the IATA and not besmirch its heritage and reputation by fraternising with the Arabs. Such instances of Boston-Brahminism, with Indians condescending to talk only to God, have been altogether too many. As the world has commenced to come to an end since October 1973, the Indians have begun to repent; but perhaps it is already too late, perhaps this exhibition of repentance is being regarded as out-and-out phoney.

As you wait for your next plane in the antiseptic airport lounge, and engage in conversation with the person sunk deep in the chair next to yours, you will be told politely, but in no uncertain manner, where the excellent Indians had gone wrong. They wanted to eat the cake and have it too: they demanded the right to be the permanent irremovable leader of the Third World, at the same time they expected to protect their prerogative to strike private after-hours deals with the Westerners. The brother-confessors wanted to be commission-agents, and wanted a rake-off from the former imperialist-colonialists as price for the sound management of the affairs of the Third World.

Brother-confessor, commission-agent, either role is played out. The former imperialist-colonialists will continue to pay you a commission only so long as they are sanguine that the outlay on the commission is worth their while, that you in fact can deliver. Once you have lost your footing in the Third World, your leverage vis-à-vis the West is also gone. You are a part of the IATA, but that has ceased to be reason enough for the airlines of the Middle

East and South-East Asia to conform blindly to the oligopolistic whims of the Association. You cannot even think of abdicating from the Conference Shipping Lines dominated and manipulated by the imperialist-colonialists, but other nations of the Third World do not owe it to you not to start their own independent Conference Line. As Billie Holiday sang the blues, way back in the forties, lover-boy, these other nations will get by, reasonably well, without you.

Nobody is anybody's keeper. The world does not owe India a living, despite its allegedly grand tradition and civilisation, despite its six hundred million inhabitants. You are on your own. For some limited time, you can manage to lead a parasitic existence, by taking a cut from x, or some hush-money from y, but the international market-place is becoming increasingly more perfect, the role of intermediaries is being increasingly de-emphasised and in any case distributive margins have plummeted way down. Since the market has almost ceased to create value—even the so-called exchange value—for a living, the lover-boy has to return to the arena of production, which is the source of all values.

Howsoever reluctantly, those who take the crucial decisions will have to come face to face with this reality. There is no substitute for hard work, for the unpleasant chores that need to be completed, if the rate of economic growth on the home front is to be lifted from the level of near-zero. These chores will involve an overhaul of the production structure itself, and therefore of the class relations underlying this structure. Each of these statements is a cliche, but then cliches are hard to substitute. They lack glamour; truth usually does.

1975

Section Three

40 The Only Hindu Kingdom in the World

It is pure Kafka: wherever you go, whichever way you turn, never mind which poor country you are currently in, there is no escape from courses and seminars on economic development. The more the frequency of such courses, the less perhaps is the rate of economic growth in the country concerned. But such cynicism cannot deter the style of a world suffering from an excess supply of economists, quite a number amongst whom, on a fair guess, must also be moonlighting as espionage agents for this or that nation. The other day, at one such course catering to officials of the Nepalese Government, there was an intense debate over the motion: If I were not born in the heavenly Kingdom of Nepal, I would then rather be born in China than in India. The motion failed to carry, but just by the skin of the teeth; the verdict of the congregated bureaucrats was six to seven, with two abstentions. The minions of the Indian embassy, anxiously waiting in the wings, must have heaved a sigh which reverberated beyond Raxaul.

The vote on the motion about sums up the situation here. The Indian presence still tilts the political balance, but just marginally. Once more, it is pure Kafka: whichever way they turn, the people here cannot get away from India. Ninety per cent or more of the country's recorded exports go to India: more than four-fifths of the recorded imports come from there. More than one-fifth of the Government's budget is contributed by aid funds from

India. The vast, uninterrupted stretch of the lower *terai*, all five hundred and odd miles of it, beckons to India, shades off into India, is enticed by India, is repelled by India. It is a smugglers' bonanza. Nonetheless, you talk with politicians and government officials, they cannot quite make up their mind whether to hate or hug the smugglers: rice is spirited away to India, which is bad, since scarcities develop on this side of the border, but which is also good, since there is an accretion of Indian rupee balances. Smugglers also bring in quantities of raw jute from India, which again leave the country dressed up as exports, and provide one major source of non-Indian rupee foreign exchange earnings. There is, of course, also the well-known case of synthetic yarn and of Chinese pens and textiles. Nepal survives on the wit and resourcefulness of seedy Indian smugglers. And, going by the articulations of the ruling elite, Nepal hates it; she hates her state of helplessness. At any given moment—was it Cyril Connolly who said something of the sort—one hates oneself; the sum of these moments is one's life. Scratch the heart of Nepal: the chances are you will find more or less the same inscription etched all over.

This feeling of claustrophobia on the part of a landlocked country has psychosomatic sanction. But sustained boorishness across the border from the south has aggravated the phenomenon. Indians as a community have tended to take for granted the only Hindu Kingdom in the world, particularly one where the roost has been traditionally ruled by waves of migrants led by the Rajputs and the Kumaon Brahmins. Jawaharlal Nehru, having extricated the hereditary king from the clutches of the scheming *Ranas*, gave no further thought to Nepal, which, for the residual duration of its life, became as insubstantial as any distant outpost of, say, the Gorakhpur division. Now that the so-called democratic revolution has been unwrought and the Nepal National Congress mercilessly cast away, those who are entrenched in power never cease enjoying a few tangential shafts at India's expense. Any Indian discomfiture, whether in the war with China or in hockey with Pakistan, provides an emotional release. This is not the prodigal son who is straining to return; distant history is distant history, and who migrated from where is an episodic accident Nepal's establishment would rudely brush aside; they demand proper respect for Nepal's separate personality, something which, they suspect, ingratiating occasional visits by Indira Gandhi notwithstanding, India is altogether niggardly in offering.

And yet, Nepal has so few options. For a country hemmed in by alien land on all sides and high mountains on most, and whose major exportables consist of boulders and timber, blind fury is an expendable luxury. A Nelson eye has therefore to be turned upon the marauding of the Rajasthani merchants, however brusque the demeanour of the Sardars who have taken charge of almost the entire road transport. It has to be put up with for, as far as one can look ahead, developing a counterpoise of a meaningful economic relationship with China will remain a pipedream. The road to Lhasa, despite recent attempts to improve transport and communications, is remote enough, but the goods the Nepalese are interested in have to travel from much further north, from the eastern heartland of China. Whatever wares have been coming from China in recent years have in fact travelled by sea via Hongkong to Calcutta, and from there in sealed wagons to the Nepal border. These too have come mostly under unilateral commodity grants by the northern neighbour, or in lieu of the local currency grant for the road project sponsored by China.

There is a multiplier effect of the Chinese gesture, for the fountain pens and textiles thus received have been sneaked into Bihar and West Bengal, adding to Nepal's Indian rupee balances. But this is small change. For the present, there is scarcely one commodity which China would be interested in picking from Nepal; even if any such commodity could be located, the transport cost is bound to pose an insuperable problem.

Nepal, weary and dejected, therefore returns to India. Every few years, the hassle over the trade arrangements heightens the tension, disputations occur over the space to be kept reserved at the Calcutta docks for goods in transit to Nepal or over what constitutes, or does not constitute, trade deflection. But these alarums have a preordained ending: in the manner of a small-time operator in an Eric Ambler novel, Nepalese officials grab whatever little additional dispensations the big neighbour chooses to throw their way, and come home to sulk. Bangladesh can offer an attractive outlet to the sea, but she would be in no position to offer better terms than India, and take a much less kindly view of any shenanigans along the border involving raw jute. The Americans could have come, but did not, and, instead, went to that other kingdom, Thailand, which was next to both Vietnam and the open sea. The Soviet Union would, in other circumstances, be a worthwhile surrogate, but the Chinese, unfortunately, would not like it. Even if one were to ignore the negligible nature of the likely economic pay-off, a closer involvement with China herself has complex political implications: suppose China catches on and develops into a domestic epidemic, the kingdom might then be in danger. Till now, the Brahmins and the Newars and the Shahs have monopolised all the fertile tracts in the lush *terai* regions and in the Kathmandu valley, they are entrenched in the bureaucracy and the professions. Till now, the tribes such as the Gurungs and the Gorkhas and the Thakalis have continued to be treated like serfs and have not demurred. But nobody knows what might happen if the northern wind starts to blow, particularly since, meanwhile, many members from these tribes have been abroad, serving in the ranks of the army and the police in other lands, and travel can broaden the mind. The ruling oligarchy in Nepal cannot afford to take the risk.

The dominating mood in Kathmandu is therefore one of sullen despondency. There is as much squalor here as you can discover in Katihar or Kidderpore; that does not yet touch the palace-dwellers nor the transient foreign advisers ensconced in Hotel Soaltee's. But one never knows how late it is. The American boys and girls—who in any case represent the dregs of the tourist traffic—still come by the plane-load in search of hashish, but here too, diminishing returns have obviously set in. Disturbing reports flock in of the galloping price rise in India. Nepal has theoretically an average annual surplus of around three hundred thousand tonnes of rice, which goes to India and pays for the import as much of luxury and semi-luxury consumer goods for the rich as of essential articles. In this year of scarcity, India might, there is now the danger, suck in more foodgrains, which would leave so much less for the tribal peoples in the inner *terai* region and up in the distant hills. In the past, a shortage of food for the servile poor did not matter. From now on, it might.

1973

41 Plastic Surgery Gone Waste

One comes across, at Hong Kong airport, a professor of sociology from Australia. You can judge the current state of the economy of any of these countries, the professor chimes along, by the rate quoted by prostitutes. In Bangkok, in one quick year, the hourly rate for a call girl has tumbled from twenty to ten dollars; the massage parlours, like the banquet halls of yore, are all deserted: the occupancy rate in the hotels is down to thirty per cent; work in progress on several new hotels has stopped; those who piled money during the great Vietnam boom of the late 1960s are sustaining a construction programme, but once this has been phased out, things will be much, much worse: to compound everything else, the export price of rice has fallen steeply.

The house that Lyndon Baines built Richard Milhous, for the grievously selfish reason of getting re-elected as President, is now destroying with great alacrity. The war in Vietnam has not been wound down, but it has been turned capital-intensive. The American boys would not fight any more, they refused to be drafted: if they were compulsorily shipped to Vietnam, they conspired against the defence establishment, or took to heroin. The war could not be subcontracted to the local gooks either. 'Vietnamisation' was soon reduced to a shambles: the Saigon chappies took the money and the arms all right, but they did not have the fight in them, and the arms were totally lost to the enemy. The story was repeated, in Cambodia and Laos. A desperate situation needs a desperate remedy. Nixon is converting the war into an exclusively air-based operation. It is expensive, but it cuts down the deployment of troops. It wastes resources and makes nonsense of McNamara's famous exercises of 'cost-effectiveness': you use up perhaps $1,000,000 worth of bombs, time-disposition of air-troopers and pilots, depreciation of planes, *et al* to demolish a ten-dollar worth of a village hutment, or to kill a stray buffalo or dog. But at least you save on numbers, you are enabled to ship the bulk of the boys back home well before sundown on the second Tuesday following the first Monday in November 1972.

The war goes on, the great little people of Vietnam, their spirit unconquered, battle along, but the Americans have mostly gone home, or are going. In the wake of their departure, a severe crisis is gripping the pokey little countries in the Far East who have, for the past ten years, subsisted, literally as well as otherwise, on the immoral earnings skimmed off from the Americans. Whether it is Bangkok, Saigon or Manila, the story is the same. The decrepit prostitute in Saigon has been reduced to near-starvation: her income has slumped to as little as one-tenth of what it was in the halcyon days of the great American whorings, but the house madam would not agree to reduce the absolute amount of her take, nor would the pimp or the police. And the Americans have left behind a rich crop of illegitimate offspring, who have to be brought up. Here and there, tucked away in odd street corners in the capital cities in the Far Eastern countries, one can see modest offices opened by Pearl Buck's outfit, which aims at arranging the adoption of this illegitimate flock by kind-hearted, God-fearing families in Akron, Dayton or Kansas City. Considering the magnitude of the problem, the effort is piffle. Where, one wonders, are the women's libbers of the United States of America? Is their fight entirely within the narrow confines of Wasp or quasi-Wasp society, woven around the triviality of dropping the r from the expression 'Mrs'? Is the be-all and end-all of liberation the ridiculous equivalence of shedding the claustrophobic shackle of a Maidenform brassiere? Do the women's libbers have at all the awareness that of all the crimes the Americans have perpetrated around the world since the end of World War II, in terms of sheer brutality, none can compare with the cynical, wholesale, systematised violation of women in country after country in the Far East? American foundations and the U.S. administration glibly talk of the sanctity of the human soul: they have the mendacity to talk of cultural freedom: the war in Vietnam, the media are made to convey the message, is for preserving and sustaining the right of free choice. Such sanctimonious nonsense-mongers deserve to be reincarnated as willowy, frightened female offspring in peasant families in Thailand, Philippines or South Vietnam. Carnal knowledge, the Americans have assumed, is, like food and drink and ranch cattle, a tradable commodity, and can be dissociated from the dignity of the human soul, or, for that matter, the human body. Pursuant to this theory, and supported logistically by wads and wads of money, land after land has been turned into a fiefdom of whoring. Walk down the waterfront of Manila, an unbelievable concentration of pimps and prostitutes, you would almost come to believe that trafficking in women must be a major national industry; at least it must be one of the principal foreign exchange earners. It could hardly be otherwise: the ruling oligarchs in each of these countries, succumbing to the lure of the dollar, leased out the economy to the Americans. The product mix had therefore to be in consonance with American desires. The Americans demanded bases and terminal facilities, girls included. The Americans got all the girls they needed, for 'rest and recreation'. The economic and social systems of the countries were geared in entirety to the impulses of the American war machine. If, in the process, your original economic occupations got disrupted, so what? If the structure of your family collapses, so what? If you convert your country into one vast network of fleshpots, so what? The Americans are paying you hard cash, aren't they: so what is griping you?

But now everything has been rendered shaky by Nixon's opportunistic avarice to be returned as President a second time. The soldiers are going home, the marines are going home, the American military bases are closing down, the American off-shore purchase of *materiel* is declining, it is difficult to obtain work in American households, institutions such as the Joint United States Military Advisory Group or the American Army Support Element are shrinking. And, of course, once the soldiers have departed, there could be no occasion for getting them 'rested' and 'recreated'. The hotels are empty: the massage parlours and assorted 'temples of health' are offering eighty per cent concession: yet custom is hard to come by: the bar girls no longer dream of thick wads of greenbacks, lavish dress and French cosmetics, they worry about the wherewithal for buying the next meal ticket. The whores have aged nearly ten years in the last six months: for them, there is but scant chance of an alternative occupation. There is also the tragedy of investments which are now a total waste: several of these girls, through plastic surgery, had raised their breasts or smoothed the slant of their eyes so as to suit American tastes. What economists coyly describe as 'frictional' unemployment thus has assumed an acute relevance. Every day, the queue of the unemployed lengthens even as the economy, structured, for nearly ten years now, on diverse kinds of prostitution, plaintively looks for an escape hatch, just any type of escape hatch.

You hop from one airport to the next, from one desolate capital to another. Each one is a specimen of panic: the panic is at some place overt, at another, still below the surface. Some are running for cover, others are thinking up desperate strategems. The boom of Walker Hill is a bygone past. South Korea is cautiously exploring a *modus vivendi* with the poor man's Mao Tse-tung, Kim II Sung. Japan has unceremoniously ditched Taiwan, and Tanaka, having profusely apologised to Chou En-Lai, is praying that China will not be too harsh in dealing with the erstwhile sinners. In Hong Kong, the three-quarters drunk journalist in Steve's, or Gene's, or Neil's Bar will inform you with a half-wink that it is all arranged: once old man Chiang Kai Shek passes from the scene, even Taiwan will quietly return to the allegiance of Mother China. In Thailand, too, one has to break out these days, the living relic of Seato notwithstanding, into *a la mode* neutralist talk, in the hope that China is listening. Malaysia and Singapore are still brazening it out, but—shades of India—suddenly the plight of the poor has become, in records and discussions, the chief concern of the ruling rich. President Marcos of the Philippines has ventured even beyond. With national elections barely six months away, the opposition relentlessly gunning for him, and the rate of inflation running at thirty per cent despite a recent devaluation, he has clamped down a military rule. It may be entirely coincidental—or it may be not—that the Constitution was suspended and the military rule enforced within a month of the country's supreme court deciding against the legality of American ownership of Philippino real estate. But, obviously, Marcos is in dire need of further buttressing! These days, in the neighbourhood, it is a well-known ploy: the Philippine President has launched his version of a *garibi hatao* programme, and, in particular, is trying to play on the ethnic emotions of the Malayan elements, who are generally way down in the socio-economic hierarchy compared to those who are of Spanish extraction. The Americans are thus no longer the saviours: the new talisman is the catechism of cliches and slogans. We Indians have been here before, during the past few years: all of a sudden, one comes to find the Far Eastern climate altogether homely.

1972

42 The Rich Have Inherited the Earth

After you have been to the Ibirapuera Park, had your fill of the Picassos, the Cezannes and the Di Cavalcantis at the Museum de Arte Assis Chateaubriand, and sipped coffee on Terraco Italia forty-three floors up in the sky, they are bound fo shove you off to a day trip twenty miles away to the beaehes of Santos in the world's leading coffee port. Much more than its export of coffee, it is perhaps its football club which sustains the reputation of Santos. For, it is the club which Pele adorns. Pele, the national hero, at the incantation of whose name young girls swoon and young boys experience a tautness in their muscles. There is no getting away from Pele in this province of Sao Paulo. Whatever wares you might want to sell, from coffee to cosmetics, at least a one-and-a-half word testimonial from Pele is a must. Brazil has only one god—a living one at that—and his name is spelled Pele.

The bizarre part of the story is that Pele is black, as black as one could be. True, on the surface, Brazilian society looks reasonably integrated. Unlike the British country squires, who colonised the lush cotton tracts of Alabama or Louisiana, the Portuguese settlers did not have the black woman only for the night's pleasure, to be cast away in the morning, but offered her quasi-legal status. Random events, however, are random events, and the big mass of Negroes who were imported as slaves during the seventeenth and eighteenth centuries could but watch the economic opportunities pass them by. Their descendants continue to be on the periphery. They faithfully dance the samba, provide the quintessential vigour of Brazilian music, ensure the country's near-supremacy in football; but otherwise they do not quite belong. They rarely own the land; they only work on the land. In industry, they provide the bulk of the unskilled labour. In offices, they constitute the vast army of menials and messenger-boys. You will be hard put to come across a black face among the academic elite. The Negroes make up the base of the entertainment and other service sectors; the country, however, is owned by the Latins. In a society basically organised on the principle of from those who need to those who have property rights, the blacks do not stand much chance. Pele is *non pareil*

Not that anybody is seemingly losing any sleep over it. The early Indian tribes—or whatever remain of them—are certainly much worse off in economic terms than even the Negroes, but nobody is worrying his head off on account of that either. Particularly in Sao Paulo, you have plenty of other things to think of, and the poor and the so-called underprivileged will have to wait a while before some radical agitator comes up and leads the black people away from the mindless samba and into political activism. For the present, topsyturviness wins all the way. Brazilian army generals, whose cause has always been dear to the heart of the US Department of State and the Central Intelligence Agency, were taught the rudiments of the theory of unbalanced growth by American economists in the early 1960s. There has been no looking back since. Of Brazil's ninety-odd million people, not more than a quarter live in the south-eastern tip, represented by the triangle of Sao Paulo-Porto Alegre-Rio de Janeiro. So what? In any case, this quarter constitutes the Latin cream. Resources have been squeezed from the rest of the country and heaped several times over, flooding the triangle. The other parts may raise the coffee and the cotton and the sugarcane and the soyabean and the tobacco, but these must all come here for processing; the climate here is temperate, almost Mediterranean, so let the resources concentrate. Investments from the northern hemisphere—some governmental, but mostly private—have come in abundance. Naturally, the country—or this part of it—is booming. Perhaps, outside of the province of Sao Paulo, not much of national income statistics exist. But you have no objective basis for refuting the suggestion that currently the economy is expanding at the rate of ten per cent per annum. It will be not at all grotesque to suggest that this growth is being exclusively cornered by the top three or four per cent of the population. The *cavalheiros* had never had it so good. One son of the family joins the army and becomes a general, another stays back to take care of the ten to fifteen thousand acres of lush prairie land, a third son perhaps collaborates with the Americans or the Germans and emerges as a leading luminary in the industrial world with offices strewn all over Praca da Republica and Largo do Paissandu. Assets breed assets, connections breed connections.

Sao Paulo was not much more than a marshy heap fifty years ago; it is South America's largest most crowded city today, with skyscrapers jostling against each other, huge, wide avenues curling away from each other, intricate flyovers and even more intricate traffic jams, cars of all conceivable descriptions making life miserable for each and every driver. The shops are literally crammed with goods; there are 600 night-clubs, 150 cinema-houses, 25 theatres, and thousands of restaurants and bars to swing away in. Who cares if, barely fifty miles away, people live on bananas and there is squalor which can compare with what one would see in the most wretched Bihar township, or if subterranean bitterness abides within the blacks and the remnants of the aborigines. The part, the theory of unbalanced growth asserts, is always greater than the whole; the part indicates the whole. Sao Paulo, with its marble structures and gay apartments, is real; the squalor, which is beyond the nose of the dainty *senhores* and *senhoras*, is, in the true existential sense, not real. So do lap it up, this good life, while you are able to.

How much time do these Latin squires have? For Sao Paulo and the skewed structure of Brazil's economy are an anachronism—an anachronism which yet presents itself in a modern garb. The Latin girls are pretty, some of the mulatto girls are prettier. Till as long as the Americans are kept happy and the generals can swiftly and efficiently deal with incipient dissent, the girls will be able to stretch themselves languidly along the exquisite beaches and the girl-watchers will have their fill of the bikinis. But can it really last? Those who dilate upon the virtues of planned imbalance refer to certain linkages which will help to transmit the message from the particular to the general. Till now, apart from the curious case of Pele, there is little evidence that any such thing has started to happen. And Pele is an accident of history; he does not represent its instrumentality. Once he passes from the scene, the Santos club will be forgotten, the taut black face will disappear from the cinema slides and street-side hoardings advertising cocoa, polo shirt, or tranquillisers, and is not likely to be substituted by any other black face.

Celso Furtado, the economist who had a grand design for revolutionary reforms for the downtrodden and undernourished ones in the north-eastern parts, was hounded out of the country the day President Goulart lost power and the generals took over. There is no more talk of land reforms in this country, or, if the subject crops up, the context is the consolidation of holdings, so that the small peasant can be dispossessed of his little plot—all in the cause of a ten per cent rate of growth. The rich shall inherit the earth; they have inherited it. Whether they will be able to hold on forever, is the question.

It is little use talking of a Cuban model. Batista's hordes were never as efficient as the present group of generals in Brazil; the US Department of State, too, once bitten twice shy, has set up a vigil which is pretty thorough-going. The multinational corporations, such as the ITT, are not going to slip up on the job either. Brazil is also altogether different from Chile; the army here has learned enough by now not to allow any indolent continuance of the parliamentary game. Working a populist coup from within the military establishment, as occurred in Peru, is a feat difficult to reproduce: the army generals in Peru committed the blunder of pursuing a rather lax policy of recruitment into the officer cadre. Once young men from peasant and lower-middle-class stock were allowed in, the class consciousness of the top brass got diluted, and the identification between the interests of the landed gentry and the military establishment suddenly became less than valid. No such calamity is going ro befall here: Brazil's generals have maintained, ferociously, their policy of closed shop. What about, then, a revolution in the style of Argentina, where the army, despite its seventeen years of opportunity, failed to kill off the Peron mystique, and, instead, itself gave in? What if an evangelist figure suddenly blazes across the Brazilian sky, and dancing the *danca das banderiolas*, brings forth the revolution? If it can happen in Buenos Aires, why not in Rio?

One can point out several flaws in such reasoning, beginning with the one that Peron himself is, after all, no messiah out to deliver the masses, but an old-time demagogue who has succeeded in obtaining excellent mileage out of radical slogans. Even in the latter respect, he is not unique. Moreover, the strength and the homogeneity of the Argentine working class are the product of trade union assiduity spreading over three to four decades. In contrast, whether at the wharves or on the plantations, in the processing units or in the export-import firms, Brazilian labour is still overburdened by paternalism: given the huge reservoir of the unemployed and under-employed, it could hardly be otherwise. Thus, for the Latin elite, the high life is more than likely to continue uninterrupted for some more while: a whiff of nineteenth-century Europe will mingle with the briskness of Yankee culture, colonial-baroque architecture will provide a twist to Moorish elegance, the samba houses will be doing business till the early hours of the morning and the underpaid Negro performers will sing full-throated *bossa nova* along with hot numbers; the rich, confident that they have all the time in the world, will unendingly gulp down the *batidas* and *guzzle feijoada*; their women will dutifully visit the autumn fashion soiree in Paris and the spring one in New York; the per capita income in the state of Sao Paulo will threaten to touch $5,000 per annum. Negro and mulatto women will, however, still be discovered picking rags round the corner from the luxury hotels on Avenue Ipiranga, and, in the north-east, barely fifty miles up from Recife, squalor and pestilence will remain stamped on each single face as you stare down from the antiseptic isolation of the air-conditioned tourist bus.

But does not all this make you feel somewhat homesick?

What has Sao Paulo got which New Delhi has not, apart from such trivialities as that a restaurant like the Cabala here will serve 200 different kinds of whisky—a feat Connaught Place is unlikely to match? As for insensitivity to the intimations of the fire that will begin to burn tomorrow, fiercely, all engulfingly, New Delhi certainly could hold a candle to Sao Paulo. Even at this distance of 12,000 miles, chauvinistic pride, if that is what it is, must, therefore, obtain its just desserts.

1973

43 An Integrated Society . . .

The man from the tourist agency managing the herd is straight out of Graham Greene. He can tell you dirty stories in eleven languages. Instead, he confines himself to circumspect jokes. Perhaps it is his past which is casting its long shadow. If you press him hard, he would perhaps own to a Hungarian ancestry. What dark history lies hidden behind the deep scar on the right cheek, the saturnine smile and the slightly angular walking gait? The man, it could be a fair guess, was perhaps a young, up-and-coming lieutenant in the early 1940s in Horthy's fascist militia. An equally fair guess, he is a scion of one of those Hungarian landowning families, given to hunting, wenching and oppressing the peasants, for whom the termination of World War II came as the apocalypse. A period of confusion, flight across perilous borders and seas, and many such people ended up, initially perhaps in Argentina, subsequently in other Latin American lands.

Brazil is full of such men. Former Nazis and fascists, soldiers of fortune, mercenaries have all discovered a great ethnic convergence in the Brazilian elite now busy colonising the country's northern territories. The frontier is being pushed back, the hinterland of the deep, mysterious Amazon is being opened up for civilisation, and who can perform the job better than the venturesome former Nazis from Europe of the pure breed? The tourist beat will tell you precisely how this great mission has been taken in hand.

The first hop on the plane will take you to the fantasy of Brasilia, the brash new capital on which 80 billion *cruzeiros* have been expended, and which remains generally unpopulated once you leave out the minimum administrative paraphernalia. The mandarins from Rio and Sao Paulo come and go, taking pride in Brasilia's architecture, but the fast jets are intended to transport them speedily back to the temperate havens in the south. The plane lands in the midst of a desert. Even as it is losing height, you can see the high-rise buildings set up in a weird geometry on the vast expanse of red soil. Funds were no limiting factor; Oskar Neimeyer was given *carte blanche* to fashion the capital in whatever manner he liked. He indulged in the extravaganza of a luxury rarely proferred in history to any other architect. It is dazzling brilliance. If you could isolate your instincts from the rest of Brazil's problems, from the tragedy of the impoverished peasants, the negroes and the mulattoes and the Indians, if you could, for some fleeting moments, turn yourselves away from the other realities, you could then enjoy the utter sensuousness of it: a continuous riot of sheets and plate glass, spires and domes, marbles and solidified concrete.

Everything is planned in a grand manner. There are residential blocks and superblocks, markets and supermarkets, a widely dispersed embassy row, but few people. Only the superior breed of civil servants and plutocrats have been provided with residential plots in the main township. The residences are built, but scarcely lived in. The mulattoes and the negroes are elsewhere, in the satellite towns. The ministries are located in United Nations-kind of match boxes which in their collectivity, however, put to shame the building at Turtle Bay. A visit to the Congress National is laid out for you, the Anexo do Senado and the Anexo da Camara are magnificent examples of compositions in marbles, steel and domes: Plato's Republic is having its apotheosis here. Even the walls of the Anexo do Senado are inlaid with carpet, the lighting is concealed and prismatic; the air-conditioning has a purring smoothness. The gods, if they had access to modern architecture, would have loved to live in such surroundings, from where, very thoughtfully, the people are expelled.

You will, with great courtesy, be led into the distinguished visitors' gallery to watch the senate at work. Barely half a dozen out of the total tally of 66 senators, each one hand-picked by the military regime, are present. One senator is declaiming into the microphone, his voice pitched at a thunderous octavo. You ask the interpreter what the hullabaloo is about. The *senhor* senator, you will be informed, is very cross with the government; the elite of the land had a substantial chunk of their other assets converted into industrial and commercial shares; the shares had boomed: the plutocrats had never been happier. But, of late, the authorities have been behaving funnily. The share prices have apparently slipped by one or two percentage points in the course of the past fortnight: this could not be; nothing could be more shocking; stockholders of the world, unite. The senator was warning the government; any further encroachment on the privileges and the rights of those who are the mainstay of the Brazilian miracle, any further dip in share prices, and the end of the miracle could no longer be avoided.

You soliloquise amen, and move on. The tourists are treated to a languid meal under the star-studded sky in the Churroscaria do Lago and are made to catch the midnight flight—a straight thousand miles—to Belem, capital of the northern state of Para, founded, way back in 1616, by the eminent pirates Franceisco Caldeira and Castelo Branco. When you land, it is steaming hot; the equator reminds you that it is around. It could be anywhere along the Coromandel coast, a bit of Goa spliced with a bit of Gibraltar. There is perspiration in the air. The beggars and tramps are out on the pavement in front of the hotel, the touts sidle up, the girls behave as they would in any southern European town ridden by sailors. An aroma of tropical fruits begins to hurt your nasal tracts. You hurl your suitcase on the floor of the dusty, musty-smelling hotel room and, groggy, try to cope with the weariness of tropical humidity. The pick-pockets and scroungers are already swarming outside, but you leave early in the morning to visit the plantations which are coming up fast. It is a cattle ranch you are taken to, all 2,300 hectares of it. The rancher has come from down south, the cattle have been mostly imported and the labourers too are either mulattoes or negroes shipped across from the north-east. Ask no questions and you will be told no lies. You look for the Indians, original settlers around these parts, they are not to be found anywhere. Those who were foolhardy enough to resist eviction have been taken away elsewhere, maybe are in concentration camps, or maybe have even been shot. The rancher treats you to a sumptuous lunch, barbecued chicken, beef and pork, papaya and pineapple, water melon and banana, beer and orange juice and *guarana* and coconut water, which, as the song goes, is good for your daughter. With food and drinks, contentment descends fast. You have your picture taken with the rancher, his wife, his lovely children; somehow, they forget to call in the black servants and hired hands

Next morning, there is a chartered flight to Altamira. After arriving, you are driven deep into the interior to see at first hand the programme of land clearance and land settlement furiously in operation. The *modus operandi* of the settlement follow the familiar pattern. The highway joining Belem with Brasilia is the pivot around which the new civilisation will unfold. Newspapers in West Germany and Japan carry discreet insertions on behalf of the Government of Brazil; lush virgin land is available in Mato Grosso, Para and Rondonia almost for free, at one American dollar per hectare, provided the migrant comes in with an investment packet of at least 10,000 dollars. It is selective breeding, as much of man as of capital. The Germans and the Japanese have begun to flock. Official facilities are made available to them. The Indians are picked up from the distributed lands and despatched to their fate. The bulldozers keep throbbing away and clear the land. In area after area, once the clearance is complete, seeds and power and labour are arranged for. Exterminate the Indians, if need be, with the help of official resources; appropriate the land; get it cleared by negro labour; from then on, it is all yours; you can raise cane, or cotton, or coffee. The North American version of the opening of the wild west is thus being re-enacted in Brazil, quietly, and with perhaps a greater finesse. The Indians are for burning. If you kill an Indian, you merely kill a vermin or an insect. An iguana you can occasionally keep as a pet; now and then, you also do the same with an Indian. But it does not really matter if you don't.

You take all this in, are treated to more and more lavish barbecues and feel like escaping. But the ex-Nazi from the tourist agency is watching you; it is *verboten* to break ranks. You give up, and, the next day, are flown to the brisk inland port of Manaus, where you see Brazil's sole jute mill furiously at work. This is supposed to be the archetypal frontier town, the ultimate point reached by the early settlers in the seventeenth century; if you will, there is a certain romantic langour about it. The motor launches chug-chug away along the River Negro. There is a busy floating market; you can come upon a stray Sindhi textile merchant; curios and antiques are a-plenty to be picked up by the tourist. At night, there is music and square-dancing at the parks, which are many. You are right in the heart of Amazonas, a state which in size is perhaps as big as the whole of India, with barely a million people, of which one-half are likely to be in Manaus itself. It is still mostly unconquered forest land; the fauna is still largely undisturbed; and the Indians, along with the animals and beasts, still a-hiding.

But the Tarzans have begun to come, and the tourists cannot be far behind. The frontier, who can doubt, will be pushed back further and further, man will vanquish Nature, man will liquidate and decimate other men. The black are visible and tolerated in Amazonas as they are tolerated elsewhere in the country; because without them the process of land clearance, as much that of industry and agriculture, will come to a halt. They represent the embodied labour which makes Brazil tick. In the new society being built up and down the Amazonas, the blacks, along with the mulattoes, have only one role to play. They are, in the literal sense, the hewers of wood and the drawers of water. In addition, in sad night clubs, they do the singing and the fixated dancing. As the forests are cleared away, it will be more of the same. The Indians will die, and the negroes will be at work in order that the whites can live it up. Brazil is an integrated society.

Leave it to your Hungarian guide. He will arrange for you to go out on an excursion up the River Negro where it merges into the Amazon, where the River Solimoes first meets the Negro and the two together enter the majestic Amazon. The water of the Negro is dark, as mysteriously dark as the long tresses of a medieval princess. The water of the Solimoes is bright, silverish white. The black water, they say, is heavier than the white water. At the confluence, one can see, next to one another, the splash of the black water of the Negro unable to mix with the sparkling white water of the Solimoes. The black water struggles for a while to cope with the other water from the Solimoes on equal terms. It struggles hard, but fails. After a while, the black water goes down under, and the water of the Amazon appears white, impeccably white. In Brazil's society, it is the same; the black and the mulatto go under and it is only the white who stay on top. And, of course, soon there will be no Indians left in and around Amazonas, unless it be for the sake of the tourists, or for the sake of a shooting sequence in a Hollywood movie. Indians will be a lost people, and Amazon a lost river.

1973

44 Lord Kitchener is Alive and Kicking

The festival of form-filling starts right at the airport. It could hardly be otherwise. The British had been here for more than fifty years: once the British came, would forms—to be filled in triplicate—be far behind? This is still Kitchener-Gordonpasha land: this is still Condominium land. The imperial-colonialists are gone, long live the ethos of imperialism-colonialism. Fill the forms, push the files: if you have to involve yourself, take care to do so only at the margin; shadow must continue to be the substance of your existence. The song of imperialism-colonialism is a sad song, hi lili, hi lili, hi lo.

Under the Condominium Agreement, the British ruled the Egyptians for more than half a century. But the fiction was preserved: they ruled only as 'trustees' of the Egyptians, who, supposedly of their own volition, transferred the burden of ruling to the white man. The Neguib-Nasser revolution swept the British out of Egypt. But, never say die, a few rearguard manoeuvres continued in Sudan, at least for a while. He who plots, prospers; he who divides, rules. So keep whispering to the tribes down south, dispersed over Beher el Ghazel, Equatorial and Upper Nile, that they were Africans, not Arabs; keep whispering to the young Arab subaltern from the Khartoum suburb of Omdurman that the *kaffirs* from the south need a bit of straightening out: keep the Ansars posted with the nefarious goings-on between the Khatmiyyas and the Egyptians; tell the Khatmiyyas about how the rich Gezira land was being gobbled up by the Ansars; urge the Ummas to battle with the Ashiqqas, warn the Ashiqqas that the Umma-Mahdists were going to exclude them from the ranks of the army and the administration.

These are familiar pieces of the puzzle: whatever the country, the British, always correctly conservative, preferred to play the invariant game. Shuffle the names—Sayed Abd al-Rahman al-Mahdi could have been Mohammed Ali Jinnah, Ismail al-Azhari could have been Tej Bahadur Sapru, Abdallah Khalil could have been Motilal Nehru. Imperialism-colonialism was always a bit like Hindu architecture—repetitive, predictable, with a predilection for pitting one native elite against another native elite. Meanwhile, of course, the cotton tracts in the confluence of the Niles turned lusher and lusher; and that other investment in empire, the single track rail line between Khartoum and Port Sudan, carried away the rich haul of raw fibre, to be duly shipped to Lancashire.

Alas, all good stories have to come to an end, the flag has to be brought down from the mast-head, and it is all over. The British had to quit in 1956, and it was Independent Sudan. Or was it? For it is still Kitchener-Gordonpasha land. In the near-twenty years since Independence, the Sudanese elite have forgotten none of the British lessons, and have since picked one or two of the American ones. This has been, for them, season for mutual hatred and intrigue, season for plots and counterplots—both during hours and after hours. Time as a dimension never entered in the British scheme of things: it has not intruded into the consciousness of Sudan's ruling groups either. Theoretically, Sudan remains Africa's largest country, the land mass exceeds India's, but the total population would barely reach sixteen million, of whom at least one-tenth are huddled together in the sanctuary of Khartoum-North Khartoum-Omdurman. Outside of the triangle around Khartoum, formed by the interstices of the Blue and the White Niles. it is a horrendously poor country.

The rains do come in the south, but nobody has till now bothered to harness them, and the southern provinces remain alien outposts, condemned to quasi-pastoral sub-existence; the nomads out in the west are left to their own devices, at least most of the time, unless irrigation makes some of their land ripe for appropriation and mechanisation, when trouble arises. Independence came in 1956, but economic development has not yet quite arrived in Sudan. The ruling groups in Khartoum schemed and plotted, coalesced and divided—all the time, the gleam in their eye was exclusively for the government spoils and the surplus extractable from the rich, limited, mechanised cotton-cum-sugar tracts in the neighbourhood of the capital.

For a while, the parliamentary game was on—the usual permutations and combinations of political groups and religious sects and foreign lobbyists. He who was with X in the morning became his grimmest enemy by sundown: he who on Tuesday was Y's implacable enemy was—by the grace of Allah the Merciful—come Wednesday high noon, his sworn lieutenant and comrade-in-combat. Now and then, some elections were held, perfunctorily, with a casually worked-out suffrage, and the elite knew how to manipulate them where. By the beginning of 1959, the army pushed aside the politicians, but the pattern did not change: the army had its sects and sub-sects, intra-command jealousies and heart-burnings. From time to time, much in the manner of sudden parliamentary manoeuvres, counter-coups followed coups; some colonels and brigadiers got shot, some got promoted. In the mid-sixties, there was a reversion to rule by the political parties. Obviously, it failed to meet the criteria of the Pareto Optimum, and the army moved back—this time, egged on by the radical students of Khartoum University and a fledgling communist party basing itself on the support of the low-paid peasant-workers in Gezira and the linesmen and pointsmen of Sudan Railway.

The students were soon driven back inside the University. And the communists, after trying a half-hearted coup of their own—a coup that failed—appear to have been altogether obliterated, barring a few half-whispers in run-down eating places in Omdurman. Meanwhile, though, a southern group, the Anya Nyas, disgusted by the fact that all the dates that are munchable and all the gum Arabic that is chewable are being munched and chewed by the rascals from the northern provinces, mounted a rebellion. Some two years ago, it was patched up. For the first time, there is a regional government for the South operating from Juba, whose head is also a Vice-President of the national regime in Khartoum. A university, again located in Juba, has also been thrown in as part of the package deal.

So, there you are. Sudan for the moment has no open civil unrest to cope with. There is, naturally, a certain stillness in the air. Go round to the offices of the Sudan Socialist Union which is the formal name for the junta which currently rules and, if you can obtain a pass, go round to the army barracks. The crisis in confidence has arrived. Power is an inheritance, but what does one do with it, particularly if one does not want to disturb overly the existing correlation of forces? To tinker with an equilibrium situation—howsoever precariously perched it might be—entails a risk. For, especially in the case of a society which continues to be ensnared by tribal diversities, you can soon lose control over the second-order consequences. The British, wizened by experience, forsook experimentation; they stuck to their standard modality: they didn't do altogether badly for more than half a century; so why not follow their example—and last out for at least another half-a-century

The radical rhetoric in the vicinity of the Sudan Socialist Union is, therefore, neither here nor there. This is a hieroglyphics which need not be deciphered, as every student of the Egyptian Wafd party and the Indian National Congress knows. Discretion is the better part of valour, more so since the discretion is helping to line the right pockets. Filling forms in triplicate, and organising an 'armed services day' every month have, thus, their crucial uses. Such stratagems keep the population engaged, who does not know that an empty mind is the devil's workshop. True, the economy has practically stagnated in the past two decades. True, since the frontiers of mechanised agriculture—expanding even during this period of national stagnation—have led to the displacement of labour and the concentration of earnings in the hands of affluent farmers and contractors, sizeable segments of the population must be experiencing progressive immiserisation. But the ruling groups do not dare to tinker with the by now established set of priorities. Over-mechanised agriculture has been combined with a certain mindlessness. Not even the most obvious, and the easiest of all, import-substitution possibilities have been thought of: the bulk of the cotton continues to be exported, and nearly two-thirds of the needed textiles continue to be imported. And this is not an individual accident; it is not even a species of 'policy' it represents an entire genre of economic philosophy. Thus the south and the west remain cut off: the roads are not there. Isolation can give peace. If only some boats and launches were to be put on the Nile, the various populations which constitute this nation could have come together; but are you sure that would be proper, would not that stir up more trouble, speed up the processes of history, what a dangerous thing to do? In the educational sphere, the same *dirigisme* is furiously at work. Forget about the south and the west, which do not really 'belong'; even for the 'triangle', the outlay on education is a fantastic inverted pyramid: elementary education and literacy drives do not get the funds, but every year the couple of Khartoum universities are encouraged to turn out a liberal quota of arts graduates. These are still limited in numbers, you can still bribe them; all graduates are carried on the government payroll. It is really very simple; all you have to do is print some more currency notes, and design some more forms, to be filled in triplicate, which will keep the graduates engaged.

Till now, this has been a placid story. Suddenly, of late, there are intimations of dynamism—from Kuwait, Riyadh, Abu Dhabi. The oil-rich Arab brothers from those quarters do not know what to do with all their recently acquired wealth, they might be willing to pass on a few billion dollars for the amelioration of the plight of their less fortunate brethren, such as the Sudanese. Excitement and speculation are the staple of the day. How much would they offer? How generous are the terms going to be? In case the money comes gushing in, where do we put it? The southerners are really not Arabs, why should they get any part of this essentially Arab bonanza? Would we have enough to import a thousand tractors a year, or two hundred harvester-combines, so that we could do without the wretched nomads in the busy season? Would there be funds enough, too, for jazzing up the army—some more brilliantly—shining, silently-rolling tanks, a score or so of fighter planes, a modest stockpile of ground-to-air missiles?

From beyond Port Sudan, right across the Red Sea, is Saudi

Arabia; look hard, Kuwait and the rest are not too far away either. Suddenly, the scent of money is filling the air, it is a-coming, a-coming. Logic demands that Barclays Bank should have been around to handle all this money. It is not, but never mind, the good Americans are very much on the scene, the Grand Hotel is overfull, and there is a Nile Hilton fast coming up. The petro-money must be recycled to the United States. The Americans, working through international agencies and otherwise, are here to ensure that whatever Arab funds flow down to Sudan do not get frittered away on silly idealistic causes, but are appropriately 'channelled' into capital-intensive projects which could make good use of high-priced, obsolete equipment from the United States.

The song of neo-colonialism is a sad song, hi lili, hi lili, hi lo. The British have departed, but have left behind a mile-long, cemented embankment along the Blue Nile, right in front of the Grand Hotel. As dusk falls, cars pack up chaotically next to the hotel, the expatriates begin to drown their physical discomfort in gimlet and shandy, and desultorily talk about which ministry to convert to their point of view the following morning; there is not much stirring on the embankment, the breeze mostly plays truant, an irrigation pump occasionally stutters from the other side of the river; the embankment is generally lonely, now and then an unemployed young man, perhaps from Omdurman, perhaps from further in the interior, aimlessly ambles by, a certain sadness in his gait; he does not know where he is going, to whom his rulers propose to barter away his destiny the following morning. All he can cling to so far is the faith that the sun also rises. But as twilight blankets the Nile, even this faith sometimes thins out in memory. Colonialism is dead, long live colonialism!

1975

45 A Certain Charm in the Old Rascal

Call him by the most vicious names, there is still a certain charm in the old rascal. And of course a certain endurability. There is an historical grandeur about him. Thirty years, twenty-five years ago, drums would beat through the villages: the boats would wind their way against the fairly strong current into the interior canals of Vikrampur or Kishorgunge and carry the tiding: the Maulana was coming to the market-place ten, fifteen, twenty miles away, your chance of a lifetime to listen to him, to be blessed by him, to be enlightened by him. Men, women and children would begin to flock from all over: they would tuck their victuals for three, four, five days in towels and trek: if the food were to run out, they could buy some in any case in the marketplace. It is market day, and Bhashani would commence to speak even before the first crowing of the earliest rising cock. Discard all notions you ever had about what constitutes a speech. It is invocation to God, religious discourse, political economy, agricultural practices, story-telling, rabble-rousing all rolled into one. In the beginning would be the prayer. The vast congregation, spread in an unplanned, untidy formation all over the field abutting the marketplace, would join in : the atmosphere would be both eerie and peaceful, and the Maulana's enormously rich voice would throb against the sky. With the prayer over, he begins on a low, matter-of-fact pitch: it is the story of the Prophet, his glory and his exploits, his saintliness and nobility, his mission, his love for the poor, the Maulana is narrating the story of the Prophet who was the first and the greatest of all socialists, Islam being the religion of socialism. It might be all theology, but you listen to it spellbound: the Maulana's charm grips you. All of a sudden, from the concept of Islamic socialism, the theme shifts to the nefarious practices of the British colonials, or to a reference to the degree of oppression let loose by the Hindu landlords: the landless peasant and the share-cropper, the Maulana thunders, must come together and rise in revolt; it was their religious obligation to do so, for it is a sin to put up with inequity. Prayer again, perhaps the time has advanced to seven or seven-thirty; adjournment for nashta and market transactions. The crowd would reassemble after about a couple of hours; the Maulana would be back, white cloth-cap, a tidy little towel on the right shoulder, to be used from time to time to wipe away the perspiration; prayer again; during this session, the first topic would perhaps be agronomic practices, tips on the transplantation of paddy, some pearls of homely wisdom on water management, a few eminently sensible comments on husking and drying operations, or on the retting of jute. A sudden riot of indignation; the Maulana has, to all appearances, gone berserk. Nothing of the sort: his wrath is boiling over at the evil doings of the Rajasthani *faria* who cheats the innocent, defenceless Bengal peasant and squeezes him dry; which brings the Maulana back to the cussedness of the local landlord who is wont to double up as the village moneylender; all usury, he roars, is sin, so said the Prophet; the Prophet must be avenged. Prayer again, an all-encompassing hush, meticulously followed by break for midday meal and rest. The congregation returns to hear their Maulana around four in the afternoon: prayer, a discourse on the drift of Indian politics, the significance of the movement for Pakistan, a masterly and succint comment on the permutations and combinations of the mutual relations between Fazlul Huq's Krishak Praja Party and the Muslim League, ending with what Maulana thought about either; the parallel between the current situation and what happened during a particular episode under the first Caliphate; one story, with a quasi-religious base, leading on to others; Maulana the soothsayer at his scintillating best; once more, intermission for prayer; the shadows lengthen; very soon, it is dark; another theological tale, and adjournment for the evening meal. The children are lullabied into sleep; fires light up here and there, mostly dehydrated jute stalks which ignite in a brilliant, if ephemeral, glow; the atmosphere is one of gay carnival, religious concourse and political barn-storming spiced together in an improbable pistachio. A relaxed Maulana resumes late at night; the bright stars look down from the ponderous sky, a languid breeze wafts along; more narrations, about crop conditions in the other districts; the state of rack-renting in the neighbouring villages; how to thatch a hut properly before the rains come down really hard; how much grain one should try to stock up for the difficult months; the tales of the maladroit Rajasthanis and the stuck-up Bengali Hindu *bhadraloks;* the lesson of the Holy Book, how you must sacrifice your all for the sake of truth and equality; roar, roar, roar; the Maulana reaches a crescendo, frenzy all around; you must rise in revolt and smash the centuries-old dungeon. Suddenly the Maulana reverses the pitch; prayer; the communion is over for the night; he would resume at the crack of dawn, so have a good night's rest; prayer. The people disperse, they find their way under the banyan trees and elsewhere; they would be up in the morning before the crowing of the first cock.

And this routine would continue for days on end: two days, three days, one week, ten days. Some amongst the crowd would trek back to their villages; but fresh groups would flock in with every day. A patriarch, a philosopher, an agronomist, a family doctor, a religious head, a political prophet, a grandfather chanting stories in the indolent evening, the Maulana was a bit of everything. The decades have passed. East Bengal and Assam donned the identity of East Pakistan, East Pakistan has shaded off into Bangladesh, but the Maulana has succeeded in remaining what he always was; a bit of everything.

This particular style, call it got-up, call it flummery, call it a sham, has remained immaculate over the years. The part-time savant has also come to exude the shrewdness of the *mofussil* politician. A man of many moods, the Maulana has always been impossible as an organisation man. His impulses have carried him in awkwardly different directions. He has revelled in Whitmanesque contradictions. But a man is a man for all that. The charm and the charisma are, to this day, undiminished. Crowds still flock whenever he decides to address a meeting. They roar at his repartee, applaud his righteous indignations, are entertained by his salty jokes. A deeply religious individual, he can get away with blasphemy; the Maulana remains the indeterminate element in Bangladesh, frustrating the nicely laid-out plans for non-zero sum games, yours as well as mine.

Call him a rascal, but grant him his charm. His current bout of fasting may end in tragedy, but it could even end as a fiasco. He has not concealed his intention to embarrass the Sheikh. He is quite unabashed in his determination to see the last of the Indo-Bangladesh Treaty. With a twinkle in the eye and a flourish of his remarkable beard, he would tell his crowd that today and for-ever, India is Bangladesh's worst enemy. The Soviet Union would be thrown in too, for she had the temerity to team up with India. There is nothing wrong with Islamic socialism, for, he would confide to his listeners, a vast majority of the Hindus are religious and will support Islamic socialism, there being no difference between Allah and Ishwar. Besides, come what may, none could prevent the establishment of the greater Bengal of his dreams, which would come in the course of the next twenty years. The movement for greater Bengal, he would confidently assert to his bed-side visitor, will intensify within the next five years, for had not New Delhi's oppression of the Hindu Bengalis been much more barbarous than Pindi's treatment of the East Pakistani Bengalis? Scan his recent speeches, there is no mistaking the continuity of the style: the same ingenious blend of religiosity and unscrupulousness, a dash of homespun brotherly advice interspersed with carefully laid-out political incendiaries.

There is perhaps a logic tucked away in the Maulana's tantrums. The authorities in Pakistan could never take him terribly seriously. There precisely lay the rub. The Maulana was not taken at his face value. But it became difficult to avoid facing the particular reality which a more pragmatic-minded disciple like Mujibur Rahman brought about once he was able to combine pent-up emotions with proper grass-root organisation: once *that* reality too was flouted, the country came apart. A repetition of the story is possible. The Maulana may fade away, but he would still leave ideas behind. His programmatic theme could be taken up by somebody with a greater flair and patience for organisation. Where petty-bourgeois passions dominate the power of the State, the demand for escape hatches registers a secular gain. The kind of seemingly rumbling complaints which the Maulana is mouthing could, with a time-lag, prove to be ideal escape hatches for some. Put the blame on me, said the old Rita Hayworth song. In Bangladesh, sooner or later, the pressure would indeed be irresistible to put all the blame not upon themselves, but, across the border, squarely on the Government of India. The long-run cost-benefit analysis of Bangladesh would then turn out to be a bizarre indeed arithmetic for the lip-smackers on this side.

1973

46 One Revolution is Enough?

One almost wishes Sheikh Mujibur Rahman had more than one face. Wherever you meander in this half-composed, semi-arranged city, you cannot avoid the face: it stares down at you from all sundry walls: the wall of the hotel lobby, the wall of the senior civil servant's drawing room, the wall of the corridor of the cinema hall, the wobbly wall of the restroom of the steam boat you take to visit your ancestral place, across the river, twenty miles away from Dacca. The face, with the slightly benign, slightly vacuous smile frozen on the lips, infests the electric poles, the street-corner hoardings, the ramparts of the football stadium. There is hardly a chance that you will be allowed to forget, even for a single moment, that you have entered the land of the Patriarch. The rest is, for the present, one is reluctantly led to conclude, altogether irrelevant.

Except, perhaps, the all-pervading fact of poverty. The posh habitats of Dhanmandi and Gulshan are deceiving beyond measure. Bangladesh, once you rip apart the thin facade, remains a frighteningly poor country. The new university complex certainly dazzles. Depending on the mood, it could well gladden the heart to see the modern-looking structures along what was, a quarter of a century ago, vast stretches of paddyland, known to the local ones as Nilkhet. As you move up and down the university buildings or take a stroll along Elephant Road or the Motijheel area, we-have-come-across-this-one kind of slogans keep entertaining you. The university has nurtured a new generation of students who can at least claim partial credit for making the liberation possible; true to expectations, they are riven by as many divisions—or perhaps even more—as their counterparts in West Bengal. There is the same adherence to Marxist-sounding slogans, the same desperate effort to discover parallels between internal situations and episodes which had happened in faraway lands in faraway times. Dacca is still a stodgy place and social mores inhibit the mixing of the sexes. The university, however, suggests a different picture, with young girls full-throatedly shouting away the same slogans as are being mouthed by the young boys. What further assails one is the overwhelming presence of the Bengali language. Beginning with the number plates of cars and road and shop signs, ending with detailed official correspondence, almost everything is in Bengali. And it is Bengali of a particularly rich variety, sonorous, full of poetry, full of music, full of elegance, full of imagination. It is as if the insurgent Bengali middle class, a-twirl with frenzy, is indulging in its newly discovered ego. The identification is total both ways: the ego is the Bengali language, the Bengali language is the ego.

But Dhanmandi, Gulshan, the university and the Motijheel surroundings constitute only the superstructure. The mass is different. To discover its contents, you only have to wend your tortuous path through the old town barely a mile away. It is teeming with people, carts, cycle-rickshaws, vendors, more people, more cars, more cycle-rickshaws, more vendors. The musty smell of decadence hangs all over. There has been hardly a fresh construction during the past twenty-five years in the old town. Patchworks here and there have not been able to rob the old town of its aura of crowded death. And yet, life flows on in the old town in an unending hum. It is an asymptotic conundrum. Real estate continues to be further fragmented with every day. The roads continue to be further piled up with dirt and rubbish and multitude. Transport becomes with every day an even more hopeless exercise in nightmares. But, somehow, the equilibration of life refuses not to click.

The story is repeated in the countryside. Leave your car behind and take a boat into the interior of Vikrampur or Manikgunge. The land looks even more desolate than a quarter of a century ago. It could scarcely be otherwise. In Bangladesh, the rate of growth of population currently exceeds three per cent, and the rate is certainly higher in the villages than in the urban areas. Over the decades, agricultural growth has not even been able to keep pace with the growth in numbers. Nine-tenths of the total cropped area is given to paddy; nonetheless, rice has been, and remains, in short supply. The cultivation of jute can provide the cash, but the smart Punjabis had so tilted the terms of trade between jute and other commodities that the farmers got very little out of the bargain during the past twenty-five years. The East Bengal Estate Acquisition and Tenancy Act of 1950 got rid of the Hindu landlords and *jotedars*, and a ceiling of a sort was imposed at 33 acres. Under Ayub, the ceiling was raised to around 125 acres; it has now been brought back to 33 acres once more. Even so, the distribution of arable land is certainly less uneven than in India and considerably less so than in West Bengal. Only 20 per cent amongst the cultivators are without any; the corresponding percentage is as high as 37 per cent in West Bengal. The average size of a family farm is little more than three acres in Bangladesh. If the land were evenly distributed amongst all cultivators, it would come down to only two. If, as some economists are pleading, you impose a ceiling at 12.5 acres and distribute the excess land amongst those who are without land, each hitherto landless family would get barely half-an-acre or thereabouts. And, as population keeps mounting, the average size of the farm would shrink to still smaller proportions.

Despite all this, the shape of agriculture could have been somewhat different if investments of even a minimal order had taken place over the years. This did not come about and ironically perhaps because, following the ejection of the *zamindars*, East Bengal was unable to set up, in the interregnum, its own class of kulaks who could counterpose their will against the thrust of the industrialists from West Pakistan. You can travel for miles and miles along the unbelievably beautiful Bangladesh countryside and not come across a single example of improved agricultural technology or a reasonably modernised irrigation system. Even the ramshackle farm sheds look as if they are relics from the pre-1947 era.

The planners, sitting at Dacca, dream of diversifying away from jute into gas, fertilisers, other petro-chemicals, paper, oil extraction, steel processing, *et al*. Ideologues at the other end dream of a more drastic land reform combined with a perfectionist socialist endeavour for every nook and corner of the economy. The major problem for Bangladesh agriculture will, however, remain: that of raising the productivity of the small plots, that of injecting some precious capital investments across-the-board. Even if land reforms are pushed to the limits of feasibility, there will be need for nurturing economies of scale, if not anywhere else, at least in the provision of services and in the marketing of output. Some surplus has to be put together from somewhere and pumped into land. Meanwhile, if one believes—as the Sheikh understandably does—that one revolution is enough, the social tensions will have to be contained. If thievery continues and those with relatively big farms clamour for remission of land revenue, the surplus will simply not be there. Political exigencies may then make it all the more alluring to accept the overture of outsiders to provide the wherewithal: the Americans, for one thing, are more than ready to pay cash in expiation of their 1971 follies.

The Sheikh is a hard-headed practical politician and one who is not at all ashamed to harness a dose of demagogy to the cause. He is also particularly enamoured of the strategy put to good use by the Prime Minister of the neighbouring country. He will radicalise his slogans, but will not radicalise his party. Talk of reconstruction of the economy within a socialist framework will be accompanied by a ten-year holiday for private industrialists, including the foreign ones. A certain stance of non-alignment in foreign policy will be matched by an open-door policy toward external assistance; by now, each little country knows almost by heart the drill of playing one rich nation against another and extracting the maximum of bargains thereby.

Since the Awami League is about as polyglot as the Indian National Congress, land reforms cannot seriously be on the agenda. The ideologues within the party will thus be disappointed. Sooner or later, they will melt away from the League and swell the ranks of assorted radical groups. A la West Bengal, these groups will quarrel amongst themselves on the dialectics of the objective situation from severely subjective angles. American funds will flood the country. Even though the Americans will not quite be able to control each nuance of the political process, they will have the satisfaction of seeing the decimation of those groups who are congenitally anti-West. The people at large will grow increasingly more anti-Indian; all imaginary as well as genuine difficulties will continue to be ascribed to the machinations of the Indians. But this is Indian destiny catching up. One has to atone for the sins of one's exploiting forefathers. India, consisting of the prototypes of Marwari *farias* and Bengali Hindu landlords, should not have expected a different denouement. The people of Bangladesh will therefore continue to write charming Bengali poetry and spout hatred toward India. The Sheikh will, on ceremonial occasions, preach eternal friendship for India and allow elements within his party to fulminate all the while against the conspiracy indulged in by Indians.

Talk of socialism will proliferate, but the administrative machinery will turn increasingly more authoritarian. All told, Bangladesh will pass through an economic experience not altogether different from what India has encountered during the past quarter of a century. Even that, however, will not bring the two nations together.

Meanwhile, the Sheikh's picture will stare down at you as you discuss the parallel between what took place on Topkhana Road on 1 January 1973, with what obtained in Berlin in October 1927, or was it in April 1932.... It is no matter, the Sheikh will take care of each and all, including the minor discrepancies.

1973

A COMMENTARY ON *CALCUTTA DIARY*

Dr Ashok Mitra, economist, civil servant, essayist, politician, journalist, and now finance minister of the Government of West Bengal, India, is a man of many parts held together by an ardent social conscience. The book under review testifies both to his versatility and to his commitment.

All but eight of the forty-six essays in this collection are about India. As the title indicates, it is a perspective viewed from Calcutta and related as a sequence of observations—a diary—between 1968 and 1975. The place and the time are both important ingredients of this discourse: they provide it not merely with its context but also its meaning.

A view from Calcutta. This is inaugurated by an article—'Calcutta Every Day'—a four-page virtuoso exercise in 1,750 words packed into a single paragraph written for *Frontier* in 1969. Only another of his numerous contributions to that militant weekly and nothing else written in that particular year have been included here—a two-fold lacuna which affirms, by means of a solitary representation, a stance, a point of view. Calcutta, the author insists, this city denounced so often as a tissue of contradictions, is as good a place as any other in the subcontinent from where to appraise the fabric of the republic. It is the puddle that mirrors the sun. There is much in these pages to demonstrate the strength of this vision. It helps to test out all-India generalizations in terms of the realities of a particularly sensitive region and evaluate broad official claims in terms of a specific set of local tensions.

And tensions abounded in the period covered by the *Diary,* written mostly as a column in the *Economic and Political Weekly* of Bombay in 1972–75. Taken together, these articles can be read as a most lucid introduction to the history of the last years of the rule of the Nehru dynasty. It is almost universally recognized that West Bengal had already witnessed in 1972–75 a dress rehearsal of what India as a whole was to experience in the 19 months of the Emergency proclaimed on 26 June 1975. One knows of the terror generated by Indira Gandh's son and his thugs in Delhi in those dark days. For a close parallel, read how already in 1973 the hoodlums of her Congress Party—euphemistically called the 'Youth Congress'—met at a convention to divide up Calcutta into zones of operation between its different factions in the manner, says Dr Mitra, of the parcelling out of Chicago at a conference of gangsters presided over by Al Capone in 1926. The killing of critics and dissidents by torture in police custody and shooting them down in jail shocked the world about the realities of the world's largest 'democracy' in 1975–76. There was nothing in this that West Bengal did not know in the preceding eight years. Read, for instance, 'Facism Shall Not Pass' for the story of two brothers, both students, murdered by the custodians of law and order sometime before the Emergency: one of them died of 'internal haemorrhage' during police interrogation and the other was shot dead in Calcutta's Presidency Jail. 'Law', under the Emergency, came to be clearly identified with lawlessness, because of its blatant perversion by Indira Gandhi and her party. For some evidence of its earlier use as an instrument of oppression and exploitation in West Bengal read 'The Emancipation of Kamal

Bose' and 'The Story of Indra Lohar'—two of the essays where the author is at his very best in his combination of sympathy and sarcasm. The first reports an authentic case of a lower-middle-class citizen held by the police for 16 months on false criminal charges in defiance of as many as six court orders for his release. The other is the true story of a sharecropper evicted from his tiny holding by a landlord and prevented from recovering it by means of an astute manipulation of the law on the part of the bureaucracy, the police and the landlord all working together.

The failure of the rule of law is matched, in Dr Mitra's critique, by the failure of the administration under the Congress raj to cope with the most pressing of India's economic problems in such areas as employment, prices, family planning and food. On the last of these topics he is particularly illuminating. I can think of no better guide to the intricacies of India's food problem than the five entries (nos. 30, 32, 33, 35, 36) of the *Diary* devoted to this subject. The power of these essays derives directly from an amalgam of the author's expertise as one of our leading economists, his vast knowledge (acquired at the highest levels of the civil service) of the processes of policy-making and the administration of economic affairs, and above all his radicalism. One of the incidental delights of his commentary on such matters is the irony and scorn with which he exposes the utter uselessness of the economic 'experts', indigenous and foreign, who thrive on India's economic maladies. As one of the tribe himself, Dr Mitra should know, and his castigation is no less true for being a sort of self-castigation.

Yet another theme which figures prominently in the *Diary* is the state of the intellectual culture of Bengal, a region which has produced many able economists but none more involved than Dr Mitra in its vast and brilliant range of literary and artistic activities. Some of the best writing in this volume represents his concern for and interest in these activities. Tuned to the somewhat pessimistic mood of these essays (I am not complaining, for what was there for an Indian democrat to celebrate in 1972–75?) many of his reflections on this theme are written up here as obituaries, both in a figurative and a literal sense of the word—the death of Bengali-language little magazines, Calcutta's dying film industry, etc., as well as real deaths such as those of an eminent anthropologist, an outstanding poet, a humble singing girl who made her way to the top, a highly talented and popular artiste who ended her days as a pauper forgotten by all. Read together these obituaries stand as a record of the conflict between Calcutta's vibrant intellectual culture and the harsh conditions of its material existence. However, one does not have to be distinguished to merit a notice of this kind in this *Diary*, for one of its most sympathetic entries is about the passing away of 'An Ordinary Man'—a homoeopath. If this reviewer may be allowed to conclude with a wish, it is that when he, an ordinary Bengali intellectual, dies the death of an emigre in a cold, alien land, Ashok Mitra, a younger man, will remember him in a few sad lines.

Ranajit Guha

First published in *Journal of Peasant Studies*, 5, 4 July 1978, pp. 525–27 and is now included in *The Small Voice of History: Collected Essays* edited by Partha Chatterjee.

THE AUTHOR

Ashok Mitra has been Chief Economic Adviser to the Government of India and Chairman of the Indian Agricultural Prices Commission. He is the author of *The Share of Wages in National Income*, has edited a volume of essays, *Economic Theory and Planning*, and his most recent book is *Terms of Trade and Class Relations*.

9 789384 439224

Printed at Repro India Ltd.